Advance praise for *7/7: The London Bombings, Islam and the Iraq War*

'Milan Rai's book about the July bombings in London is clear, scholarly, analytical, powerful, persuasive—and very readable.

'Seeking the real explanation for those events he completely destroys the illusion spread by the prime minister that they had nothing to do with Britain's illegal aggression against Iraq, which no-one really believes.

'The author, a man committed to peace, holds no brief for the violence in those attacks and the suffering they caused, but patiently takes us through the circumstances that played a part in motivating those who carried them out.

'This is a book that everyone with a serious interest in the crisis we face must read if they are to hope to understand it, its causes, its effects, and how we might resolve it.'

    Tony Benn

'Clear, interesting and very well-informed.'

    Revd Canon Prof. Martyn Percy,
    Principal of Ripon College Cuddesdon, Oxford

7/7

Also by Milan Rai:

Chomsky's Politics
(Verso 1995)

War Plan Iraq
Ten Reasons Against War on Iraq
(Verso 2002)

Regime Unchanged
Why the War on Iraq Changed Nothing
(Pluto Press 2003)

For more information about 7/7,
please visit the website for this book:
www.thelondonbombings.info

7/7

The London Bombings, Islam
and the Iraq War

Milan Rai

Pluto Press

London • Ann Arbor, MI

First published 2006 by Pluto Press
345 Archway Road, London N6 5AA
and 839 Greene Street, Ann Arbor, MI 48106

www.plutobooks.com

Copyright text © Milan Rai 2006
Copyright engravings © Emily Johns 2006

The right of Milan Rai to be identified as the author of this work has been asserted by him
in accordance with the Copyright, Designs and Patents Act 1988.

British Library Cataloguing in Publication Data
A catalogue record for this book is available from the British Library

ISBN   0 7453 2564 5 hardback
ISBN   0 7453 2563 7 paperback

Library of Congress Cataloging in Publication Data applied for

10 9 8 7 6 5 4 3 2 1

Designed and typeset for Pluto Press by JNV.
Printed and bound in the European Union by
Gutenberg Press, Malta

As a vicar's daughter and former theology student, I am asked about evil. I think the bombers were not born evil: it is because they fell into a trap of hate and despair and alienation. I believe that any of us could fall into the same black hole, but there is a way out of the darkness.

My way is to admit I am afraid, and to ask for help, to draw strength from my fellow humans instead of fearing them and drawing away from them.

Rachel North
survivor of the bomb on the King's Cross train[1]

Contents

Tables

Abbreviations

CE	Common Era (replaces AD *Anno Domini*)
CIA	Central Intelligence Agency (US)
CCTV	closed circuit television
DWP	Department for Work and Pensions
FBI	Federal Bureau of Investigation (US)
FCO	Foreign and Commonwealth Office
GCSE	General Certificate of Secondary Education
GLA	Greater London Authority; local government body
ICM	a British polling agency
IRA	Irish Republican Army; nationalist guerrilla movement in Ireland
ISC	Intelligence and Security Committee
JIC	Joint Intelligence Committee
JTAC	Joint Terrorism Analysis Centre
LRA	Lord's Resistance Army; Christian guerrilla movement in Uganda
MI5	British internal security intelligence agency
MORI	a British polling agency
ONS	Office of National Statistics
ODPM	Office of the Deputy Prime Minister
RUSI	Royal United Services Institute; quasi-official security think tank
SAS	Special Air Service; elite British Army special operations unit
TUC	Trade Union Congress; national confederation of unions
YouGov	a British polling agency

Acknowledgements

I would like to express my gratitude to the staff of the British Library in London for their assistance; to Ziauddin Sardar for initially reading an early draft of the section on Islam—I must stress, however, that any remaining errors in this area (which has undergone extensive revision) are entirely mine; to Professor David Canter, Revd Ray Gaston, Professor Ron Geaves, Toby Mayer and Gabrielle Rifkind for responding promptly and thoughtfully to unsolicited queries; to Emily Johns, Susan Johns, Cedric Knight, Martin O. and Jonathan Stevenson for their eagle eyes and wise counsel (not always heeded, alas); and to Stephen Hancock for, as always, productive conversation.

I am grateful to Emily Johns for her tulip images, commissioned as illustrations for this book; to Jennifer Johnson for permission to use her poem *Disconnection and Reconnection*; and to Rachel North for permission to use her words as the epigraph of this book.

I am also grateful to my colleagues and co-workers Maya Evans in Justice Not Vengeance <www.j-n-v.org> and Jonathan Stevenson in Pandemic Action <www.pandemicaction.net> for their tolerance, commitment and energy.

Special thanks are due to Gabriel Carlyle, Arkady Johns, Emily Johns, Susan Johns and Patrick Nicholson for their many acts of generosity, inspiration and support during the writing of this book.

Introduction

We Need Explanation, Not Narration

No Connection?

In the immediate aftermath of the bombings on 7 July 2005, one explanation for the tragedy was firmly ruled out by the British government. Tony Blair denied any connection between the July attacks on the one hand, and the ongoing war in Iraq, or British foreign policy in general, on the other. The Prime Minister failed to acknowledge the contents of secret documents leaked to British newspapers over the next few weeks, documents which demonstrated that his own government accepted exactly this connection, as we shall discover.

There is a central question: how young men born and bred in Britain, with all the rights and freedoms a British citizen enjoys, could decide to blow themselves up on London's public transport system, killing fellow citizens. The British government has ruled out holding an inquiry into this critical question, despite calls from 7/7 survivors, from relatives of those who died, and from prominent Muslims. We have been promised instead a 'narrative' of the attacks. What the British people want—both Muslim and non-Muslim—is not 'narration' but 'explanation'. This book is an attempt to supply a first draft of that explanation, an investigation into precisely the areas that the Blair government wishes to obscure and conceal.

By the time this book appears, the government's 'narrative' is likely to have been published. Different impressions have been created of quite what it might look like. One possibility is that it may be a simple recounting of events in the weeks before the bombings, and on the day of the attacks. Kirsty Morrison, a survivor from the King's Cross Underground train, responded: 'But the people on that Tube already know what happened, that is not what we are trying to understand. What is important is why it happened and how it can be prevented from happening again.'[1]

On the other hand, it has also been suggested that British intelligence is keen to publish secret documentation on the 7/7 plot, which apparently provides a detailed picture of how these young men became suicide bombers. 'MI5 is understood to have compiled a detailed picture of the influences thought to have been exerted on the bombers, and their motivations,' and is reportedly willing to share this with the public.[2]

A 'Bad, Unnecessary War'

Most commentators are extremely sceptical that an honest account will be given of the bombers' motivations. Stephen Glover, a columnist in the right-wing tabloid the *Daily Mail*, declares that the case for a public inquiry is 'irresistible'. The reason it has been vetoed by the government is that 'Mr Blair knows that any proper analysis of the events of 7/7 would lead to a conclusion that he resists against all reason. The four suicide bombers were motivated in large measure by Britain's illegitimate invasion of Iraq in 2003. This does not remotely excuse their actions, but it does help to explain them.' For Glover, the bombings were, 'at least in part, a dreadful consequence' of this 'bad, unnecessary war'. He observes:

> If you don't understand the past, you are unable to deal with the future. But because Mr Blair does not dare give us a public inquiry, we can't make sense of 7/7, and we have no basis for making any predictions about what lies ahead.[3]

A former intelligence official in No. 10, Crispin Black observes that the Blair government 'does not want an inquiry into the events of 7 July because, among other things, it does not want to face the fact that its actions put us into danger in the first place—that the prosecution of the Iraq War and the dishonest intelligence that ran up to it have caused anger and alienation and made a small number of our own Muslims more susceptible to the terrorists' message.' Black notes: 'The only people who do want an inquiry are the public—the targets of the attacks on 7 and 21 July.'[4]

Pressing Questions

What do we want to know? A columnist in the *Sun*, another right-wing British tabloid, suggested that the paramount question was: 'How did we create the conditions in which Muslim fanatics could flourish under our noses?'[5] There are two ways of approaching this question. We can seek to understand how extremism and fanaticism could reach these levels in the British Muslim community. Alternatively, we can ask how a British government could allow the Muslim fanatics that exist to 'flourish'. The second approach presumes that there will (always) be British Muslims inclined to terrorism; the problem is how to control them. The first approach makes no assumptions. It attempts to discover how British Muslims who begin their lives without being predisposed to political violence could somehow become drawn to terrorism.

On the other hand, the *Daily Mail* posed four 'pressing' questions which ranged from the technical to the political:

> Why was Britain's terror alert status downgraded a month before the bombings? Did the intelligence services have contact with the bombers before the attack? Was bomber Mohammad Sidique Khan part of a wider Al Qaeda network? Were the bombers motivated by the Iraq war?[6]

Much of this book is an attempt to find the answer to this last question. Some interim answers to the other three questions will be noted along the way.

In order to discover whether or not the Iraq war was a central motivating force in the bombers' minds, we will first consider the other factors that have been offered as possible explanations for their actions. Does the available evidence support the notion that they were 'brainwashed' by some evil mastermind? As we shall see, what is known about the bombers does not fit this picture. Does the available evidence support the idea that they were driven to violence by their 'inherently brutal' religion? Once again, we will discover that the Islam in which at least three of these young men were raised was more of an obstacle to this kind of violence than an encouragement. Were these four young men driven to violence by the cultural oppression and socio-economic deprivation of their communities? While there are indications that the conditions of community life may have tended to attract the bombers towards Islamic fundamentalism, there is little to suggest that these were motivations for the 7/7 bombings. Did an ideology of violence, a particularly brutal interpretation of Islam, and the community background of the four men play a part in their radicalization? The argument in these pages is that these were parts of the jigsaw, but that the key to this puzzle lies elsewhere. The argument in these pages is that in order to solve this mystery, we must turn our eyes not inwards to the heart of Islam or to a run-down suburb of the English city of Leeds, but outwards to the crushing realities of the global Muslim community, and in particular to the tragic realities of occupied Iraq.

This is not only my argument. It is also the argument of the British government itself, as we shall see shortly.[7] We begin our inquiry—alas, not a fully-fledged public inquiry—by contrasting the public positions taken by the British Prime Minister in the aftermath of the London bombings with the internal record of government ministries and the assessments of British intelligence.

Clarifications

Before turning to this comparison, there are perhaps a few clarifications that should be made. First, and most obviously, there were of course two al-Qaeda-related bomb attacks in London in July 2005. However, we will not be discussing any aspect of the attempted bombings of 21 July, despite their relevance and importance. There are a number of reasons for this exclusion, the most important of which is that, at the time of writing, there are trials pending for men suspected of involvement in that bomb plot.

Secondly, it may be worth defining the word 'terrorism' as it appears in these pages. The term is usually reserved solely for violent acts carried out by non-state actors such as the al-Qaeda network or the IRA. However, the dictionary definition of terrorism is not restricted to individuals and groups. The word first arose in the context of the 'Great Terror'—the state terror—of the French Revolution in the years 1793–4. The Pentagon defines terrorism as the 'calculated use of unlawful violence or threat of unlawful violence to inculcate fear; intended to coerce or to intimidate governments or societies in the pursuit of goals that are generally political, religious, or ideological.'[8] A Pentagon-commissioned study by the noted terrorologist Robert Kupperman has given a more succinct definition: the threat or use of force 'to achieve political objectives without the full-scale commitment of resources.' Noam Chomsky, citing this definition in 1991, adds: 'Kupperman, however, is not discussing terrorism; rather, low intensity conflict (LIC), a central doctrine of the Reagan Administration'.[9] This kind of military doctrine, Chomsky observes, is 'little more than a euphemism for state-directed international terrorism.' States can carry out acts of terrorism, and they can even adopt terrorism formally as a working method.

The word 'terrorism' will be used in this book in its dictionary sense of 'the use or threatened use of force for political or religious purposes'. It will be applied to the actions of individuals and, if appropriate, to the actions of governments also.

On the subject of terminology, I should also make clear that in what follows I have referred to people and places according to the names that they have adopted, or had conferred on them by legitimate authorities. So Germaine Lindsay (also referred to as Jermaine Lindsay or even Lindsay Germaine) is referred to by the name he chose for himself on converting to Islam: 'Abdullah Shaheed Jamal'. The two holy cities of Islam, usually transliterated as 'Mecca' and 'Medina', are here 'Makka' and 'Madina'. The holy book usually referred to in English as the *Koran* is rendered here as the *Qur'an* (though the pronounciation is of course the same, with the stress on the second syllable).

While it is of no relevance to the discussion of these issues, it may perhaps be appropriate to remove a potential distraction from the argument by clarifying my own religious background. Raised as a 'cultural Hindu'—participating in ceremonies without belief or, often, understanding—I have never been a believer in any religious tradition. The analysis that follows is intended to be even-handed and respectful to all the traditions under scrutiny.

Reading The *Qur'an*

It is said that many non-Muslims are turning to the *Qur'an* for some kind of explanation of the London bombings. This is rather like trying to understand the bombing of Hiroshima by reading a physics textbook. The *Qur'an*, like any scripture, can be interpreted in many different ways, for different purposes, as we shall see. Similarly, the equations of atomic physics can be used for destruction, for cosmic insights into the universe, for developing practical tools useful in daily life, or simply as a set of ideas of great beauty.

A Narrow Focus

It may be useful to state clearly that the intention of this book is quite narrow. It does not attempt to deal with the entire phenomenon of suicide terrorism, or religious fundamentalism, or the al-Qaeda network, or Islam.

The aim here is to provide a partial response to the challenge posed by Kirsty Morrison: 'What is important is why it happened and how it can be prevented from happening again.'[10] We owe it to those who lost their lives on 7 July, to those whose lives were irrevocably altered on that day, and to those who will be affected by the next such atrocity, to understand the past, and to be able to deal with the future. We can reduce the likelihood of more such tragedies, and perhaps prevent them altogether, if only we are prepared to cast aside official lies, try to understand the roots of al-Qaeda, and take the appropriate action.

The narrow focus of this book means that a great deal of important context has been set aside. Part of that context is of course the experience of Iraq itself since March 2003, which is an implicit presence throughout this book.

Robert Fisk, the veteran Middle East journalist, entitled one of his dispatches from Baghdad: 'How easily we have come to take the bombs and the deaths in Iraq for granted'. While in no way wishing to detract from the suffering of the London bombings, Fisk, one of the bravest Western reporters in Iraq, observed with an understandable exaggeration: 'The July 7 bombings would be a comparatively quiet day in Baghdad.'[11] The weekend following 7/7, nineteen suicide bombers struck in Iraq, killing 150 people. In one incident, a suicide bomber detonated a fuel truck, killing 98 people. In the month of July 2005, the Iraq Body Count database of media reports lists 26 suicide bombings—the ones that were reported—with a minimum reported death toll of 321.[12]

As is well-known, a survey-based study of the death toll in Iraq due to the invasion and occupation was published in the *Lancet* medical journal in September 2004. This report, which estimated that 98,000 Iraqis had died from direct military deaths and indirect lethal effects, has been confirmed in essence by a subsequent larger study published by the United Nations Development Programme.[13]

The tragedy of Iraq is an important part of the story of 7/7; it is the backdrop in many ways to our discussion, but it is not the focus of what follows.

1

Near Consensus

The Public Makes The Connection

The National Near Consensus

One of the extraordinary features of the debate around the 7 July bombings in London, is that there is almost a national consensus linking the war in Iraq to the atrocities, and at the same time a fierce and unyielding denial from the government on this point. This becomes all the more extraordinary when we learn that, despite the government's outward denial of any link between the bombings and the war, precisely this connection has long been acknowledged at the heart of government.

The vast majority of people in Britain have a decided view on this question. We know this because of three polls carried out for the *Guardian*, the *Daily Mirror* and the Greater London Authority. Just over a week after the explosions, the polling agency ICM canvassed over 1000 British residents for the liberal-left national newspaper, the *Guardian*. Mr Blair's decision to invade Iraq was felt by two-thirds (64 per cent) of British citizens to be one of the causes of the 7/7 attacks.[1] The *Guardian* reported that, 'Only 28% of voters agree with the government that Iraq and the London bombings are not connected.'

The next national poll in Britain was conducted for the *Daily Mirror* between 22 and 24 July 2005. Asked, 'Do you believe Britain's role in the Iraq War was the main cause of the bombings in London?', 23 per cent believed that the war was 'the main cause' of the bombings; 62 per cent believed that it 'contributed, but was not the main cause'. Only 12 per cent thought that it was 'NOT a significant cause'.[2] A total of 85 per cent thought that the war in Iraq was one of the causes of the bombings. Interestingly, a *Financial Times* survey of 64 leading businesses conducted weeks before the July attacks found that '83 per cent of respondents felt the war with Iraq had increased the terrorist threat.'[3]

A poll of Londoners was carried out for the Greater London Authority (GLA) in September. Asked 'To what extent, if at all, do you think that Britain's involvement in the Iraq war contributed towards the terrorist attacks in London?' only 8 per cent said, 'Not at all'. 74 per cent responded, 'A great deal' or 'A fair amount'.[4] An ICM poll in October found 73 per cent of those questioned believed the Iraq war had increased the likelihood of terrorist attacks in the UK. Only 2 per cent said that it made such attacks less likely.[5]

Putting all the national results together, it seems that, roughly speaking, just over one in five British people felt that the war in Iraq was in no way a cause of the London bombings, while around three-quarters of the population thought that it was one of the causes of the attacks.

Table 1. 'To what extent, if at all, do you think each of the following is responsible for the London bombings?' 'Tony Blair, for his decision to invade Iraq' (ICM / Guardian, 15-17 July 2005)	
A lot	33%
A little	31%
Not at all	28%
Don't know	8%

Table 2. 'Do you believe Britain's role in the Iraq War was the main cause of the bombings in London?' (YouGov / Mirror / GMTV, 22-24 July 2005)	
It was the main cause	23%
It contributed, but was not the main cause	62%
It was NOT a significant cause	12%
Don't know	3%

Conservative Concerns

Former Tory Chancellor Ken Clarke launched his bid for the leadership of the Conservative party by saying: 'If the Prime Minister really believes it, he must be the only person left who thinks that the recent bombs in London had no connection at all with his policy in Iraq.'[6] There were similarly scathing remarks from other senior Tories. Stephen Dorrell, the former Conservative Health Secretary, asked whether the war in Iraq had made Britain more vulnerable to terrorism, observed, 'Of course that is true. Who do they think they are kidding?'[7] Norman Lamont, the former Conservative Chancellor of the Exchequer, commented that Ken Clarke had given 'a heavyweight speech': 'Iraq has been this country's biggest foreign policy disaster since Suez, *has made Britain and the world a more dangerous place*, and yet has hardly been criticised at all by the Conservative Party.'[8]

So, the political spectrum of those making the connection ran from former Conservative Cabinet Ministers all the way to George Galloway MP of the newly-

	National polls				London poll
	Guardian	*Mirror*	*Newsnight*	National Average	GLA
Major cause	33%	23%	-	28%	39%
A minor cause	31%	62%	-	47%	33%
Total making a link	64%	85%	73%	74%	72%
Not a cause	28%	12%	24%	21%	8%

Table 3. 'Was the war in Iraq a major cause of the London bombings?' (Comparison of polls with varying questions, national and local.)

Sources: ICM/*Guardian*, 1005 adults by phone, 15-17 July 2005 <http://tinyurl.com/8ndrm>; YouGov/*Daily Mirror*, 1600 adults online, 22-24 July 2005 <http://tinyurl.com/76yc3>; ICM/*Newsnight*, 1024 adults by phone, October 2005 <http://tinyurl.com/9xfpc>; MORI/GLA, 1002 adults by phone, 22-26 September 2005 <http://tinyurl.com/8ykgg>.

formed anti-war 'Respect Party'. Former Conservative MP Matthew Parris observed that: 'You will be very far from being thrown out of a [right-wing] Derbyshire pub for suggesting that "Tony Blair asked for this".' In the pub, 'One elderly man, in other ways about as ideologically distant from Mr Galloway as it is possible to get, put it like this: "We should never have got mixed up in this business. That George Galloway was right. Who is he, anyway? Do you know anything about him?" '[9]

Blair's Evasions

The first reflex of the British government, on the other hand, was to deny any possible connection between the bombings and the war in Iraq. When George Galloway spoke out on 8 July he was simply ignored.[10] When a more tentative speech was made by the then Liberal Democrat leader Charles Kennedy four days later, however, Downing Street was forced to respond. The Prime Minister's Official Spokesperson said: 'It was not right in any way to suggest that this kind of terrorism was spawned by the Iraq war. It was something that was active before then.'[11] Tony Blair did not actually make the argument that because al-Qaeda-type terrorism had existed before the Iraq war, the war had no connection to the London bombings.[12] He was too wily for that. Blair did his best to *imply* such an argument without ever actually stating it.

Intimidating Journalists

At a press conference with President Hamid Karzai of Afghanistan on 19 July, the Prime Minister successfully intimidated journalists. He made inquiring into the possible link between Iraq and the bombings sound like a justification for the atrocities: 'Terrorists' will 'use Iraq as an excuse, they will use Afghanistan … They will always have their reasons for acting, but we have got to be really careful of almost giving in to the sort of perverted and twisted logic with which they argue.' Blair repeatedly implied that those who try to understand the causes of the violence end up justifying that violence. There was 'a kind of insidious way… that this is looked at where people say yes we entirely abhor the methods of these terrorists, but nonetheless we sort of understand what they are saying about American foreign policy, or Iraq, or Afghanistan or Palestine.' He warned of where 'that argument lead[s] you': 'what you have got to be careful of is getting into their perverted logic'. '[I]f you are not careful, where it leads you is, not obviously justifying the bombings, I am not suggesting anyone says that, but you end up in a sense compromising with the ideas.' '[M]aybe this is not something people clearly want to hear—but there is still a tendency I think to compromise too much with their argument.' 'Sometimes there is too much in this of people going along with their argument, even though they say their methods are terrible and it is absolutely appalling to kill innocent people, you can get on a slippery slope very, very quickly with this argument.'[13]

At a second press conference, a week later, these tactics brought a protest from a journalist, who said: 'I noticed at the beginning that the people who were asking about the issue of Iraq [were] made to feel, and I feel that way, as if they were justifying what the terrorist has done.'[14] This brought an immediate denial from the Prime Minister, but the words he used speak for themselves:

> Whatever excuse or justification these people use I do not believe we should give one inch to them... we shouldn't compromise with it [what they say]. I am not saying anyone says any of these things [to] justify it, but we shouldn't even allow them the vestige of an excuse for what they do....

If you try to understand what might have caused the London bombings, and this leads you to examine the role of British foreign policy, you are 'compromising' with the bombers, and 'allowing them an excuse for what they do'. 'Excuses' (and therefore explanations) are the same as 'justifications'. Blair continued:

> You have said well cannot you understand how these people justify a sense of grievance by reference to what is happening in Iraq. And my answer to you is no. What is happening in Iraq is that ordinary, decent Iraqis are being butchered by these people with the same terrorist ideology that is killing people in different parts of the world.

This is a particularly bold stroke. Are there people in Britain who feel a sense of grievance over the death toll in Iraq caused or exacerbated by the US-UK occupation? No, because *all that is happening in Iraq,* Blair implies, is that al-Qaeda is butchering Iraqi civilians.[15] No civilians are being killed—even by accident—by US or British forces. The Prime Minister continued:

> [W]hen... people talk about this as if we are doing this in Iraq, they are doing this here. There is more or less an equivalent. Until we get rid of this frankly complete nonsense in trying to build some equivalence between what we are doing helping Iraqis and Afghans get their democracy and these people going in deliberately killing wholly innocent people for the sake of it, until we

eliminate that we are not going to confront this ideology in the way it needs to be confronted and my point to you is this, it is time we stopped saying OK we abhor their methods, but we kind of see something in their ideas or maybe they have got a sliver of excuse or justification. They have got no justification for it.[16]

Tracing any possible connections between British foreign policy and the rising risk of terrorism in Britain is 'frankly complete nonsense' which undermines the fight against al-Qaeda-type terrorism. According to the Prime Minister, 'it is time we stopped' trying to understand what lies behind these atrocities.

As we shall see shortly, the British government, in secret documents leaked to the press, is itself guilty of what the Prime Minister called, 'getting into the terrorists' perverted logic', and 'in a sense compromising with their ideas'.

Blair Gives Ground

Under overwhelming pressure, Tony Blair was unable to maintain his position. On 26 July, he finally gave ground. He opened: 'I read occasionally that I am supposed to have said [7/7] is nothing to do with Iraq, in inverted commas. Actually I haven't said that. If you go back and look at the comments I have made over the past couple of weeks.'[17] This is accurate, and dishonest. The Prime Minister had not specifically denied that there was a connection between the bombings and the war, in those words, but he had strongly given this impression.

In his speech to the Labour Party Conference on 16 July, Blair said: 'This ideology and the violence that is inherent in it did not start a few years ago in response to a particular policy. Over the past 12 years, Al-Qaeda and its associates have attacked 26 countries, killed thousands of people, many of them Muslims.'[18] He performed this (accurate but misleading) manoeuvre time and again over the next week, not explicitly denying a connection between the war in Iraq and the bombings, but strongly implying that there was no such connection. But on 26 July the Prime Minister was forced into a retreat. He said: 'I am not saying that any of these things don't affect their warped reasoning and warped logic as to what they do, or that they don't use these things to try and recruit people.'[19] Untangling the double negatives, Blair was finally conceding that the war in Iraq might have affected the thinking of members of al-Qaeda, and that it might have been useful to them as they recruited suicide bombers. (A few minutes later, pressed by a journalist who said to the Prime Minister, 'you do appear to be insulting the intelligence of the British people', Blair conceded: 'I can see how these people use these issues to recruit people.'[20] It was no longer merely about 'trying' to recruit suicide bombers; the conflict in Iraq was actually *being used* by al-Qaeda to recruit people.)

On the one hand, Blair was now saying that there was a connection between the war and the risk of terrorism in Britain in that it provided a means of recruiting bombers. On the other hand, he prohibited anyone from drawing the logical conclusion that the war had increased the risk of terrorism in Britain. At the 26 July press conference, the Prime Minister was asked, 'simply as a fact, rightly or wrongly, do you accept the possibility that Britain's involvement in Iraq has increased the danger of terrorism in this country?' Blair refused to answer. His questioner returned: 'Would you accept the possibility?' The Prime Minister answered: 'I know what you are trying to do.' That was his entire answer.

In this same (very long) 26 July press conference, Tony Blair said that terrorism would only be defeated, '[w]hen we actually have people going into the communities here in this country and elsewhere and saying I am sorry, we are not having any of this nonsense about it is to do with what the British are doing in Iraq or Afghanistan, or support for Israel, or support for America, or any of the rest of it.'[21]

Legitimate And Illegitimate Causes

Inconsistently, again at this same press conference, the Prime Minister acknowledged that 'there are obviously certain things that we have to do as governments and an international community to try and take away legitimate causes upon which these people [prey].' The prime case was Israel and Palestine. Blair said he did not accept that 'they'—the leaders of al-Qaeda—'really care about these causes'. However, there was still a 'need to make progress on the Israeli-Palestinian issue, it is an important part.' Why? Because '[t]here is a legitimate concern over that'. It 'doesn't justify suicide bombing or terrorism', but 'there is a legitimate concern about that and you have to deal with it.'[22]

Those who raise the Arab-Israeli conflict as a possible motivation for al-Qaeda terrorism are raising a 'legitimate concern'. Those who raise the Iraq war as a possible motivation for al-Qaeda terrorism are raising an 'illegitimate concern'. Raising this particular grievance, according to the Prime Minister, assists the terrorists in reinforcing their justification for violence. Raising the plight of the Palestinians, on the other hand, does not assist the terrorists. The difference? In the case of Palestine, there is no controversial policy to which the

Prime Minister has committed himself, and which would wound him politically to reverse. In the case of Iraq, the Prime Minister's political life and historical reputation is tied to the validity of Britain's participation in the invasion and occupation.

To suggest that the ongoing war in Iraq—quite apart from being illegal and illegitimate and disastrous for the people of Iraq themselves—also substantially increases the risk of terrorism in Britain itself, was to strike a heavy political blow at an increasingly unpopular policy pursued by an increasingly unpopular leader. That is why Tony Blair had to resort to smearing anyone who inquired into this topic as a terrorist sympathiser.

The Prime Minister's retreat had been foreshadowed by his Foreign Secretary, Jack Straw. On 20 July, the Foreign Secretary had said unequivocally: 'It may be a comfortable thought by some people to think all this follows the military action in Iraq. It does not.' However, on 23 July, Straw told the BBC: 'It's impossible to say for certain' whether the atrocities were connected to the Iraq war.[23] The *Telegraph* observed that: 'sources said ministers had become aware that the line needed to be softened because most members of the public did not accept that nothing had changed'. Straw's comments were said to come after a *Guardian*/ICM poll found that 'two-thirds of Britons believed there was a link between the decision to support the war in Iraq and the London bombings.'[24]

In other words, the government was being forced by the weight of public disbelief to begin to concede that there might possibly be some form of connection between the war and the bombings.

2

Tony Blair Lied

The Secret Documents That Exposed
The Prime Minister's Deceit

The JIC Warning

Five weeks before the invasion of Iraq, the highest body in British intelligence warned the Prime Minister that invading Iraq would 'heighten' the risk of terrorism in Britain:

126. In their assessment *International Terrorism: War with Iraq*, dated 10 February 2003, the JIC [Joint Intelligence Committee]... assessed that al-Qaida and associated groups continued to represent by far the greatest terrorist threat to Western interests, and that threat would be heightened by military action against Iraq.

127. The JIC assessed that any collapse of the Iraqi regime would increase the risk of chemical and biological warfare technology or agents finding their way into the hands of terrorists, not necessarily al-Qaida.

This is taken from a post-invasion report by the British government's own 'Intelligence and Security Committee'.[1] According to British intelligence, invading Iraq would 'heighten' the risk of terrorism against the West by al-Qaeda (and would also 'increase' the risk that such terrorism might be carried out with chemical or biological weapons).[2]

The Prime Minister presented a rather different picture to the House of Commons on 18 March 2003 when he persuaded a majority of his own Labour backbenchers to vote for war. He argued passionately that although the association between terrorism and weapons of mass destruction (WMD) was 'loose' at that moment, it was 'hardening'. There was a real and present danger of terrorist groups gaining possession of such weapons.[3] We had to invade Iraq.

This might have been a good time to let the rest of us know that invading Iraq would actually 'harden' the association between 'terrorism' and WMD, according to British intelligence. This might have been a good time to let us know that invading Iraq would 'heighten' the risk of terrorism, according to Britain's top spies. Instead Tony Blair concealed the intelligence and advice he had received. He dissembled. He lied.

This same assessment of the danger was delivered by the anti-war movement in Britain and abroad, and by a wide range of figures including retired military personnel.[4] One dramatic intervention came from Ken Clarke, the former Conservative Chancellor of the Exchequer, who warned in a debate on 26 February 2003 that the war would simply recruit more terrorists:

> *Next time a large bomb goes off in a western city*, how far did this policy [the invasion of Iraq] contribute to it?[5]

Despite the fact that Mr Clarke made a bid for the leadership of the Conservative Party soon after 7/7, and made opposition to the war in Iraq a central plank of his campaign, this passage was not, to my knowledge, quoted anywhere in the British mainstream media. More importantly, there were only the most muted mentions[6] of the JIC warning, despite the fact that it became public knowledge in September 2003, and was remarkably pertinent to the 7/7 tragedy.

'Young Muslims And Extremism'

The JIC warning is not the only remarkable case of media amnesia. After the London bombings a series of secret government documents were released into the public domain, which sank almost without a trace. These documents were part of a government project code-named 'Operation Contest', initiated in the aftermath of the Madrid bombings. Operation Contest had as its 'first plank' the prevention of terrorism arising from the British Muslim community.

On 18 May 2004 the head of the Foreign Office, Michael Jay, wrote that while other colleagues had 'flagged up some of the potential underlying causes of extremism that can affect the Muslim community, such as discrimination, disadvantage and exclusion', one 'recurring theme' was 'the issue of British foreign policy', especially in the context of 'the Middle East Peace Process and Iraq.' According to Jay, both ministers and officials felt that 'the issue of British foreign policy and the perception of its negative effect on Muslims globally plays a significant role in creating a feeling of anger and impotence among especially the younger generation of British Muslims.' Jay wrote that foreign policy 'seems to be a key driver behind recruitment by extremist organisations (e.g. recruitment drives by groups such as Hizb-ut-Tahrir and al Muhajiroon).'[7] (Foreign Secretary Jack Straw later acknowledged that he had authorised this letter.[8])

As part of Operation Contest, the Foreign Office drew up a joint report with the Home Office entitled, 'Young Muslims and Extremism'. 'Extremism' was defined quite broadly to mean not only support for terrorist attacks against British or western targets, or for British Muslims fighting against British and allied forces abroad, but also 'arguing that it is not possible to be Muslim and British, calling on Muslims to reject engagement with British society and politics, and advocating the creation of an Islamic state in Britain.'[9]

What causes 'extremism'? The report summary listed three factors, the first of which was 'Anger', which revolves around 'a perception of "double standards" in British foreign policy', where 'democracy is preached but oppression of the "Ummah" (the one nation of believers) is practised or tolerated e.g. in Palestine, Iraq, Afghanistan, Kashmir, Chechnya'. This is accompanied by a 'sense of helplessness' over the situation of Muslims, and a 'lack of any real opportunities to vent frustration'.[10] In the main body of the report, a number of different causes are listed. Once again, foreign policy is the first factor listed:

Foreign policy issues

It seems that a particularly strong cause of disillusionment amongst Muslims including young Muslims is a perceived 'double standard' in the foreign policy of western governments (and often those of Muslim governments), in particular Britain and the US...

Perceived Western bias in Israel's favour over the Israel/Palestinian conflict is a key long term grievance of the international Muslim community which probably influences British Muslims.

This perception seems to have become more acute post 9/11. The perception is that *passive 'oppression'*, as demonstrated in British foreign policy, eg non-action on Kashmir and Chechnya, has given way to *'active oppression'*—the war on terror, and in Iraq and Afghanistan are all seen by a section of British Muslims as having been acts against Islam.[11]

Were the Foreign Office and Home Office 'getting into the perverted logic' of the bombers? Did they 'end up in a sense compromising with the ideas' of al-Qaeda? Were these top civil servants allowing the bombers 'the vestige of an excuse for what they do'?[12] Of course not. They were simply presenting the best analysis they could assemble of the causes of the growing support for terrorism amongst young British Muslims. For the Prime Minister to attack journalists for daring to engage in exactly this same process was deceitful and shameful.

The Prime Minister's attempt to avoid responsibility by saying 'we have always been a target for al-Qaeda' is contradicted by the government's own internal analysis that Muslim perceptions of British bias 'seem to have become *more* acute *post 9/11*'. Britain had been seen as uncaring towards Muslims around the world, but, with the invasions of Afghanistan and Iraq, and British support for the wider US 'war on terror', malign neglect was seen to have hardened into 'active oppression' of Muslims. Britain's aggressive foreign policy increased the risk of terrorism, just as the Joint Intelligence Committee had warned.

Media Self-Censorship

The draft 'Young Muslims and Extremism' report was published on the *Sunday Times* website on 10 July, just three days after the first London bombings, and reported in the *Sunday Times* in a front page story on that day.[13] The report was an authoritative account from the heart of government addressing the burning question of the day—how young men born and bred in Britain could come to carry out such an atrocity.[14] Its release was timely (in fact, the *Sunday Times* seems to have had the documents for over a year[15]), and its impact should have been immense, particularly as it gave the lie to the government's claim that the war in Iraq had not increased the risk of terrorism in the UK.

The British media responded with silence.

Ten days later, when a British intelligence report re-confirming this analysis was leaked to the press, the *Guardian* took the opportunity to re-publish part of the 'Young Muslims and Extremism' report.[16] A few weeks later, on 8 August, the *Guardian* ran another story mentioning the report, but without mentioning its key findings regarding the role of British foreign policy.[17] Eleven days later, the *Guardian* published the second serious article on the report in the mainstream British print media.[18] Otherwise there was a resounding silence.

On 28 August, the *Observer* published another part of the high-level corre-spondence—Peter Jay's 18 May 2004 letter, discussed above—without referring to the previous revelations or the larger Operation Contest context. Once again, the story faded away (though after receiving a few desultory notices[19]) without leaving a trace on the larger debate.

The 'Young Muslims and Extremism' report has effectively been erased from history. The British media essentially shut out this report and associated revelations, which had the potential to electrify the entire debate about the July bombings, and to expose conclusively the depths of Tony Blair's deceit over these questions. If this was incompetence, why was this incompetence so systematic? Why did it fail to pick up the *Sunday Times* story published on 10 July (apart from a few low-key mentions in the *Guardian*), *and* the *Observer* story on 28 August? This failure of the media becomes even more puzzling when we consider that other secret reports were also leaked to the media during this period, providing further opportunities—systematically ignored—to take up the story.

MI5 Realism In Public

In mid-June 2005, three weeks before the first attacks, the 'Joint Terrorism Analysis Centre' (JTAC) reported to the British government that, 'Events in Iraq are continuing to act as motivation and a focus of a range of terrorist-related activity in the UK'. (JTAC is based in the MI5 building, but is a separate organization composed of representatives from eleven government departments and agencies.[20]) This report was leaked to the *New York Times* by another intelligence agency, and published on 19 July.[21]

Nine days after the *New York Times* story broke, the London *Times* noticed another part of the British intelligence system saying much the same thing—in public.[22] When we turn to the MI5 website (MI5 is Britain's domestic intelligence agency), we find these sentences: 'Both British and foreign nationals linked to or sympathetic with Al Qaida are known to be present within the UK... Though they have a range of aspirations and "causes", Iraq is a dominant issue for a range of extremist groups and individuals in the UK and Europe.'[23]

These intelligence findings gave perfect opportunities for the mainstream media to re-consider the Joint Intelligence Committee warning to the Prime Minister in February 2003, look seriously at the 'Young Muslims and Extremism' report, and review properly the high-level correspondence in Whitehall about all these matters in early 2004. There were scattered reports, but the overall response of the media to these revelations was effectively to suppress these pertinent facts. They were effectively erased from the record—not by any command from the government or from newspaper owners, but by the self-censorship of journalists and editors.

Noam Chomsky and Edward Herman have written the classic analysis of this phenomenon:

> That the media provide some information about an issue... proves absolutely nothing about the adequacy or accuracy of media coverage. The media do in fact suppress a great deal of information, but even more important is the way they present a particular fact—its placement, tone, and frequency of repetition—and the framework of analysis in which it is placed.
>
> [T]he enormous amount of material that is produced in the media and books makes it possible for a really assiduous and committed researcher to gain a fair picture of the real world by cutting through the mass of misrepresentation and fraud to the nuggets hidden within.
>
> That a careful reader, looking for a fact can sometimes find it, with diligence and a skeptical eye, tells us nothing about whether that fact received the attention and context it deserved, whether it was intelligible to most readers, or whether it was effectively distorted or suppressed.[24]

Careful reading is needed to overcome what Chomsky and Herman have called 'brainwashing under freedom'.

British Intelligence Realism

Turning from the media representation of these events, we can now contrast the Prime Minister's public position with the internal analysis of the British intelligence system not in early 2004, but merely weeks before the July attacks. The *Financial Times* reported the day after the Joint Terrorism Analysis Centre assessment was published that: 'Tony Blair was forced on to the defensive over the London bomb attacks for the first time on Tuesday after a leaked British intelligence report bolstered claims that the Iraq war had increased the terrorist threat.'[25] Blair attempted to brush aside this authoritative intelligence assessment, but the damage was done, contributing to the U-turn later that week by Jack Straw, and then the Prime Minister's own concessions at the 26 July press conference we have discussed at such length. At that press conference, Blair said Iraq was an 'excuse', that was used by 'these people' to recruit.[26] On the other hand, British intelligence analysts actually studying 'these people', said that Iraq and foreign policy issues act as a 'motivation' (not an 'excuse') and 'a focus' (not a tool to 'use') for 'a range of terrorist-related activity in the UK'.

We have now cleared the way to consider the 7/7 bomb plot itself.

3

Disbelief

Four 'Nice' Men

The Hussain Family

As soon as they heard the news, like millions of other parents, they began phoning. Mahmood and Maniza Hussain had last seen their son Hasib the day before, when he'd said he was heading to London with 'some mates'. Now there was no reply on his mobile phone. After a fruitless, frightening day, the Hussain family watched the 10pm news for the latest on the dreadful events in London.

It was Thursday, 7 July 2005, and that morning bombs had exploded in central London, killing dozens of people. Three explosions had taken place in trains underground, making it difficult and hazardous to recover the bodies, and the exact death toll was not known. A fourth bomb had gone off on the top deck of a No. 30 bus in Tavistock Square, not far from Euston train station. Foreign Secretary Jack Straw said it had all 'the hallmarks of an al-Qaeda-related attack'.[1]

After the news, a casualty bureau phone number was shown. Mrs Hussain picked up the phone, and reported her 18-year-old son missing. At the Metropolitan Police headquarters in Hendon, London, a detailed description was taken. Hasib was 6ft 2ins tall, with a heavy build, wearing a distinctive blue jacket and jeans. Three days later, when a police officer visited the family at their home in Beeston, Leeds, to collect a photograph of Hasib, Mrs Hussain also suggested the names of two friends who might have been accompanying her son.[2]

Mrs Hussain's call was one of thousands received by the police. It turned out to be a key event accelerating the investigation. Much later, Hasib's father commented: 'I like to think that we may have helped in some way. Before we called, the police had no idea Hasib was there.'[3] By the time he made this bittersweet observation, Mr Hussain had learned what had happened to his son. Hasib Mir Hussain had indeed lost his life in the London bombings. But he was not a victim.

Uncovering Identities

At first, it was unclear whether these were suicide attacks. The bombs in Madrid on 11 March 2004 had been detonated by mobile phone. But there was one body on the No. 30 bus that had suffered massive damage, and been decapitated by the explosion. Palestinian suicide bombers have suffered similar injuries.[4] The clothing and general description of this body fitted the details given by Mrs Hussain. There were also eyewitness reports of a young man of 'Mediterranean' appearance rummaging in his rucksack before the explosion.[5]

Meanwhile, the Hussain family were racking their brains. Brother Imran went through Hasib's computer and his mobile phone memory. He phoned a 'Jamal'. There was no answer. Imran followed clues from the computer to a house in the Hyde Park area of Leeds. He knocked on the door, but was unable to enter. Two days after the bombing, Imran and some of his cousins travelled to London to ask at hospitals and police stations for Hasib. They didn't find him.[6]

One strand of the police investigation was the monumental task of scanning more than 5000 tapes of CCTV footage taken around the bomb sites on 7 July. Astonishingly, within four days, police officers discovered the footage they were seeking, taken from a camera high above the station forecourt at King's Cross railway station at 8.20am. Amongst the commuters and tourists, just off-centre, were four young Asian men with rucksacks on their backs. They fitted the 'profile'.[7] One of these men matched Hasib Hussain's description. Two of the others, also bearing large rucksacks were soon identified: 22-year-old Shehzad Tanweer, and 30-year-old Mohammad Sidique Khan, both from Leeds.

The four men spoke together in a relaxed fashion for several minutes. Without making any elaborate farewells, the group divided, and each man entered the Underground.[8] One person who saw the CCTV images said later, 'It was like the infantry going to war, or like they were going on a hiking holiday.'[9]

Another strand of investigation had been screening the identities of those who had lost their lives. None of the names appeared on 'watch lists' of people connected with terror networks. Investigators were also looking for Muslims, searching for Arabic or Pakistani names.[10] (Pakistanis make up the bulk of the British Muslim population.) At the Edgware Road bombsite, they found documents belonging to Mohammad Sidique Khan. There were no other Arabic or

Pakistani names there. At the Aldgate bombsite, they found documents belonging to Shehzad Tanweer. It was soon established that both men were from the same area of Leeds, and they were connected to Hasib Hussain. Mrs Hussain had given their names as possible companions of her son in London. 'We had three Muslim guys from Yorkshire who were together at King's Cross and then killed in separate bomb explosions,' an anti-terrorist officer said. 'There was no way that could be just a coincidence.'[11]

The fourth man on the video was 19-year-old Germaine Lindsay, known as Abdullah Shaheed Jamal (the name we will use from this point), from Aylesbury in Buckinghamshire. 'Jamal' had failed to answer Imran Hussain's call on 7/7.

The four bombers' movements were then tracked backwards. They had caught a Thameslink train from Luton at 7.48am. The four had been captured on CCTV cameras in Luton. In the multi-storey car park at Luton station, police found two abandoned cars. One had been rented by Shehzad Tanweer from a firm in Leeds. The police knew of the hired car already because a few days after the bombings an agent from a hire company turned up at Tanweer's home address to try to reclaim it—just as the house was being raided by police.[12] The other car had been rented by Abdullah Jamal—he had left a pay and display ticket on the windscreen. The DNA left on that scrap of paper by Jamal would later be used to identify his remains.[13] Police used high-pressure hoses to wash explosives out of the cars.[14] Later, photographs and X-rays of some of the devices found in the cars were broadcast on US television. One was a nail bomb.[15]

The bombers were then tracked back to Leeds itself, to a flat in the Hyde Park area of Leeds—the same flat Imran Hussain had been unable to enter. Forensic tests established that all four bombers had visited this flat. Neighbours said the men had come and gone from the flat at all hours of the day and night. Inside, the police discovered, among other things, a bathtub full of explosives.[16]

Much later, it was established that the bombs had been hand-detonated. On the No. 30 bus, the tip of the small plastic detonator lodged in the leg of survivor Louise Barry. She said later: 'At first, experts thought it was a toggle off a coat, then they realised it was the detonator. Police told me it was the best forensic evidence they had from the scene.'[17]

Disbelief

The conclusion was inescapable. Hasib Hussain, Mohammad Sidique Khan, Shehzad Tanweer and Abdullah Jamal—four Muslims raised in Britain, three of them born in Britain—had carried out the London bombings.

The police released the names of the three Leeds bombers on 12 July, just five days after the bombings.

The naming was greeted by shock and disbelief by those who knew the men. Malek Abdul Shabaz, 24, who had played soccer with the 22-year-old Tanweer, said, 'They are from our back garden, people you grew up with. They wouldn't hurt a fly, wouldn't say boo. What goes into people's heads to make them do something like that—killing themselves, killing innocent people, killing their own families?' Shabaz posed the central problem: 'We live here. This is our country. I don't understand it.'[18]

In Beeston, a local man named John told *The Times*, 'The thing that frightens me most is that this would have been the last place I'd have looked for a bomber. I don't know much about these lads but by all accounts they were OK, nice people.'[19]

A neighbour of Tanweer's expressed his disbelief in forceful terms. The 37-year-old taxi driver, Yorkshire-born and non-Asian, spoke on condition of anonymity of his five years living next door to Shehzad Tanweer and his family. He had never imagined the 'polite, educated boy' who lived next door could be one of the bombers: 'It is utterly devastating. I am totally gobsmacked, I just can't believe it. I can't put into words how I feel.' He added that Tanweer 'seemed a nice enough lad, just nice and normal. He was always well spoken. He seemed like a normal teenager, he didn't have a beard, he wore sports tops, tracksuit bottoms and trainers—like anybody else, really... He just seemed like a well-educated, polite, young man.' The Yorkshireman added: 'His father, Mumtaz, is a lovely bloke, a really nice fella. He just seems like a family man who thinks a lot about his family and runs his business... I can't really describe how I feel. I would never have thought in a million years he was anything at all to do with this. They are such a nice, decent family, always pleasant and well-spoken. Especially in the Asian community, their traditions are a lot to do with the family and respect, and they are a very well-respected family within their community.'

One of the most extraordinary aspects of the 7/7 story is the general consensus that all four bombers were 'nice people'. Rebecca Whitaker, who trained with Aldgate bomber Shehzad Tanweer in athletics at South Leeds Stadium, said: 'He was a "straight A" student who had everything going for him. It just makes me feel anyone is capable of anything. Perhaps nice people are easily brainwashed.'[20]

The most respected and apparently the 'nicest' of the four men was Mohammad Sidique Khan.

4

Mohammad Sidique Khan

The Beloved Teaching Assistant

Mohammad Sidique Khan

Until only months before 7/7, Mohammad Sidique Khan, 30, had been a teaching assistant at Hillside Primary School in the Beeston area of Leeds—a 'learning mentor' for children with learning difficulties, and for children of immigrant families who had just arrived in Britain. The teaching staff are united in describing Khan as gently-spoken, endlessly patient, and immensely popular with children—who called him their buddy. He is known to have taught hundreds of children.[1] The head teacher at Hillside, Sarah Balfour, told reporters after the bombings, 'Sidique Khan was a member of staff at Hillside Primary School and he was employed here between March 2001 and December 2004 as a learning mentor. He was great with the children and they all loved him. He did so much for them, helping and supporting them and running extra clubs and activities. Sidique was a real asset to the school and always showed 100% commitment.'[2]

Parents at the school said Khan had been highly regarded by both children and parents. 'He was a good man, quiet,' said one parent, speaking outside the school. 'When I told my daughter, she said, "No, he can't do something like that". I had to go and buy the paper and show her.' Another parent, Sharon Stevens, said he had been a 'big supporter' of both pupils and parents: 'He was really understanding and he did work for the children and parents.' Even the right-wing *Daily Mail* could find only praise among parents: 'The children loved him and looked up to him,' said one mother. 'He showed a lot of enthusiasm in the classroom and knew how to get the best out of children. I could not believe it when I heard he was involved in this. He must have been living a double life.'

Tina Head, 33, a local parent, described him as a father figure. 'His baby was due three months before mine last year and we used to talk about that. He seemed a lovely person,' she said.[3] One child who was taught by Khan at Hillside said, 'He seemed a really kind man, he taught the really bad kids and everyone seemed to like him.'[4] 'I liked him. He was nice,' said another pupil, Billy Sandersen, 13. He and other former pupils said that though they were shocked to learn Khan was one of the bombers, they still liked him. 'Just a little bit, but not for what he's done—killing innocent people,' said Sandersen. 'I still like him,' said Sean Woodham, 13, another former pupil, 'because he always helped me with my homework.'[5]

One reason for Khan's popularity with parents was his 'breakfast club', taking children to school. Each weekday morning at 8am, Khan called at the home of local resident Deborah Quick to pick up her two daughters, Harley and Robyn, and take them to Hillside Primary. The *Wall Street Journal* reports, 'As word spread of his kindness, other parents in Beeston, a deprived and drug-blighted district of this northern English town, asked Mr. Khan to pick up their children, too. Unable to fit them all into his small, navy blue Vauxhall Corsa, Mr. Khan started walking them to school.' The purpose of the 'breakfast club' was to help the children of parents on state benefits to reach school in time for an 8.30 breakfast and 9am start. Conscientious and cheery, Khan was 'brilliant', Deborah Quick told journalists.

Part of the reason for accompanying the Quick children was that Khan was carefully observing their development for government social services. In a detailed report to social services in November 2003, Khan wrote, 'They are both chatty and will talk to me as well as other children on the way down to school. Harley has a stronger character and will look after Robyn's needs.' Khan continued to take the Quick children, then 6 and 4, to school until they moved away.[6]

During its last Ofsted inspection in 2002, Hillside Primary School's learning assistants were singled out for special praise in dealing with a transient pupil population from a socially deprived area. Mohammad Sidique Khan spoke about his work to the *Times Educational Supplement* at the time: 'A lot of [the pupils] have said this is the best school they have been to,' he said.[7]

As well as being a learning mentor who worked well with kids, Khan won respect as a social worker committed to ridding the streets of drugs. He took a part-time job with a local government agency working with troubled youth in Beeston in the late 1990s. Unemployment had soared to 40 per cent among men of Pakistani and Bangladeshi descent. During the summer holidays he ran workshops for children. Afzal Choudhry, a community worker who took part in the summer sessions, said Khan was 'always ready to get involved.' At that time, around 1997, Khan was not particularly religious. He sometimes got 'what we call the Friday feeling', and would go to mosque for Friday prayers, but 'he otherwise didn't pray much', said Choudhry.[8] It was Choudhry who invited Khan to work on a government-funded study of Beeston's substance abuse problems. Khan co-authored the resulting study on fighting drug use. In a note appended to the 2001 report, he wrote, 'I have tried to support and help local drug users in the past, but at best this has been haphazard. I feel that the knowledge and experience on drugs and community research that I've gained through the training and the field work has been invaluable.'[9] We will learn more of this.

Such was the regard for Khan that he was invited to the home of Hillside Primary's head teacher, Sarah Balfour, whose husband, Jon Trickett, is a Member of Parliament. In July 2004, one year before the bombs went off, Khan and some of his students were shown around the Houses of Parliament by Jon Trickett MP.[10]

The Good Neighbour

Towards the end of 2004, Khan prepared to move into a new house in Dewsbury, a town 10 miles southwest of Leeds. He rented the two-bedroom home from the local council and started to redecorate. 'I thought he was a really nice guy and thought "He'll be good for our neighborhood," ' said Imran Zaman, who lives two doors away.[11] Zaman told the *Daily Mail*, Khan was a 'quiet person': 'He kept himself to himself. He was a nice bloke, but who would have thought he would have done something like this? I never knew he had a religious background. I go to the local mosque and have never seen him there.'[12] Another neighbour said: 'He didn't seem to be an extremist. He was not one to talk about religion. He was generally a very nice bloke.'[13]

Reporting is very hazy as to Khan's final months. As part of the move, one newspaper suggested that Khan became a liaison officer in another local school.[14] Another paper claimed that before the bombings, 'Impeccably professional, Khan warned his employers that he would not be coming in to work on Thursday.'[15]

The Youth Worker

Local people interviewed after the bombings testified to Khan's popularity amongst the young people of Beeston. Mohammad Farouk, a community health worker at the *Hamara* youth centre, said, 'You know the children here—if they had a problem—they went to him [Khan]. That's why I can't get my head around it. I could never contemplate that he had those tendencies in him because it wasn't in his bones—it baffles me.'[16]

Nasir, a 22-year-old Bradford University student, who was a good friend of Shehzad Tanweer, one of the other bombers, told reporters that Khan had had a huge influence on many young men in the area: 'He was a father figure to lots of young kids round here, they looked up to him. He was a youth worker who used that centre and he used to play football with the young kids. Personally I didn't respect him as a father figure, but lots of kids did. It looks to me like Sidique was the older figure who was influencing them [Shehzad and Hasib].' Nasir added: 'I never knew that Sidique and Shehzad and Hasib knew each other well. But I have heard since they had been quite close through this centre and I was really shocked, to be honest. If someone can get Shehzad to do such a thing, to leave his little brother and his sisters behind, they must have really got inside his head. It's the guys who did this to him who are the real terrorists.'[17]

The Husband And Father

Not only was Khan a respected member of the staff at Hillside Primary School (until December 2004), and a well-known social worker with a new home, he was also a married man and a father. A former colleague told the *Wall Street Journal* that Khan met his wife, Hasina, a Muslim whose parents are of Indian descent (and who moved to Britain from South Africa), at Leeds Metropolitan University. 'The university says Mr. Khan's wife attended the college, but it has no record of Mr. Khan himself taking courses.'[18] Their daughter Maryam was born on 14 May 2004, fourteen months before her father killed himself and six other people on the London Underground.[19]

It was reported that at the time of the bombings, Hasina Khan was four months pregnant.[20]

The Times summarizes Khan's situation at the end of 2004: 'At 30, Khan was the oldest of the trio, and in many ways the oddest: no naïve and angry youth, but a professional, married man, with a steady job, a pregnant wife, a baby daughter, a new council house, a season ticket to the gym and a silver Honda Civic.'[21] Khurshid Drabu, an adviser provided to the Khan family by the Muslim Council of Britain, said, 'If Khan could be turned, it means anybody could be turned. That's what's terrifying.'[22]

But what was it that 'turned' Mohammad Sidique Khan?

Family Statement

'The Khan family would like to sincerely express their deepest and heart felt sympathies to all the innocent victims and their families and friends affected by this horrific and evil act. We are devastated that our son may have been brain-washed into carrying out such an atrocity, since we know him as a kind and caring member of our family.'

'We urge people with the tiniest piece of information to come forward in order to expose these terror networks which target and groom our sons to carry out such evils.'[23]

Edgware Road

Mohammad Sidique Khan exploded his rucksack bomb at 8.50am on the London Underground. He was in the second carriage of a Circle line train, which had just left Edgware Road station heading west for Paddington. His bomb went off on the floor of the carriage, close to the forward set of double doors.

Six people were killed by the blast. Their names were: Michael Brewster, Jonathan Downey, David Foulkes, Colin Morley, Jennifer Nicholson, and Laura Webb. One hundred and twenty people were injured by the explosion.

Michael Brewster

Michael Brewster, 52, was married to Sandra, a hairdresser, with whom he had a daughter Katie, 20, and a son Mark, 17. Mr Brewster was a council highways engineer, and a keen amateur footballer. Mr Brewster's funeral may have been the largest ever seen in Swanwick, Derbyshire.

Jonathan Downey

Jonathan Downey, 34, was also a council official, working in human resources for the London borough of Kensington & Chelsea. Mr Downey's family issued this statement: 'He was a kind, caring, considerate and supportive son, husband and friend. He will be sorely missed by his wife, family and many friends.'

David Foulkes

David Foulkes, 22, worked for the *Guardian* in the North-West, visiting local shops to promote the newspaper. Stephanie Reid, Mr Foulkes' girlfriend, said: 'He was my world. As soon as we met, we knew that was it. We made plans, and he was never shy about being affectionate and romantic.'

Colin Morley

Colin Morley, 52, worked with both charities and businesses in advertising and marketing. He was survived by his wife Ros, and their three sons. 25,000 words in tribute to Mr Morley were posted on the 'Be The Change' website after his death.

Jennifer Nicholson

Jennifer Nicholson, 24, also worked in advertising and marketing. Her passion in life, however was music. 'She was a talented, beautiful and vivacious young woman whose life was stretched out before her and we are not going to see that fulfilled,' said the Rt Rev Mike Hall, Bishop of Bristol.

Laura Webb

Laura Webb, 29, from north London, worked in advertising as a personal assistant. Her brother Robert, a Cardiff council public relations officer, spent a week in London searching for his sister. He said later: 'She was always there for us. She was fantastic, and I will always remember her smiling.'

5

Shehzad Tanweer

The Popular Cricketer

Shehzad Tanweer

Shehzad Tanweer, 22, was another unlikely suicide bomber. *The Times* remarked of his family, 'If ever there were model immigrants, they were the Tanweers.'[1] A close-knit family, originally from Pakistan, the Tanweers ran the local fish-and-chip shop in Beeston, as well as a butcher shop and a restaurant. Mohammed Mumtaz Tanweer came to Britain to study, became a police officer, then built up his businesses.[2] Other Beeston merchants said he was widely admired for being able to turn a profit, while providing services to customers who didn't have a lot of money to spend.[3] Mumtaz Tanweer gave legal and business advice freely to friends and neighbours, and helped fill out official forms. 'If you wanted to borrow anything, he would help you,' said Mohammed Ali, a Beeston shopkeeper.[4]

Shehzad Tanweer 'appeared to be the epitome of assimilation into British society', formerly an ambitious college student, who excelled at cricket and just about any other sport he tried.[5] Tanweer's uncle, Bashir Ahmad, said that his nephew had a passion for sport, especially cricket, and would spend hours discussing the game, but had never talked about politics so far as he knew. 'The news is just unbelievable. It's very hard for me to believe Shehzad did this because I can't believe he's capable of it.'[6] He added, 'Shehzad had never been in trouble before. So what drove him to do it? It can't be him. It must be something else behind him.'[7] Bashir Ahmad believed that his nephew was 'proud to be British'. He said if he had known Tanweer was involved in any fanatical groups or organisations he would have put a stop to it. Asked what may have driven his nephew to commit the atrocity, he said, 'There is no explanation I can come to.'[8]

Completely Integrated

The day before Tanweer put on his rucksack bomb, he went to the park and played sport, as he did most days. 'He was laughing and joking like normal,' Saeed Ahmed, 29, later told reporters. Tanweer was the most unlikely of the four bombers, according to friends. 'He seemed to enjoy everything British and Western, and had the means to do so.'[9] There is no evidence of Tanweer being personally hostile to white people or to non-Muslims. 'He was my best mate growing up,' said Chris Whitley, who lives across the street from the Tanweers, and who is white.[10] Tanweer's classmate at Wortley High School, Sunny Lotta, said: 'He got on with everyone and had lots of friends who were white, Sikhs, whatever.'[11] At school, and then at Leeds Metropolitan University, where he studied sports science, Tanweer was popular and apparently never experienced the racism that older Asians felt. 'He felt completely integrated and never showed any signs of disaffection,' according to Safina Ahmad, his cousin.[12]

Neil Kay, a white family friend (a business partner of Tanweer's father), was disbelieving when Tanweer was identified as one of the bombers: 'I've known Kaki [Tanweer's family nickname] since he was two. He was always praying. He'd even get up at 4am to pray. He's a very religious lad, but a lot of his friends are white. He never put a white man down. He called me his uncle Neil. I can't believe he could be a religious fanatic.'[13]

Tanweer was not religious during his childhood. He did learn passages of the *Qur'an*, but only after some arm-twisting.[14] 'He was more British than Muslim up until he was 18,' according to his boyhood friend Chris Whitley. 'He started going to mosque a lot more. We grew apart.'[15] (Incidentally, would anyone say: 'He was more British than Jewish', or 'more British than Catholic until he was 18'?[16])

Bashir Ahmad said after the bombings: 'I saw him the day before he went to London. He was completely calm and normal, just his normal self. He was playing cricket in the park with his friends until quite late in the evening.'[17] According to Safina Ahmad, his cousin, Tanweer's boyhood dream was quintessentially British: to become a professional cricketer. He wore tracksuits and T-shirts so he could play cricket or football at a moment's notice.[18] Chris Whitley confirms: 'He couldn't go a day without playing cricket.'[19] Tanweer was reportedly outstanding at sports at Wortley High School, excelling at cricket, triple jump, long-distance running and football.[20] His bedroom was a shrine to sport, with a shelf full of trophies for the long-jump, football and cricket.[21]

Safina Ahmad said that, so far as she knew, Tanweer was never interested in foreign policy or politics. She never once saw him reading a newspaper or watching the news. To her knowledge, he never attended any protests against Britain's involvement in Iraq or Afghanistan, or against Israeli policies.[22] She added: 'Shehzad grew into a calm and peaceful young man. Nothing could anger him. I cannot recall the last time I heard him even raise his voice.'[23]

Sound As A Pound

Speaking to reporters from *The Times* on the day that it was revealed that Tanweer had been one of the bombers, his friends Mohamed Ansaar Riaz, 19, and Azzy Mohamed, 21, said Shehzad was 'the best lad you could ever meet'—'He was a sweet guy who gets on with everyone.'[24] Azzy Mohamed said, 'Shazzy is the best lad I have ever met. He's a top guy and a top lad. We play cricket together, he's a bowler and a batsman. He wouldn't do anything like this. He's from a very strong family... Shehzad is a very kind person who would get along with anyone and anybody. He's the kind of guy who would condemn extremism.'[25] He told another reporter on 12 July that Shehzad was as 'sound as a pound.' The idea that he was involved in terrorism or extremism was 'ridiculous'. The idea that he went down to London and exploded a bomb was 'unbelievable': 'I only played cricket in the park with him around 10 days ago. He is not interested in politics.' Tanweer gave the impression to his friends that he was not even that interested in Islam: he 'went to a few mosques around here but he was more interested in his jujitsu. I trained with him all the time; he is really fit,' said Azzy Mohamed.[26]

Another friend said that both the two younger bombers were respected in the area: 'Shehzad was the sort of person who would always tell the young kids that they should stay out of trouble and make something of their lives. Hasib [Hussain] was also someone I looked up to, even though he was a year younger than me. He was a real gentle giant.'[27] Malik Abdul Shabaz, 24, told reporters: 'If you met Shezzy, you'd love him. He was really calm and humble. Very intelligent. All them boys was. That's why this is so shocking.'[28]

Two young Muslim men from Beeston, who knew Tanweer, expressed their astonishment: 'Why him? Why not me? I've gone to the same schools, gone to the same mosque, done the same things.' CNN reporter Henry Schuster comments: 'He and others don't speak with anger—but rather incomprehension, confounded by the investigation unfolding in their hometown.'[29] 'I don't understand where his hatred came from,' said Saeed Ahmed, Tanweer's friend.[30]

Shehzad Tanweer and his fellow bombers had hidden the most important part of their lives from their parents, their families, and from many of their friends.

Family Statements

Shehzad Tanweer's uncle Bashir Ahmad described how his family had been left 'shattered' by news he had been involved in the attack. 'It must have been forces behind him,' Ahmad said.

Tanweer's cousin wrote: 'My heartfelt apologies go out to all those who lost someone in the attacks. If there was anything I could have done to prevent this, I would have done it. I know that goes for all my family. We didn't want to lose our Shehzad, we believe he was taken from us. I have no doubt in my mind that Shehzad was merely a tool of somebody else's evil ideology. I am certain somebody got to him, and duped him. I will not rest until that person or group is caught and brought to justice.'[31]

Aldgate

Shehzad Tanweer exploded his rucksack bomb at 8.50am. He was in the second carriage of a Circle line Underground train, which had just left Liverpool Street station, travelling east to Aldgate. The bomb was on the floor at the very rear of the second carriage. The explosion killed three men and four women, in addition to Tanweer himself. Their names were: Lee Baisden, Benedetta Ciaccia, Richard Ellery, Richard Gray, Anne Moffat, Fiona Stevenson, and Carrie Taylor. One hundred people were injured by the blast; at least ten were injured seriously.

Lee Baisden

Lee Baisden, 34, an accountant for the London Fire Brigade, had recently moved in with Paul Groman, his boyfriend of three years. Mr Baisden spent much of his time helping his widowed mother, Denise, who has multiple sclerosis. His friend Helen Lasky described Lee as a 'shy, reserved person'.

Benedetta Ciaccia

Born in Rome, Benedetta Ciaccia, 30, a business analyst, was engaged to be married to Fiaz Bhatti, a 29-year-old Muslim. Ms Ciaccia had planned a wedding uniting Catholic and Muslim rites. Her body was flown to Italy, and she was buried in her wedding dress.

Richard Ellery

Richard Ellery, 21, worked in Jessops camera shop in Ipswich, where he lived. On 7 July, he was on his way to a training course at the firm's Kensington branch.

Mr Ellery's family released a statement saying: 'Richard was a fun-loving boy—full of enthusiasm for life.'

Richard Gray

Father to Adam, 11, and Ruby, 7, and husband to Louise, Richard Gray, 41, was a chartered tax accountant with two real passions: his family, and hockey. Co-founder of the Ipswich & East Suffolk Hockey Club, he was regarded as a pacy midfield or forward with an eye for goal.

Anne Moffat

Anne Moffat, 48, was on her way to work at 'Girlguiding UK', where she worked as head of marketing and communications. Former colleague Muriel Dunn, said: 'I will always remember her quiet manner, her professionalism, her expertise in her work area and her charm and warmth when working with others.'

Fiona Stevenson

Fiona Stevenson, 29, was a duty solicitor in court and police stations, specialising in fraud and extradition. She had recently taken a four-month unpaid sabbatical in Belize to help develop a staff training manual for child care proceedings. A human rights lawyer, Ms Stevenson marched against the war in Iraq.

Carrie Taylor

Carrie Taylor, 24, was a finance officer at the Royal Society of Arts, organising grants for young artists. Ms Taylor, who was secretly writing a novel later found in her bedroom, was looking forward to a 25th birthday trip to Hawaii in May 2006, with her parents and her brother, Simon.

Disconnection and Reconnection

That Thursday had started off so well.
I was going to get to work early.

Bang! Screams that for months woke me early.
Victorian brick dust and modern peroxide filled our lungs.
We didn't want to breathe this contaminated air
but there was no other. Trapped in that Tube, alongside
a carriage without doors, we talked until breathing got too hard.
Then, the dust cleared a little and we could see those in the dark,
who minutes before might have been reading about love,
now lying on the floor, their bones and muscles exposed
to pictures taken on mobile phones. Half an hour later
doctors shouted 'Keep your head still' over and over.

Kept for an hour because 'debris had to be removed'
we, sickened, like some animal's innards, then spilt towards
the daylight at the end of our darkness,
passed buckled Tube doors and more pieces of glass
than you could imagine: glass like that
we had caught our reflection in so many times before.
We realized body parts were the 'debris' they removed.
When we reached Edgware Road, staff handed us
paper towels to wipe off the dirt but there was blood
on the steps and so many with bandaged heads
sitting on the concrete, waiting... I walked on past police,
ambulances and phoned my boss, shouting above the sirens.
I then walked and walked feeling rootless, disconnected.
Some I'd left behind had families who'd miss them.
I, who live alone, had walked away, found myself lost,
exhausted, but had to keep going somewhere ...

I kept busy for a week answering calls of concern, of curiosity.
The two-minute silence, though, dissolved my defences.
I couldn't stop crying, wanted to do myself in,
as if the bombings were retribution for my past wrongs.
The police came round for four hours, made me go over
that dark hour. Later, I threw up, wretched for three days,
remembering others who'd tried to kill me,
my mother when I cried beyond her endurance,
someone who, in a row, had tried to strangle me
and muggers who'd once left me for dead.
With each call to The Samaritans I kept rubbing those sores
but needed them to help me connect my present self
to the one out of reach with good memories.

We met up again. Now I use the same Tube line reconnected.

Jennifer Johnson

6

Abdullah Jamal

The Teenage Convert

Germaine Lindsay/Abdullah Shaheed Jamal

Germaine Lindsay, 19 years old, is the least well-known member of the group. Born in Jamaica, he spent his teenage years in Huddersfield, less than 20 miles from Leeds. Lindsay changed his name to 'Abdullah Shaheed Jamal' after converting to Islam in 2001, at the age of 15. He grew a beard, asked for permission to pray at school, and exchanged his jeans for Muslim dress. He even persuaded his mother, Mary McLeod, the daughter of an evangelical Christian, to embrace Islam.[1] Like the other bombers, Jamal seems to have been devoted to sports. A natural athlete who played soccer, ran and did the long jump, Jamal was a regular at the gym and took up boxing.[2] Reports differ as to the effects of his conversion to Islam at the age of 15. Some say that Jamal changed strikingly, rejecting some of his old friends.[3] He apparently stopped smoking, listening to music or playing soccer, and sometimes sat in class listening to Islamic tapes on his personal stereo. According to one report, Jamal 'shut himself away.' Others say he attempted to convert his friends to Islam, trying to persuade them to reject Western vices and amusements. 'He was really passionate about his religion and it seemed like he wanted to pass it on to other people,' said Antoinette Crook, who attended his school. However, another former classmate said of Jamal's conversion: 'We were surprised but he didn't make a big deal about it. He was just a regular guy. He was bright but quiet. He was keen on athletics and we used to go out running together.'[4]

Theresa Weldrick, who was in the year below Jamal at the 400-pupil Rawthorpe High School in Huddersfield, said, 'Everyone who knew him is shocked.

He was really nice—one of those people who didn't get into trouble. He was so good. I just can't think what could have possessed his soul.'[5] Another former school mate said: 'Now you tell us he was one of the London bombers. He was just about the last person you could imagine doing such a thing.'[6]

Jamal frequently attended prayers, first at the Omar Masjid (mosque), across the street from the apartment in Huddersfield where he and his wife lived before moving to Aylesbury. The *imam* there, Nazeeb Albi, told reporters that Jamal often worked at the neighbourhood open-air market selling mobile phone covers.[7]

The Husband And Father

In 2002, Jamal met Samantha Lewthwaite, then aged 19, at a college in Luton. Despite the objections of her parents, Ms Lewthwaite married Jamal in an Islamic ceremony shortly after they met (the couple apparently never registered the union with the authorities). A few months before the bombings, they moved to Aylesbury, where Ms Lewthwaite had grown up.[8] (In interviews after the bombings, Ms Lewthwaite retained her pre-conversion first name, rather than use her adopted name, Sherafiyah.) At the time of the London bombings, the couple had one fifteen-month-old child, and another baby on the way.

Nigel Lindsay, Jamal's father, a 45-year-old carpenter from Mandeville, north Jamaica, later described how he had been contacted by his son out of the blue in September 2004. Jamal had feared that his father might have been affected by Hurricane Ivan, which had devastated parts of Jamaica. There had been no contact between the two for the previous eight years—since Jamal's mother, who left Jamaica for Britain in 1986, last brought him to the island. 'Since the hurricane last year I have been in touch with him at least weekly,' Mr Lindsay told Radio Jamaica. 'I think he was quiet and calm.' Their conversations suddenly stopped, at about the time that Jamal is believed to have moved to a rented flat in Aylesbury, Bucks.

'I tried contacting him and didn't get any answer,' said Jamal's father. It is now thought that this loss of contact might have been a sign of the activation of the plot, two months before the attack took place. 'He seemed like a young man who had got his priorities right,' said Mr Lindsay. 'He sounded like he was happy with his life and his religion and gave away no signs that he was up to anything bad. It felt like he was enjoying life and was really on top of things. He was settled with his woman and kid. I thought he was mixing with the right set of people in that religion—people who could guide him along and keep him on the straight.' Nigel Lindsay asked: 'How could I have not known this was going to happen so I could put a stop to it? I only wish I could. My heart goes out to the victims and their loved ones in London. I am so sorry.'[9]

Mary McLeod, Jamal's mother, who was in Jamaica at the time of the bombing, said she was stunned that her son was suspected of carrying a bomb onto the Piccadilly Line of the Underground in London. 'I haven't stopped crying for all the people who died,' she said. 'And I cried for my son. I have to deal not only with his death but with the fact that he may have killed all those people.' She found it incomprehensible because 'after September 11, I was devastated, and so was Germaine': 'We cried for all the people who died and wondered how Muslims could do this.'[10]

The Widow

At first, Jamal's widow was disbelieving. While in protective custody, Samantha Lewthwaite said she could not believe that her husband was involved: 'I won't believe it until they show me the proof. I'm not going to accept it until they have his DNA.'[11] Later, after seeing the CCTV footage of her husband in King's Cross station, Ms Lewthwaite said that trips to radical mosques had 'poisoned' her 19-year-old husband's mind.

Having by this time given birth to a daughter, she said Jamal had turned from a 'peaceful man who loved people' into someone whose character she did not recognise, after meeting a group of men at a prayer meeting in 2004. She said that he had begun disappearing for days at a time, visiting mosques around the country. 'How these people could have turned him and poisoned his mind is dreadful,' she said. 'He was an innocent, naive and simple man. I suppose he must have been an ideal candidate.'[12]

Family Statements

In a public statement Samantha Lewthwaite said she 'never predicted or imagined that he was involved in such horrific activities.' She said: 'My whole world has fallen apart and my thoughts are with the families of the victims of this incomprehensible devastation.'[13]

A statement issued by Jamal's relatives Andrew, Sabrina, Allan, and Carly, said Germaine Lindsay 'had a kind, caring and calming presence about him'; 'He was a good and loving husband and a brilliant father, who showed absolutely no sign of doing this atrocious crime. We as a family had no idea of his plans and are as horrified as the rest of the world.'[14]

Russell Square

Abdullah Shaheed Jamal, formerly known as Germaine Lindsay, exploded his rucksack bomb at 8.50am on a London Underground train on the Piccadilly Line, travelling south from King's Cross station to Russell Square. He was in the front carriage of the train. His bomb was positioned next to the rear set of double doors.

Twenty-six people, other than Jamal himself, were killed. Their names were: James Adams, Samantha Badham and Lee Harris, Philip Beer, Anna Brandt, Ciaran Cassidy, Rachelle Chung For Yuen, Elizabeth Daplyn, Arthur Frederick, Karolina Gluck, Gamze Gunoral, Ojara Ikeagwu, Emily Jenkins, Adrian Johnson, Helen Jones, Susan Levy, Shelley Mather, Michael Matsushita, James Mayes, Behnaz Mozakka, Mihaela Otto, Atique Sharifi, Ihab Slimane, Christian Small/ Njoya Diawara-Small, Monika Suchocka, Mala Trivedi. Many more people were injured.

James Adams

James Adams, 32, a deacon, was a mortgage adviser. His parents said later: 'James was a deeply loved son and brother, who lived and loved life to the full. We do not know who is ultimately responsible for our loss but we do not hold any religion or faith accountable.'

Samantha Badham and Lee Harris

On 7 July, Lee Harris, 30, and Samantha Badham, 36, were planning a romantic dinner after work, just before their 14th anniversary. So Ms Badham, a secretary, did not drive to work, and Mr Harris, a fire brigade architect, did not cycle to work, as they usually did. Mr Harris was in a coma for eight days after the explosion, and died on 15 July. The next day, his partner's body was brought out of the train wreckage. Samantha Badham and Lee Harris were buried together on 5 August 2005, after a joint funeral service in Ledbury.

Philip Beer

Philip Beer, 22, was a hair stylist from Borehamwood, Hertfordshire. Mr Beer lived with his parents Kim and Phil, and his four sisters, Michelle, Stacy, Angelina, and one-year-old Lilymay. In a statement, his family said: 'He was so loving to everyone, even though he'd drive us all mad at times!'

Anna Brandt

Anna Brandt, 41, was a cleaner. Ms Brandt had been living in London for three years, after moving from her home in Wagrowiec, Poland. She was survived by two daughters. One of them arrived in Britain on 7 July, having come to visit her mother.

Ciaran Cassidy

Ciaran Cassidy, 22, was a print shop assistant. He had been saving for some months to pay for a planned trip to Australia. His close friend Joe Hayes later said: 'He didn't care for politics or war, but for his family, his friends, for his football and his weekend drink.'

Rachelle Chung For Yuen

Rachelle Chung For Yuen, 27, was an accountant. Mrs Chung For Yuen moved to Britain three years earlier from Curepipe in Mauritius. Her funeral service was in her homeland, attended by the country's most senior statesmen, including President Sir Anerood Jugnauth, Prime Minister Navin Ramgoolam and opposition leader Paul Berenger.

Elizabeth Daplyn

Elizabeth Daplyn, 26, worked in a hospital neuro-radiology department. Pamela Hutchinson, a friend, later wrote: 'She was a treasured guest at any party, thanks to her witty conversation, her home baking, and her "emergency kit" complete with corkscrew—not to mention her impish smile.'

Arthur Frederick

Arthur Frederick, 60, was a museum security guard, a former police officer, and a calypso singer whose song 'Signs of Christmas' is still played on Montserrat radio. Mr Frederick had recently returned from Grenada, where he had helped his elderly parents rebuild their home after Hurricane Ivan.

Karolina Gluck

Karolina Gluck, 29, a receptionist who had moved to London three years earlier from Poland, was, like Samantha Badham, looking forward to a romantic occasion on 7 July. She was due to leave that evening to spend a long weekend in Paris with her partner Richard Deer .

Gamze Gunoral

Gamze Gunoral, 24, came to London to improve her English after graduating from the University of Marmara, Istanbul, Turkey with a degree in insurance and banking. Ms Gunoral was buried in Istanbul.

Ojara Ikeagwu

Social worker Ojara Ikeagwu, 56, worked for Hounslow social services in London. Mrs Ikeagwu was of Nigerian descent and had lived in Luton for 25 years. She was survived by her husband, a retired doctor, Okorasor Ikeagwu, and their three adult children.

Emily Jenkins

Emily Jenkins, 24, was a trainee midwife. Christie Aumonier, a friend, wrote later: 'Few people could touch the life of so many people in such a terribly short space of time. Many regarded her as their closest friend and people flew in from around the world to say their goodbyes...'

Adrian Johnson

Adrian Johnson, 38, lived in Sutton-in-Ashfield, Nottinghamshire, with his wife Catherine, 36, son Christopher, 9, and daughter Rebekah, 6. As a product technical manager for Burberry, Mr Johnson travelled three weeks out of four. Mr Johnson was on the Russell Square train because he had broken his routine to see his family.

Helen Jones

Helen Jones, 28, an accountant, grew up in Annan, near Lockerbie, Dumfriesshire, and was a pupil there when a Pan Am jet exploded over the town in 1988 with the loss of 270 lives. She was a brilliant scholar, becoming the youngest student at Aberdeen University when aged just 16, studying divinity.

Susan Levy

Susan Levy, 53, a legal secretary, and her husband Harry had two sons, Daniel, 25, and Jamie, 23. Mr Levy's cousin Jason later said: 'They were the most tight-knit family imaginable. They did everything together. I feel for the two boys—they are absolutely devastated.'

Shelley Mather

Shelley Mather, 26, like Ms Brandt, Mrs Chung For Yuen, Ms Gluck and Atique Sharifi (see below), had been living in London for three years. Temping as an administrator, Ms Mather was planning a trip to Greece. When she went missing, her parents John Mather and Kathryn Gilkison flew from Auckland, New Zealand, to search for her.

Michael Matsushita

Mike Matsushita, born in Vietnam and raised in New York, moved to London in June 2005 to settle down with his new British girlfriend. Mr Matsushita's family and friends launched a new charity in his honour, to benefit orphans in Cambodia, where he had worked as a tour guide.

James Mayes

James Mayes, 28, was an analyst at the Healthcare Commission. Robert Irons, a colleague said later: 'James was one of the most honest, kind people I have ever met, always willing to listen and give advice (not all of it good!) and was well liked by everyone he met.'

Behnaz Mozakka

Behnaz Mozakka, 47, was an Iranian-born biomedical officer at Great Ormond Street Children's Hospital. Mrs Mozakka's husband Nader said: 'She was a very peaceful person.' Their daughter, Saba, 24, and son, Saeed, 22, said: 'She had time for everyone, she had a big heart, and now this has left us destroyed.'

Mihaela Otto

Mihaela Otto, 46, (she preferred to be known as Michelle) was a dental technician. She moved to London from Romania in 1984, following her sister Dania Gorodi. She lived in Mill Hill, north London, with her mother Elena Draganescu, 78, and her sister Dania and her family.

Atique Sharifi

Atique Sharifi, 24, lost his parents to the Taliban. He left Afghanistan for Britain in January 2002, and started studying English at West Thames College. College tutor Harminder Ubhie said: 'He was a delight to have in the group. I knew he would be one of our high achievers.'

Ihab Slimane

Ihab Slimane, 24, had come from France weeks earlier to improve his English. Of Tunisian heritage, M. Slimane was a waiter, but he had just completed an IT engineering degree from the University Institute of Technology near Grenoble. He planned to work in computer programming. M Slimane was buried in Tunis.

Christian Small/Njoya Diawara-Small

Christian Small, 28, who worked in advertising sales, decided after a trip to Africa to call himself Njoya Diawara ('strong in spirit') Small. His mother Sheila issued a statement saying that no one should be deflected by the bombings from supporting Mr Small's ideals, such as educating young people about Africa or campaigning for fair trade and debt relief.

Monika Suchocka

Monika Suchocka, 23, had moved to London from Poland only two months earlier. Ms Suchocka worked at an accountancy firm in West Kensington. Three Metropolitan Police officers carried her ashes back to her homeland.

Mala Trivedi

Mala Trivedi, 30, like Behnaz Mozakka, worked at London's Great Ormond Street Hospital for Sick Children—in the X-ray department, with skills in imaging IT. Dr Cathy Owens, on behalf of the department of radiology said: 'Mala was kind and empathic, and, for her, work was a vocation.'

7

Hasib Hussain

The Gentle Giant

Hasib Hussain

Hasib Hussain, only 18 when he blew up the No. 30 bus on 7 July, had had a dramatic and visible 'conversion' experience which had turned his life around two years earlier. His father, Mahmood Hussain, a retired foundry worker, said after the bombings: 'The boy I see on the TV news, the boy I see in the papers, is not the child I knew. He was the perfect son.' There were plans for his life: 'He was due to start university in September. He had also agreed to an arranged marriage with a young woman from Pakistan, though no date had been set.'[1] Before his conversion experience, however, Hussain had been something less than a 'perfect son' in the eyes of his parents—and the neighbours. Paula Baker, a neighbour of the Hussains, said: 'Hasib was trouble at school and was known as a fighter at Matthew Murray [School], which he and Imran [his elder brother] went to.' Those who knew him at school tended to remember him differently, according to their race. 'He was a very good lad; he kept himself to himself,' said 18-year-old Jameel Hussain (no relation), who went to school with Hussain. 'There had been riots at school but he just stood and watched; he was a good lad,' said Billal Hussain, 15 (also no relation). On the other hand, Danny Thomlinson, aged 20 said: 'He was a bit argumentative'. 'He got on with his work but he had a short fuse,' said 18-year-old Dale Bingham, who claimed that Hussain often got into fights with non-Muslims. Other non-Muslim schoolmates at Matthew Murray remembered him as an occasional bully.[2] One former schoolfriend observed: 'It was always whites against Asians and there were so many fights. Hasib was really quiet and didn't get into any fights himself but he was in the thick of gangs that did. Maybe that played a part in making him feel alienated from the country of his birth and western society.'[3]

It is difficult to form a coherent story from the mess of conflicting reports, but it seems clear that at one time Hussain was highly Westernized, known for his sense of humour and sense of style. He is said at one point to have worn blue contact lenses and long hair parted in the middle. 'It fell like a curtain on his head,' said a friend, who identified himself only as G.[4] It was after he left school almost without qualifications, according to neighbours, that Hussain 'went a bit wild'.[5] It has been reported that he was arrested by the police for shoplifting,[6] and that he started going to pubs, fighting and swearing. Hussain's parents are said to have despaired of him for a time. It is said they made 'desperate attempts to instil discipline into him'.[7] The exact nature of these 'attempts' is not spelled out. It has been widely reported that he was sent to an Islamic study school or *madrasa* in Pakistan, thinking that this might give him more of a focus.[8] According to his brother, however, Hasib Hussain's only visit to Pakistan since he was an infant was a four-week, non-religious trip to the outskirts of Islamabad for a wedding in 2002.[9]

The Setbacks

The *Independent* observed that, 'A series of setbacks in Hussain's life may be behind a sudden change from a British Asian who dressed in Western clothes to a religious teenager who wore Islamic garb and only stopped to say salaam to fellow Muslims.'[10] One major set-back was the closure of the local Holbeck Hornets football team that Hussain was involved in.[11] It has been reported that when the Hornets' pitch was closed, Hussain withdrew into himself, and his grades plummeted.[12] The other major set-back came almost simultaneously, when Hussain was withdrawn by teachers from his GCSE examinations, leaving school on 20 July 2003 with a single GNVQ certificate in business studies.[13] After the 7/7 bombings, the school released this statement about Hussain: 'He was a good attender and there is nothing unusual about his school records except he was withdrawn by the school from all of his GCSEs, except GNVQ business studies.'[14] It is difficult, now, to know what to make of the claim that Hussain was involved in an incident in which he hit out at a group of girls. It is said that this incident may have contributed to the decision by teachers withdraw Hussain from his GCSEs.[15] This may put a different light on his 'gentleness'.

In addition to football, Hussain was also passionate about cricket. He belonged to a local cricket team and was often seen playing in his whites—often with Shehzad Tanweer.[16] Former classmate, Matthew Judge, 18, recalled how, towards the end of his schooldays, Hasib underwent a dramatic change: 'He liked playing cricket and hockey, then one day he came into school and had undergone a complete transformation, almost overnight. He started wearing a topi hat from the mosque, grew a beard and wore robes. Before that he was always in jeans.'[17]

A friend of the family, who wished to remain anonymous, claims that the move towards fundamentalism initially worried Hussain's family: 'Imran [his elder brother] was worried because Hasib seemed to be getting into some kind of gang and started wearing white robes but he thought the worst thing they were doing was praying and decided there was no harm in him becoming religious. He didn't realise that there might have been something more sinister to it.'[18] We will learn more of this 'gang' later in our investigation.[19]

Quieter and less confident than Tanweer, Hussain was somewhat awkward, not very bright, and rather overshadowed by his glamorous older brother, Imran.[20] He has been described as 'a born follower'.[21] For many, Hussain was yet another 'nice' young man. His uncle said: 'He was a nice lad. He was really nice. He wasn't the type of guy to do it. He wouldn't do it. I wish in my heart he was still alive.'[22]

Another friend said, 'Hasib was someone I looked up to. He was a gentle giant. He went on the *Haj* [pilgrimage to Makka] a couple of years ago and grew a beard for that, but he never came across as any kind of fanatic.'[23] It seems that 'gentleness' was a genuine strand of his complex nature. Hussain's father recalled after the bombings, with bemusement:

If a fly came into the house, he would catch it and take it outside. If there was a caterpillar in the garden, he would make sure it was safe. I keep thinking that this must be some kind of mistake. That it must have been someone else who did this. I can only imagine that he was brainwashed into doing this. If I am wrong, then my son will face his reward in the next life.[24]

Hussain's elder brother Imran said: 'Two weeks before he disappeared he called my mother to his room. He was sitting on the bed and asked her to get rid of the spider in there. He was so gentle. He was built like me physically, but people got the wrong idea—he was a big softie.' Imran and his parents are at a loss to explain how a soft-hearted, unassuming 18-year-old, who was afraid of spiders and refused to kill flies or any insects, turned into a mass murderer.[25]

Tavistock Square

Unlike the others, Hasib Hussain did not detonate his explosives at 8.50am. Just before 9am, he left King's Cross station and phoned the other bombers. He is reported to have said: 'I can't get on a train. What should I do ?'[26] After a period of aimless wandering, he boarded a double-decker No. 30 bus. Various theories have been given for Hussain's delay in triggering his bomb. The most likely is that his repeated attempts still failed to set the bomb off. This would explain the observation of fellow bus passenger Richard Jones, who reports that the bomber was jumpy and anxious in the minutes leading up to the explosion, fiddling incessantly with a bag in front of his feet: 'This young guy kept diving into this bag or whatever he had at his feet, and it was like he was taking a couple of grapes or a bunch of grapes, both hands were in the bag. He must have done that at least every minute, if not every 30 seconds. He was getting annoyed, the only reason I noticed it was that he was annoying me.'[27] It may be that the reason for the delay, and the 'annoyance', was that the detonator mechanism was not working. Hussain may have thought initially that the other bombers had also been unable to trigger their explosives at the agreed time, hence his phone calls to them.

Whatever the reason for his delay, Hasib Hussain finally detonated his rucksack bomb at 9.47am. He was on the top deck of the No. 30 bus at the junction of Tavistock Square and Upper Woburn Place in central London, not far from Euston station. The bomb seems to have been on the floor at the back of the upper deck. The explosion killed thirteen people in addition to Hasib Hussain himself. Their names were: Anthony Fatayi-Williams, Jamie Gordon, Giles Hart, Marie Hartley, Miriam Hyman, Shahara Islam, Neetu Jain, Sam Ly, Shyanuja Parathasangary, Anat Rosenberg, Philip Russell, William Wise, and Gladys Wundowa.

Anthony Fatayi-Williams

Anthony Fatayi-Williams, 26, was an executive developing new business for the company Amec in the oil and gas industry in Africa. His father, a Muslim, is one of Nigeria's leading medical practitioners. His mother, Marie, a Catholic and a senior oil executive, made a powerful memorial speech in Tavistock Square.

Jamie Gordon

Having stayed over at a friend's after a party, Jamie Gordon, 30, caught the No. 30 bus instead of his usual train. After living together for four years, he and

Yvonne Nash had recently decided to marry. Photographs of Ms Nash desperately searching for Mr Gordon were among the most distressing images of 7/7.

Giles Hart

A BT engineer, Giles Hart, 55, was a campaigner for social justice, and a former chair of the Polish Solidarity Campaign of Great Britain. His wife Danuta, daughter Maryla, 21, and son Martin, 17, said: 'Giles was always a champion of liberty and human rights and a campaigner against political injustice and bigotry.'

Marie Hartley

Marie Hartley, 34, worked at the greeting card firm Hambledon Studios. David Dean, the managing director, said that Ms Hartley's colleagues became so distressed after her death that counsellors had to be called in. Her mother Barbara Targett said: 'When Marie walked into a room the whole place lit up, it was impossible to miss her presence.'

Miriam Hyman

Freelance picture editor Miriam Hyman, 31, phoned her father, John, only minutes before the explosion, to tell him that she was all right after being evacuated from King's Cross. Andy Bodle, a friend, remembered her as a bubbly young woman who laughed a lot and was the life and soul of any gathering.

Shahara Islam

Shahara Islam, 20, was a British Bengali Muslim who attended her local mosque every Friday. A cashier at the Cooperative Bank in Islington, Ms Islam also loved shopping for clothes, handbags and shoes in London's West End, and was always impeccably dressed. Her family issued this statement: 'She was an Eastender, a Londoner and British, but above all a true Muslim and proud to be so.'

Neetu Jain

Neetu Jain, 37, a Hindu born in Delhi, lived for her job as a computer analyst, which took her around the world. A former colleague of hers, Mike Kelly, wrote later: 'I can truly say that I never once heard her complain about work, about colleagues, about anything at all.'

Sam Ly

Sam Ly, 28, a computer professional, was born in Vietnam; in 1980 his family escaped in a boat to Australia, where Mr Ly grew up. He came to London with his girlfriend in 2003 for a working holiday. He died in hospital one week after the blast.

Shyanuja Parathasangary

Born in Sri Lanka, Shyanuja Parathasangary, 30, came to the UK at the age of one. She worked as an assistant buyer for the Royal Mail, and had recently bought a house with her sister, which she was very proud of. She left for work later than usual on 7 July because she had been feeling unwell.

Anat Rosenberg

Anat Rosenberg, 39, had been worried about going back to her native Israel to visit her parents, because of the threat of suicide bombings. The charity worker, 39, died while speaking on the phone to her boyfriend, John Falding. He said later: 'Anat was gorgeous and outrageous. She was a one-off.'

Philip Russell

After university, and a four-month trip to South Africa, Australia and New Zealand, Philip Russell, 28, began work in the City. He was said by colleagues at investment bank JP Morgan to be 'on the threshold of a brilliant career'. His father, Grahame Russell, said: 'He always had time to listen.'

William Wise

William Wise, 54, was a senior software developer and IT specialist at Equitas Holdings in St Mary Axe, near Liverpool Street. He has been described by friends as a quiet, gentle and intelligent man.

Gladys Wundowa

Gladys Wundowa, 50, had a husband Emmanuel Wyndowa, daughter Azuma, 16, and son Zakari, 14. She was a cleaner at University College London, and a volunteer for the African Development Agency in north London, a charity and community centre. Dr Adu Seray-Wurie, head of the Agency, said of Mrs Wundowa: 'I have never seen her angry, and when people came in with problems with housing or immigration she was always happy to help.'

8

Self-Brainwashing

Not Coercive Brainwashing
But Self-Radicalization

The 'Brainwashing' Model

One way of explaining how such 'nice' young men could have carried out these atrocities was 'brainwashing'. Rebecca Whitaker said of Aldgate bomber Shehzad Tanweer: 'Perhaps nice people are easily brainwashed.'[1] As we have seen, the families of other bombers used similar language.

'Brainwashing' means radically changing a person's beliefs and behaviour by coercive techniques. The term came into currency after the Chinese Revolution with the Communist 'thought reform' campaigns against both Chinese intellectuals and Western prisoners. The classic treatment of this phenomenon was Robert J. Lifton's 1961 *Thought Reform and the Psychology of Totalism*.[2] Lifton observed that the 'most basic feature' of 'thought reform', 'the psychological current upon which all else depends', is 'the control of human communication':

> Through this milieu control the totalist environment seeks to establish domain over not only the individual's communication with the outside (all that he sees and hears, reads and writes, experiences and expresses), but also—in its penetration of his inner life—over what we may speak of as his communication with himself.[3]

Lifton commented that 'the Chinese Communist prison and revolutionary university produce just about as thoroughly controlled a group environment as has ever existed.' For Western prisoners, 'thought reform' involved chains, sleep deprivation, humiliating toilet and feeding practices, and so on. For students at 'revolutionary universities', such violent methods were not necessary. The all-encompassing group living, and constant denunciation and self-accusation in group meetings, were quite sufficient.

Kathleen Taylor, author of *Brainwashing*, has pointed out that 'five core techniques keep cropping up: isolation, control, uncertainty, repetition and emotional manipulation'.[4] We are familiar with the idea that religious cults gain control of their recruits by separating them from their family and friends, and isolating them physically in a strictly-controlled communal environment. This did not happen with the 7/7 bombers. Hussain and Tanweer, for example, continued living at home with their parents till the day of the attacks. Kathleen Taylor suggests that, a potential suicide bomber would be groomed by giving them:

> fewer aspirational Hollywood fantasies and adverts promoting western consumer lifestyles; more about the west's selfish greed, its neglect of its own disadvantaged, and the atrocities that emerge whenever Europe or the US bungles[5] foreign policy.

But who was in the bombers' homes limiting their viewing of Hollywood blockbusters and Western advertisements? The bombers continued their normal lives without arousing suspicion among their family members or employers.

Atrocity Videos

According to an unnamed friend of the three Leeds bombers, 'it was in a back-street bookshop that the trio "turned religious" ' about four years earlier. (2001, the year of the 11 September attacks, and the worldwide anti-Muslim backlash.) Iqra, a new Islamic bookshop in Beeston, opened up an alternative, radical, communication channel. 'I think the shop is innocent,' said the bombers' 'friend', 'but I think it sold under-the-counter stuff, videos of what was happening in Bosnia, Iraq and Chechnya. Stuff the television could not show. Rapes, murders, mutilation, all saying: "Look what is happening to your Muslim brothers and sisters." You see that and you start to get angry. That was the beginning.'[6] The 29-year-old, who refused to give his name, added: 'From that, you feel you want to learn more about religion, about your Muslim brothers and sisters around the world getting murdered.'

This makes sense as an explanation of how someone could start down the track of political extremism, but it is a world away from 'brainwashing'. The 'friend' continued with an explanation of the process: 'Then people get to know you, invite you to private meetings in their homes. Once they start to trust you they get on to extreme views. Some people get brainwashed by it. Then they find out how far you are willing to go.' This is not coercive brainwashing.

Former US naval intelligence official, Malcolm Nance, author of *The Terrorist Recognition Handbook: A Manual for Predicting and Identifying Terrorist Activities*, puts another perspective on the same process. Nance writes: 'al-Qa'eda's security is very good these days: you don't ask to join them, you have to be asked'.

> To be picked for such a mission, he believes, would be considered an enormous honour. 'The fact that they could not tell a soul will have made it all the more exciting. One can see how this could be seductive to some: you see something similar in the special ops and intelligence communities of Western armies. The fact that your operation is so secret makes them feel special. For a young 19-year-old it will have felt the equivalent of being recruited into the SAS.[7]

This is not about coercive 'milieu control', but something quite different.

Going back to Robert J. Lifton's discussion of 'thought reform', he contrasts two possible modes of 're-education'. One is frankly coercive: 'you *must* change and become what we tell you to become—or else'. The alternative might be death, social ostracism, any kind of physical or emotional pain. This method is based on fear. (The classic appeal might be: 'salvation through us - or eternal damnation'.) The other mode is 'exhortative': 'you *should* change—if you are a moral person—and become what we (in the name of a higher moral authority) tell you to become.' This approach seeks disciples and converts, and uses shame and guilt to transform individuals into followers. Lifton comments that 'It is the method par excellence of religions and of pseudo-religious secular ideologies'.[8] The mobilization described by the Leeds bombers' 'friend', and by Malcolm Nance, seems more to the 'exhortative' end of the spectrum.

A Failed Recruitment

There are more testimonies concerning this video-led recruitment process. The *Daily Mirror* reported one failed attempt:

> [O]ne evening I attended a gathering in a home in London. After everyone else had left the two men took me aside and asked me if I was angry about the West's persecution of *Ummah*, the Islamic nation. They pulled out a video

cassette and slipped it into the machine. The tape started with masked men talking in Arabic. I didn't understand everything so they paused the tape to translate and explain what was going on.

Then I watched in horror as grotesque footage was played of Chechen fighters being executed by Russian soldiers. The men were shot in the head, with blood going everywhere. It was the first time I'd seen such horrific things and I felt physically sick, hardly able to watch.

"You see what's happening to your brothers and sisters?" one of the men told me as other images of Muslims being killed in Palestine and Iraq flashed up. "But these people are going instantly to heaven." The other added: "Imagine how it feels to be one of these brothers, to know you are about to be rewarded with eternal life and the highest place in *Jannah* [Heaven]." After the video had ended the two men sat on either side of me and began to discuss how glorious it would be to die for the great cause.[9]

After the sexual advantages of Paradise were outlined, 'Muhammed' was tempted with the prospect of seeing his recently deceased father by becoming a suicide bomber. He told the *Mirror* that he felt 'drawn into their discourse, feeling the pain of my Muslim brothers and sisters around the world who were being killed and maimed unjustly.'

There was no attempt (at this point) to coerce Muhammed or convert him to a particular set of beliefs. Muhammed was not approached on the basis of 'ideology'. He was approached on the basis of (a selectively-portrayed) reality. Where 'reality' becomes 'ideology' is, firstly, in portraying this suffering as the deliberate result of an anti-Muslim 'crusade' by the West, and, secondly, distorting Islamic law to justify suicide terrorism against civilians.

This process is not based on 'milieu control', but on a powerful reality-based emotional appeal allied with an equally powerful (though distorted) analysis. The watching of these videos does not take place (by these accounts) in a physically coercive atmosphere. Having watched them, and heard the recruiters' appeal, the target individual is not isolated or permanently separated from family and friends. They may be advised to remain outwardly 'normal'.

This kind of 'thought reform' gains control over the external and internal life of the target individual—'over what we may speak of as his communication with himself', as Lifton puts it[10]—but without coercion. According to Nance, the recruitment process is one of selection and seduction—drawing in potential volunteers with secrecy, elitism and acceptance, rather than humiliation.

Former CIA field agent Robert Baer presented a series of documentaries on British television entitled 'The Cult of The Suicide Bomber' in the wake of the July bombings. In a newspaper article accompanying the series, Baer wrote:

> Like all cults, the cult of suicide bombing feeds upon itself. Log on to the internet or visit a militant Islamic bookshop and within a few minutes you will find enough inspiration in CDs, ranting sermons, DVDs, for a hundred suicide bombs. It swirls across the Islamic world as an expression of rage against the West for the invasion of Iraq, support for Israel, and for Western dominance of the world economy.[11]

Stephen Ulph, from the Jamestown Foundation, an American think-tank, observes: 'The internet has replaced Afghanistan as a source of training and inspiration for militant Muslims.' The *Telegraph* adds: 'Websites and satellite television channels supply images and incendiary rhetoric from any location on Earth where Muslims are fighting non-Muslims. Once Chechnya was the battlefield of choice for armchair viewing; now Iraq is the focus.'[12]

The Opposite Of Brainwashing

There is no need for a 'recruiter' or a 'preacher of hatred' in this scenario. This is the complete opposite of classical brainwashing. This is consumer-led, in the surroundings and the company chosen by the potential recruit. It is not the Grand Inquisitor holding a prisoner isolated in a dungeon, or the Communist commissar orchestrating waves of denunciation from a group of political robots. This is not brainwashing. It is 'self-radicalization'. At the time of writing, there is no evidence of outside recruiters playing a role in the development of the Leeds bomber cell. The picture is one of self-radicalization in which, had inflammatory materials not been available through the bookshop, the group might have pursued the same path via the internet.

A close associate of Mohammad Sidique Khan revealed to a BBC journalist that the bombers and he were part of a tightly-knit group of young Muslims from Dewsbury, Leeds and Huddersfield who would watch atrocity videos and play 'paintball' (a military-style game). There were no radical mosques involved:

> Before we would leave the house, there would sometimes be a video reflecting what's happening in Palestine or Chechnya or other places where Muslims were affected. Looking back on it now I do find it a bit weird that we had such

a viewing. I can see why some youth would be affected by this—they get fired up, they get stirred up—and having the airing of that video might not have been in the best interests of certain people.

[Mohammad Sidique Khan] was there but someone else was introducing the videos.[13]

We know what this anger led to. But was it anger managed and escalated and channelled by some terrorist mastermind? George Kassimeris, a terrorism expert at the University of Wolverhampton, has said of the 7/7 and 21/7 attacks: 'Far from requiring large amounts of money, training and co-ordination, the attacks appear to have been largely spontaneous and self-generated.'[14]

An Explanation That Made Sense

This reading of the plot is not compatible with 'brainwashing'. These conclusions may yet be overturned, but at the time of writing all the evidence is pointing in one direction, a direction summarized by Jason Burke, author of *Al Qaeda*, just one month after the 7/7 attacks: 'The 7 July bombers were not "brainwashed" by anyone. Radical Islam provided them with an explanation of what was happening in the world and suggested actions that made sense to them.'[15] Notice that the al-Qaeda ideology explains *what is happening in the world*. The suffering of Muslims in Chechnya, Palestine, Iraq, Thailand, Kashmir, and so on is real. The question is what interpretation one puts on it. Al-Qaeda has a diagnosis and a prescription that makes sense to some young Muslims. This interpretation is something that some young Muslims themselves seek out, by video cassette, by personal contact, or over the internet. It is not forced on them. It is 'self-radicalization', 'self-brainwashing'.[16]

Shane Brighton, a security analyst with the Royal United Services Institute in London, observed shortly after the 21/7 bombing attempts that 'self-radicalization' is a growing concern: 'If you already accept that there's a historic struggle between Muslims and the West and that the only resort is violence,' he says, 'you don't need to sit at the feet of an imam for months. You just need to watch the news to have your mind-set reconfirmed.'[17] This is not even the atrocity videos of the underground communications system, or the internet: this is just 'watching the news'.

The question is not, then, one of how al-Qaeda recruiters managed to brainwash 'nice' people into carrying out atrocities. The question is how a 'nice' person could conceivably come to choose such a path.

Khan took a lot from me. I can't grab hold of him and shout.
But I only feel anger towards him, and not to the Muslim religion
or Muslims. I channel my anger into getting my life back.

Danny Biddle,
who lost both legs, his left eye and hearing in his left ear
on the Aldgate train. (Taken from a news report.[1])

9

Islam Is Not To Blame

Inside The Sacred Writings

The Growing Fear Of Islam

A poll by the *Telegraph* newspaper on the day after the bombings found an astonishing degree of fear and anger towards British Muslims. The proportion of British people believing that Islam itself—*as distinct from fundamentalist Islamic groups*—poses a threat to western liberal democracy had risen from 32 per cent shortly after 9/11 to 46 per cent on 8 July 2005. Roughly half the adult population of Britain believes that Islam itself, as a religion, is a threat to liberal democracy in Britain, an increase of nearly 50 per cent since 2001. Furthermore, the proportion of people believing that Islam poses a *major* threat to Western liberal democracy nearly doubled, to 20 per cent of the British population. One in ten believes that 'a large proportion of British Muslims feel no loyalty at all to this country and are prepared to condone or even carry out acts of terrorism'.[1]

For non-Muslims living in the West, after centuries of fear and hatred, it is not easy to think rationally about Islam. But rational thinking is needed now more than ever before. What is needed is the ability to apply the same standards and the same categories of language to all the three main monotheistic religions—Judaism, Christianity and Islam.

'Christianist' And 'Islamist'

It is common to refer to those who are committed to the establishment of brutal and repressive legal systems based on a harsh reading of the *Qur'an*, and/or the use of violence to achieve such an end, as 'Islamists'. (Indeed, this is the name they take for themselves.)

It is not common to refer to someone who is committed to the establishment of the brutal and repressive legal system in parts of the Old Testament, or who is committed to the use of violence to see such laws enacted, as a 'Christianist'.

The implication is that Islam is inherently brutal, repressive and violent, and the 'Islamists' are committed to a pure or 'extreme' form of Islam, whereas Christianity is inherently not brutal, repressive or violent, and someone who showed an equal dedication to the harsher laws inscribed in the Bible is 'anti-Christian'.

LRA 'Christianism'

This is not an academic question. In Uganda, the Lord's Resistance Army (LRA) is fighting precisely to impose the laws of the Old Testament. History conducted something of a laboratory test when two relevant events were reported in the same issue of the *Observer*, possibly the most liberal newspaper on social issues in Britain. These two short items appeared, just as they are printed below, one above the other on page 21 of the newspaper on 25 September 2005:

> Lord's Resistance Army rebels killed in bloody gun battle
> Ugandan troops killed 15 rebels from the Lord's Resistance Army (LRA) in a gun battle in remote southern Sudan, the military said. For 19 years the cult-like LRA has terrorised isolated communities on both sides of the border, uprooting 1.6 million people in northern Uganda alone and triggering one of the world's worst humanitarian crises.

> Algerian rebels kill 10
> Al-Qaeda-aligned Islamist militants have killed 10 people, including seven soldiers, in separate ambushes in Algeria, newspapers reported yesterday. The attacks came a week ahead of a national referendum on a partial amnesty aimed at rebels fighting for a purist Islamic state.

Assuming that these reports are accurate, why are the Algerian militants 'Islamists', but the LRA not described as 'Christianist'? Why are the Algerian militants described as fighting for purist Islam, when the LRA are not described as fighting for purist Christianity? Why are there two references to Islam (as well as one to al-Qaeda) in relation to the Algerian militants, but no reference at all to Christianity in relation to the LRA (who are instead described as 'cult-like')?

These short reports encapsulate, in around 100 words, the poisonous assumptions which skew reporting, and deepen public fear and hatred of Islam.

In an earlier report, the *Telegraph* noted that LRA leader Joseph Kony 'says only that he wishes to rule Uganda according to the Ten Commandments.' The LRA is described as 'a fanatical cult rather than a political movement'.[2] Why not a 'fanatical Christian cult'? Or 'fanatical Christian terrorists'? As Joseph Kony says, there is a basis in the Christian Bible for this kind of behaviour:

> Moses saw that the people were out of control, for Aaron had let them get out of control, so that they would be vulnerable to their enemies. And Moses stood at the camp's entrance and said, 'Whoever is for the Lord, [come] to me.' And all the Levites gathered around him. He told them, 'This is what the Lord, the God of Israel, says, "Every man fasten his sword to his side; go back and forth through the camp from entrance to entrance, and each of you kill his brother, his friend, and his neighbor." ' The Levites did as Moses commanded, and about 3,000 men fell dead that day among the people. Afterwards Moses said, 'Today you have been dedicated to the Lord, since each man went against his son and his brother. Therefore you have brought a blessing on yourselves today.' (Exodus 32:25-9 Holman Christian Standard)

One response to this kind of behaviour, and to the 'Christian' justification offered by Kony, might be to divide the Old Testament very firmly from the New, and to focus on the sayings of Jesus and his apostles as the real heart of Christianity, quite divorced from the massacres of earlier Jewish history. Unfortunately, this would fly in the face of quite explicit statements by Jesus himself:

> Think not that I have come to abolish the [Jewish] law and the prophets; I have come not to abolish them but to fulfil them. For truly, I say to you, till heaven and earth pass away, not an iota, not a dot, will pass from the law until all is accomplished.
>
> (Matthew 5:17-20 Revised Standard Version: RSV)

> [I]t is easier for heaven and earth to pass away, than for one dot of the [Jewish] law to become void.
>
> (Luke 16:17 RSV)

If we adopt the literal, ungenerous approach to the Christian Bible that non-Muslims tend to take towards the *Qur'an*, this appears to mean that all pre-existing Jewish law, and prophetic precedent, is therefore part of Jesus' teaching.

One of the particular features of the LRA is the use of child soldiers, who are often forced to kill their own parents before being abducted into the army. Twenty thousand children are said to have been abducted by the LRA.[3] It may seem unbelievable, but it is possible to relate these acts to the words of Jesus himself. Encouraging the Apostles to be confident in their speech if they are put on trial, he predicts these consequences of their divinely-inspired preaching:

> When they deliver you up, do not be anxious how you are to speak or what you are to say; for what you are to say will be given to you in that hour; for it is not you who speak, but the Spirit of your Father speaking through you. Brother will deliver up brother to death, and the father his child, and children will rise against parents and have them put to death; and you will be hated by all for my name's sake. But he who endures to the end will be saved.
>
> (Matthew 10:19-22 RSV)

It is not difficult to see how Joseph Kony could comfort himself with these frightening words, which he no doubt regards as instructions, from Jesus himself. A literal reading suggests that the Apostles will trigger bloody conflict, but will not themselves engage in violence. It is easy to see how Kony could regard the giving of orders to his followers to organise the killing of parents by children as his version of the divinely-inspired preaching urged by Jesus.

Now we come to the questions of orientation, which help us move towards a rational discussion of Islam. Can the behaviour of the LRA be used to condemn all Christians? The answer is obvious. Can these violent passages from the Christian Bible (both Old and New Testament) be described as 'the essence' of the religion, and used to condemn Christianity itself? Again, the answer is obvious. Can the (likely) Kony interpretation of the words of Jesus be regarded as definitive? Once again, the answer is obvious.

The problem is that even among the most liberal Western non-Muslims, it is difficult to apply the same standards to Islam that we apply to Christianity.

Jesus And The Law

Before proceeding to discuss Islam and violence, let us take a closer look at Christianity and violence. We have already seen Jesus' firm stance on the continuing validity of Jewish law. As is widely known, the death penalty is prescribed for adultery (Leviticus 20:11); for male homosexuality (Leviticus 20:13); for witchcraft and for being a medium (Leviticus 20:27); for friends and family who try to entice you into worshipping another god (Deuteronomy 13:6-10); for anyone who worships another god, or the sun, or any heavenly body (Deuteronomy 17:2-7); and for anyone who disobeys a priest (Deuteronomy 17:2-7). Many more laws could be cited here which to modern eyes are appalling.

These are some of the laws Jesus himself said would not become void until the end of time (on a literal and naïve reading). One particular law is actually mentioned by Jesus himself. The law itself says: 'For every one who curses his father or his mother shall be put to death' (Leviticus 20:9 RSV). When challenged over his dietary practices by the Pharisees, Jesus said:

> And he said to them, "You have a fine way of rejecting the commandment of God, in order to keep your tradition! For Moses said, 'Honor your father and your mother'; and, 'He who speaks evil of father or mother, let him surely die'; but you say, 'If a man tells his father or his mother, What you would have gained from me is Corban' (that is, given to God)—then you no longer permit him to do anything for his father or mother, thus making void the word of God through your tradition which you hand on. And many such things you do."
>
> (Mark 7:9-13 RSV)

On a literal reading, Jesus is saying that the Pharisees were wrong not to put all disobedient and defiant children to death. (See also Matthew 15:3-7 RSV.)

Now there are no doubt a variety of ways of interpreting this passage. That is the diversity of belief. Within any religion, there will be different ways of absorbing the messages of holy writings, and different elements will be stressed or censored by different communities within the one faith. Somehow, this plurality is thought to disappear with Islam. Outsiders believe that they know the true 'essence' of the scriptures and therefore of the religion.

Ferocity

Simon Carr, the sketchwriter, made one of the plainest statements of this belief a week after the London bombings—in the *Independent*, one of the most Islam-friendly newspapers in Britain. Carr criticised the leader of the Opposition for his statement that the bombers' version of Islam was a 'perversion of Islam'. Carr wondered, 'what if it isn't a perversion of Islam? What if it's a distillation of it? ... There is a desert-dwelling, Old Testament ferocity in the Koran that is very comfortable with violence.'[4] It is absolutely true that there *is* ferocity in the

Qur'an. However, to focus on this element, and to regard it as the 'distillation' of Muhammad's revelation is a political choice, not a textual fact. Karen Armstrong, a former Catholic nun, has suggested that, 'Like the Bible, the *Qur'an* has its share of aggressive texts, but like all the great religions, its main thrust is towards kindliness and compassion. Islamic law outlaws war against any country in which Muslims are allowed to practice their religion freely, and forbids the use of fire, the destruction of buildings and the killing of innocent civilians in a military campaign. So although Muslims, like Christians or Jews, have all too often failed to live up to their ideals, it is not because of the religion *per se*.'[5]

The Sword Verse

It is true that the *Qur'an* contains a violent passage known as the 'Sword Verse'.

> Do not think that I have come to bring peace on earth; I have not come to bring peace, but a sword. For I have come to set a man against his father, and a daughter against her mother, and a daughter-in-law against her mother-in-law; and a man's foes will be those of his own household. He who loves father or mother more than me is not worthy of me; and he who loves son or daughter more than me is not worthy of me... He who finds his life will lose it, and he who loses his life for my sake will find it.

This speech does indeed seem to encourage violence, strife of the most intimate kind, and, in fact, suicidal devotion. However, it was not delivered by Muhammad, but by Jesus (Matthew, 24:34-39, RSV).[6]

Another version of this speech is rendered in Luke:

> I came to bring fire to the earth, and how I wish it were already kindled! I have a baptism with which to be baptized, and what stress I am under until it is completed! Do you think that I have come to bring peace to the earth? No, I tell you, but rather division! From now on five in one household will be divided, three against two and two against three; they will be divided: father against son and son against father, mother against daughter and daughter against mother, mother-in-law against her daughter-in-law and daughter-in-law against mother-in-law.
>
> (Luke 12:49-53, RSV)[7]

Jesus wishes ardently for the world to be set on fire. Most modern Christians would no doubt wish to read that metaphorically, but, troublingly, the following sentences urge 'division' and conflict rather than 'peace'. Earlier in Luke's account, when a Samaritan village rejects Jesus, two disciples ask: 'Lord, do you want us to bid fire come down from heaven and consume them?'[8] This does not sound metaphorical. (Jesus 'rebuked them', by the way.)

Adopting a naïve, somewhat hostile point of view, if we take into account the consistently apocalyptic tone Jesus takes in relation to the imminent[9] end of the world, we can take these words out of their context and marry them to such incidents as Jesus calling on his disciples to sell their clothes in order to buy swords as he is on the way to the Mount of Olives (Luke 22:35-36). We can create a literal reading of selected passages which encourages Christian violence .

It is common to find non-Muslims making exactly this kind of literal, selective and harsh interpretation of verses in the *Qur'an*. The real 'Sword Verse' in the *Qur'an* runs thus:

> Then, when the sacred months are drawn away, slay the idolaters wherever you find them, and take them, and confine them, and lie in wait for them at every place of ambush. But if they repent, and perform the prayer, and pay the alms, then let them go their way; God is All-forgiving, All-compassionate.
>
> (*Sura* 9:4-5, Arberry translation[10])

What does this mean? Juan Cole, Professor of Modern Middle East and South Asian History at the University of Michigan, and (at the time of writing) President of the Middle East Studies Association of North America, comments that references to 'unbelievers' in the *Qur'an* are 'almost always' to the idolaters of Makka, who are 'characterized by *kufr* or the ingratitude of active disbelief'. The *Qur'an* enjoins Muslims to fight back against the idolatrous Makkans who were attacking Madina, *not* all other non-Muslims.[11] The injunction to attack the 'idolaters', therefore, was made at a specific point in the history of the new Muslim community, when it was in grave danger of extinction at the hands of the people of Makka ('Mecca', which Muhammad and the Muslims had had to flee from in order to survive). The term does not, and cannot, refer to either Christians or Jews, in Professor Cole's view, because they do not worship idols.

However, Michael Cook, Professor in Near Eastern Studies at Princeton University, says that the word used in verse 9:5 is *mushrik*, meaning 'polytheist'. He notes that the term could be used of those Christians or Jews who allied with the idolaters, thereby proving that they were not really true 'People of the Book'.[12]

Whatever the room for reasonable disagreement on the interpretation of this verse, if it is read literally (as Islamophobes tend to), it is difficult to understand how either of the terms 'polytheist' or 'idolater' could be used of Jews and Christians in general.[13]

According to one reasonable view, the Sword Verse applies to the particular historical circumstances in which this revelation was received, and to those circumstances alone. There is indeed a general approach to the *Qur'an* which holds that each revelation must be understood in the historical context in which it was received by the Prophet. Juan Cole comments:

> I contend that virtually the only Koran verses that commend violence are referring to the need to defend against the Meccan siege of Medina [where the Muslims had found refuge from the Meccans] and the machinations of the Meccans' allies. Since the pagan Meccan civilization no longer exists and since aggressive Meccan polytheism is not a force in today's world, it is not clear that any of these verses have any relevance whatsoever any more. There are no Koran verses that commend violence against anyone but the Meccan pagans and their allies. Jews, Christians, even the Mandaean gnostic sect of the Sabeans, are all granted freedom to practice and to live in peace.[14]

As we have seen, Michael Cook has a less restrictive and more violent interpretation of the Sword verse. However, even Cook observes that the second half of the 'Sword Verse' ('if they repent, and perform the prayer, and pay the alms, then let them go their way; God is All-forgiving, All-compassionate') compares favourably with parts of the Christian Bible: 'Such a prescription for dealing with people outside one's religious community is considerably gentler than, for example, the stipulation in the Biblical law of war that "of the cities of these people, which the Lord thy God doth give thee for an inheritance, thou shalt save alive nothing that breatheth" (Deut. 20:16).'[15]

The fact is that an ungenerous and literal reading of the sacred texts of any major religion will pull out uncomfortable strands of thinking and behaviour. It is a political decision to choose which strands to emphasise. In the Hebrew Bible, we also find the pacifist vision of Isaiah, which foresees the beating of swords into ploughshares, and spears into pruning hooks, and the end of war (Isaiah 2:3-5, RSV). In the Gospels, we find, of course, the Sermon on the Mount, when Jesus calls on his followers to love their enemies (Matthew 5:38-46, RSV).

In the *Qur'an* we not only find divine commandments to nonviolence (reviewed below), we find a record of Muhammad's living nonviolence. For the first thirteen years of his revelation, Muhammad and the early Muslims suffered considerable discrimination and abuse, and even physical attack, from the non-Muslim majority in Makka. Karen Armstrong observes: 'Constantly [the *Qur'an*] urges the Muslims to be patient and to endure their present sufferings with fortitude and dignity.'[16] For example: 'And if you chastise, chastise even as you have been chastised; and yet assuredly if you are patient, better it is for those patient' (*Qur'an* 16:126, Arberry[17]). It is better to suffer harm than to take revenge. 'Not equal are the good deed and the evil deed. Repel with that which is fairer and behold, he between whom and thee there is enmity shall be as if he were a loyal friend' (*Qur'an* 41:34-35, Arberry). This is akin to Jesus.

Muhammad did not take a pacifist position, but while living in the city of the enemy, the Prophet did hold back the rage of his followers, despite severe provocations. Karen Armstrong relates the following stories:

> His neighbours started to play very nasty tricks with a sheep's uterus: they used to thwack Muhammad with this disgusting object while he was at prayer and one joker even popped it into the family cooking pot. One day, while Muhammad was walking in the city, a young Qurayshi threw dirt all over him. His daughter burst into tears when he returned home in this state and wept as she washed it off. 'Don't cry, my little girl,' Muhammad comforted her, 'for God will protect your father.'[18]

Muhammad bore these insults with a Jesus-like fortitude.

Later, of course, Muhammad accepted the idea of self-defence, then a 'just war' theory, and finally a broader concept of war which launched the astonishing military successes and empire-building of his immediate successors. The turning point came with his flight from Makka to the largely Jewish enclave of Madina (the name is Aramaic, not Arabic, according to Armstrong). This strategic withdrawal from Makka is known to Muslims as the *Hijra*, and the Islamic calendar is dated from this event. After this point, Muhammad was no longer simply a teacher, but a political and military leader, forced to condone violence in order to ensure the physical survival of his new super-tribe.

It should be pointed out, however, that even after this turning point in Islamic history, two of the most crucial steps in the development of the Islamic state were the negotiations by which the Muslims formed a coalition with the warring tribes of Madina; and the extraordinary decision to march almost unarmed into the lion's den—Makka—in order to lay the basis for a bloodless end to the Qurayshi-Muslim war. These acts of nonviolence and peacemaking were critical to the laying of the foundations of the new Islamic state.

Let us consider the latter case. After winning a war of survival against the Quraysh, and after successfully blockading them, Muhammad could have destroyed them militarily. Instead he led his followers in a nonviolent pilgrimage (virtually unarmed, carrying only short hunting swords[19]) into the hands of the Quraysh, during the holy months when armed violence is forbidden. Muhammad signed a generous peace treaty with his former persecutors, and abandoned his economic blockade, paving the way for peace in war-torn Arabia.[20] The Prophet did not merely risk his own life, but the survival of his entire community, with this disarmed pilgrimage. One thinks perhaps of Gandhi rather than Jesus.

Imperial Religions

This, of course, is only one part of the picture. What is misleading for non-Muslim Westerners looking back across the centuries is that Muhammad's theological move from 'patience' to 'just war' was compressed into a single lifetime. The same movement in Christian doctrine took until 313 CE when the Emperor Constantine adopted Christianity as the religion of the Roman Empire. (Constantine was then eulogised by the Christian theologian Eusebius of Ceasarea as almost the fourth person of the Trinity.[21])

It seems likely that any major religion—any 'world religion'—is, or has been at some time in its history, an imperial religion. In the case of Islam, the imperial period followed almost immediately upon its founding; as it did in Judaism, with the conquests of Moses' people as they entered 'the Promised Land'.[22] Christianity is therefore the odd one out of the great monotheistic faiths, in that the imperial period began centuries after the death of the founder. On the other hand, this period has not yet ended.

Returning to Islam, we may repeat Karen Armstrong's summary. While some Muslims, like some followers of other religions, have failed to abide by the laws of war set down in their sacred books, that is a defect of those human beings, and not necessarily a fatal flaw within the books themselves.[23]

While there is much more that could be said on these topics, and particularly on the laws of military *jihad*,[24] perhaps we have said enough about the sacred texts themselves, and we can turn to the living reality of the Muslim communities in which most of the Leeds bombers grew up.

10

Living Islam

The Religion They Grew Up With

Muslim Diversity

One of the features of anti-Muslim racism, also known as 'Islamophobia', is the homogenization of Islam. Islam is regarded as a single, uniform, monolithic belief system—which is barbaric, exotic and brutal. However, the global Muslim community—one in five people on the planet, or over 1 billion human beings—is as diverse as the global Christian community (2.2 billion people). In Christianity, there are divisions between the Orthodox and the Roman Catholic churches, and between these great powers and the many Protestant churches which broke away from them. Then there are many other fragments or fractions of the Christian community. In Islam, there are similarly deep divisions between different branches of the faith.

The most familiar categories within Islam for the non-Muslim are the divisions into Sunni, Shia and Sufi. The division between the Sunni and the Shia (also referred to as 'Shi'i' or 'Shi'ite') dates back to the early years of Islam immediately after the death of Muhammad. The immediate cause of the division was that the Shia supported the claim of Ali, Muhammad's son-in-law, and his descendants, to succeed the Prophet. ('Shia' comes from *shi'at Ali*—the party of Ali.) The Sunnis supported the claim of the Caliphs who *did* succeed Muhammad, none of whom were Ali's descendants. ('Sunni' refers to the *Sunnah*, or the path of Muhammad.) From this original point of division have grown up many other dividing markers between the broad mass of Sunni believers and the broad mass of Shia believers—as well as within these categories. Within Shia Islam, there are, for example, major demarcations between Twelver, Sevener and

Fiver Shias. The numbers refer to the number of imams or religious leaders that the different traditions believe have existed on earth since Muhammad.

Sufi Sunni Islam

Sufism turns out to be a slippery concept for the non-Muslim, as there are many different interpretations of this strand or theme in Islam.[1] One confusing aspect of Sufism is that there are Muslims who consider themselves Sunni *and* Sufi, an interpretation rejected by other Sunnis who think of themselves as more 'orthodox'. So we may speak of 'Sufi Sunnis' and 'non-Sufi Sunnis'. This makes a lot of the discussion around Islam, and particularly around Islamic fundamentalism, somewhat disorienting. We may turn to a book written by Abd Samad Moussaoui about his brother Zacarias, who trained to be a 9/11 pilot, but who was detained before the strikes took place. Abd Samad later discovered from his sister that Zacarias had turned against him on the grounds that he (Abd Samad) was 'doing *tawassul*', a 'heathen' practice.[2] Abd Samad defends *tawassul* as entirely orthodox, presenting it as a Sunni ritual:

> *Tawassul* for Sunni Muslims is an invocational formula whereby a person asks Allah to grant him a favour or help him to avoid a problem by citing the name of a prophet or saint in honour of the person cited. For example: 'I ask Allah, through the Prophet Muhammad to grant me piety.' The Wahhabis reckon that this is akin to idolatry, for, in their book, 'no one may use an intermediary to address Allah'.[3]

This is misleading in two respects. Firstly, this is not a practice of *all* Sunni Muslims, but a practice of the Sufi strand within the Sunni community (which admittedly is probably a majority of those describing themselves as Sunnis, in global terms). There is a non-Sufi strand within the Sunni community which regards such practices as non-Sunni, and even non-Islamic. It might therefore be more accurate to describe *tawassul* as a 'Sufi Sunni' practice.

Secondly, Abd Samad Moussaoui gives the impression that invocation or intercession is mainly centred on the Prophet himself, whereas in Sufism the figure prayed to is likely to be a saint, who is believed to have accumulated enormous *baraka* (divine blessing), which can be transferred to a devotee who prays to that saint or who visits the saint's shrine.

In any event, most non-Muslim readers of Moussaoui's book will have been left with the impression that 'Sunnis' are hostile to 'Wahhabis', when Wahhabism is part of the Sunni fold, and the antagonism he describes is actually between 'Sufi Sunnism' and a range of ideas (including 'salafism') that are labelled 'Wahhabism' (a harsh fundamentalist movement).

In many parts of the world, Sufi associations or *tariqas* have been missionary groups bringing Islam in a form acceptable to, and in many cases merged with, local cultures. These variants of the message are often denigrated as 'folk Islam'. Professor Ron Geaves, in his book *The Sufis of Britain: An Exploration of Muslim Identity*, argues that, 'the *tariqas* represent the most articulate and organised form of traditional Islam and command the respect of millions throughout the Muslim world.' The British academic goes further, suggesting that, 'The only places where traditional Islam has lost its predominance is in the areas where Wahhabism gained its strongholds, namely Saudi Arabia and the region adjacent to it.'[4] (Wahhabism is the state religion of Saudi Arabia.)

Traditional Islam is characterised by everyday recourse to various spirits and intermediaries—the wearing of a magical 'charm', for example, is common. In this view, Sufism should be regarded as Traditional Islam, and Traditional Islam is majority Islam, taking a global view.[5] In contrast to the usual picture of Sufism as a marginal mystical activity, Geaves places Sunni Sufism in the centre of the Muslim world, dominating it in numbers if not in influence. Everyday life for most Muslims consists of these kinds of beliefs and practices, in contrast to what has been called the 'High Islam' of 'scripturalist Islam', which is focused on the sacred texts of the *Qur'an* and the *hadith* (sayings of the Prophet), and (some selection of) the vast body of scholarly interpretation and legal judgement.

Contesting Islam

There is considerable tension between these two worlds. Osama bin Laden and the leadership and the known activists of al-Qaeda are all adherents of Wahhabism, which is one of many forms of Islamic revivalism, seeking a purification of Islam through the scouring away of all practices not approved of by what they regard as 'orthodox' sources. Wahhabism is characterized by extreme hostility to Sufism (among many other things). The relevance of this to our present discussion is that three of the bombers, including the likely lead bomber, Mohammad Sidique Khan, were raised in a Sufi Sunni community, yet they became followers of bin Laden—as we shall see in Khan's video statement.

Geaves, describing the largest community of Sufi Sunnis in Britain, points out that they prefer to be known as the *Ahl as-Sunnat wa Jamaat*: 'This title refers to the community of Sunni Muslims and indicates that the followers of the *tariqas* and their sympathisers see themselves as traditional Sunni Muslims as opposed to the new doctrines of the Wahhabi-inspired movements and their counter claims to Sunni orthodoxy.'[6] The *Ahl as-Sunnat wa Jamaat* are often referred to by outsiders as 'Barelwi' (or 'Barelvi') Muslims. Within Sufism as a whole, the central organizational form is the *tariqa* or order, centred on a spiritual leader. There may be a founder or *shaykh* of the order, and a more accessible, local *pir* or spiritual guide.[7] There are several *tariqas* within the *Ahl as-Sunnat wa Jamaat*, but, as Geaves comments:

> within the major Sufi *tariqas* the prime loyalty is not to the *tariqa* itself but to the individual *pir*. Although those amongst the Barelwis who follow a *pir* acknowledge his *tariqa*, they do not organise themselves around their identity as Naqshabandis, Chishtis, or Qadiris [three major *tariqas*]. Each group of *murids* [disciples or initiates] following a particular *pir* creates its own organisation in which membership is restricted to the *murids* and the *pir*.[8]

Barelwi *pir* Noor ul-Aqtab Siddiqi told Geaves that the Barelwi mosques are 'connected with people [and] personalities' rather than organisations.[9]

This might sound very fragmented and isolated. There is more. The largest Muslim population in Britain—43 per cent of the British Muslim population[10]—comes from Pakistan. Most British Pakistanis (70 per cent[11]) come from the district of Mirpur in the Pakistani Kashmir, and the 'vast majority' of Mirpuris are Barelwi Sufis.[12] (Sylhet in Bangladesh has produced a similarly disproportionate number of Bangladeshi immigrants to Britain, and is also a stronghold of Sunni Sufism.[13]) Geaves observes that in these communities, the most important social formations are the *biradari* or local networks of extended families which form an enclosed intermarrying group. They function in a similar fashion to the caste system in Hinduism. 'These *biradari* networks retain traditional loyalties to the villages of origin and the customs and practices associated with them.' Their primary loyalty is to a *shaykh* or a shrine closely connected to their place of origin and their family traditions. In Britain, Geaves notes, 'these groups often control the committees of Barelwi mosques and are exceedingly zealous in protecting their own status and *biradari* influence'. For this reason, 'the Barelwi tradition has been bedevilled by intra-Barelwi rivalries which continue to erect boundaries around specific localised ethnic groups.'[14] When Geaves refers to 'intermarrying' family networks, this often takes the form of marriage between first cousins. One study found that approximately one-third of British citizens of

Mirpuri descent had first cousins as parents.[15] Barelwi Pakistani communities continue to arrange marriages within their *biradari* networks—across continents—finding appropriate partners back in Pakistan. The focus of much of British Pakistani Islam is on the *biradari* network, an inward-orientation.

An Island In Society

The founding father of the Barelwi tendency was Ahmad Raza Khan Barelwi. His quietist and segregationist approach has been described by an enthusiastic British Barelwi:

> *Hazrat* [The exalted] *Imam* [spiritual leader] Raza also showed how the Muslim community could really survive safe in this World. He outlined this in his famous four-point programme of 1913. The Muslims, he said, should form an island in Society, and within that island totally preserve the traditional society that was [Sufi] Sunni Islam. They should do this by settling their own disputes among themselves, so that the Community had its own leaders, and they should also buy and sell from each other so that the Muslim community would draw closer together and provide a place for Muslims to live. And the wealthy Muslims should provide the saving to finance investment, so that this Muslim island in society could grow and develop. And the Muslims should study Islam, and revive it, so that the Muslim Community would grow ever more Islamic as time went by.[16]

There was no need for military *jihad*, for political mobilization or for material advancement in the outside (non-Muslim) world, according to the Barelwi worldview. This is the world that Mohammad Sidique Khan, Shehzad Tanweer and Hasib Hussain came out of.

The greatest concern of Imam Ahmad Raza was, in the words of a British convert, 'to defeat the evil of the Wahhabis'. The term 'Wahhabi' is used pejoratively to refer to a wide range of fundamentalist movements. In particular, Imam Ahmad Raza opposed the Deobandi and the *Alhl-i-Hadith*.[17] The Deobandi oppose, for example, the Sufi practice of 'intercession', or praying the assistance of an Islamic 'saint'. The *Ahl-i Hadith* went further; rejecting the decisions of the medieval Islamic law schools, making their own 'direct use of the *Quran* and the *Hadith*.' This is something common to all fundamentalist movements (see Joseph Kony and the LRA): the sweeping away of commentary and tradition, the claiming of a fresh relationship with the original holy texts, and the rejection of existing forms of worship.[18] This is precisely the interpretive move made by Zacarias Moussaoui as he moved towards al-Qaeda, according to his brother.

The struggle between Barelwis and Deobandis, which began in India in the late nineteenth century, continues in Britain in the twenty-first century. Francis Robinson notes that the relationships between the Barelwis and their opponents have sometimes been expressed in 'street rioting'.[19] Prominent British Barelwi Maulana Shahid Raza has 'argued that many devoted Barelwis and Deobandis believed that if their children joined a rival group it was as if they had almost lost their faith and they ceased to be a Muslim.'[20]

The Muslim Reformation

Geaves places the conflict between High Islam and Traditional Islam, between 'Wahhabism' and Sufism, between the Deobandi and the Barelwi, in a larger framework:

It has been argued that a protestant reformation is taking place in the Muslim world in which the Wahhabis and Salafis[21] represent the protestant reform movements and the *Ahl as-Sunnat wa Jamaat* are analoguous to the Roman Catholic majority that formerly existed in Europe. In this analogy the Sufis play a similar part to the intercessionary role of saints in Catholicism. The analogy is crude but it does provide some insights into the cleavage. The civil wars taking place in various parts of the Muslim world can then be paralleled to the conflicts that tore Europe apart after the Protestant Reformation.[22]

There is much more to say about these tendencies in modern Islam, and their significance for the world. For our purposes, however, what is of most significance is that three of the four suicide bombers we are trying to understand grew up in a Barelwi environment, deeply hostile to 'Wahhabism', strategically secluded from wider British society, uninterested in military *jihad* or holy war, and extremely parochial in outlook.

The Satanic Verses

It would be misleading, however, to suggest that the Barelwi community is entirely secluded and non-political. One aspect of the teaching of Imam Ahmad Raza is the intense veneration focused on the person of Muhammad.[23] So while

Wahhabis reject the idea of celebrating the birthday of the Prophet as heretical, this is an extremely important festival for the Barelwi. Imam Ahmad Raza believed that during the birthday celebrations, Muhammad himself became present in the mosque.[24] Barelwi Muslims believe that Muhammad is still alive, and hears prayers addressed to him.[25] This extraordinary devotion explains why it was Barelwi Muslims who formed the backbone of the uprising against Salman Rushdie's novel *The Satanic Verses*. They saw in this book not the disturbed fantasy of an actor in the middle of a mental breakdown (the subject of the novel), but a series of insults to the Prophet and his wives. This propelled angry Barelwis onto the streets.

Professor Tariq Modood, now of Bristol University, observed in 1990 that, unnoticed by most non-Muslims, 'the anger over *Satanic Verses* [was] not so much a Muslim response as a *South Asian* Muslim response.' It was not his exploration of religious doubt but Rushdie's lampooning of the Prophet that provoked the anger: 'This sensitivity has nothing to do with *Qur'anic* fundamentalism, but with South Asian reverence of Muhammad (deemed by many Muslims, including fundamentalists, to be excessive) and cultural insensitivity as experienced in Britain and even more profoundly in India.' Leaving aside Tehran (which was a latecomer to the scene), Modood pointed out: 'the demonstrations, whether in Johannesburg or Bradford, Bombay or Islamabad, have all been by South Asians.' There were no major demonstrations in other Muslim countries. It was Britain, the only western country to have a significant Asian Muslim working class, that had the major Western demonstrations. Modood noted: 'while fundamentalism is primarily a movement of the educated middle class, the devotion to the Prophet is strongest among the rural peasantry from which Pakistani and Bangladeshi immigrants to Britain, unlike those to the USA, originate.'[26] Geaves adds that while the Barelwis were 'particularly upset by the novel', and were 'foremost in public expressions of anger', they 'lacked the leadership to organise'. The role of organising the Muslim reaction to the novel therefore fell to 'the better educated and structured reform [High Islam] groups'.[27] This is similar to the pattern of 7/7: (former) Barelwis took the action; Wahhabis issued the later leadership statements.

So the convulsion within the Muslim world over *The Satanic Verses*—that did so much to colour the non-Muslim Western view of Islam—was very largely the product of the particular sensitivities of the Barelwi community. However, this upheaval was not at all typical of the Barelwi stance. Geaves comments that the typical Barelwi mosque 'functions more strongly as a means of reinforcing kinship and ethnic ties than as a means of intensifying the sense of belonging to the wider *ummah*, or even the *Ahl as-Sunnat wa Jamaat*, whether in Britain or in the wider Muslim world.'[28]

We are approaching a critical juncture. It turns around a word that we have encountered already in passing: *umma*. In a way the *umma* is the key to 7/7. The *umma* is the totality of Muslims in the world. It is the global Muslim population, which is considered by Muslims to be one community, just as in times past there was considered by most Christians to be such a thing as 'Christendom', and just as now there is considered by most Jews to be one 'Jewish people'—in Israel and in the diaspora.

The financial, logistical and recruiting power of Osama bin Laden lies precisely in his appeal to Muslims throughout the world to defend—or avenge—communities within the *umma* which are suffering appalling oppression by non-Muslims. Thus, to take one of bin Laden's most recent (December 2004) statements, this speaks to the prospective insurgent: 'You scare the enemy but they do not scare you, and you are well aware that the burning issues of the *umma* today are the *jihads* in Palestine and in Iraq. So be very sure to help them ' He declares. 'Remember too that the biggest reason for our enemies' control over our lands is to steal our oil, so give everything you can to stop the greatest theft of oil in history from the current and future generations.'[29] When bin Laden speaks of 'our lands' and 'our oil', he means the lands and oil that belong to the whole *umma*, and that should be used for the benefit of the global Muslim population.

Bin Laden is not only an anti-Sufi Wahhabi, a high-profile political activist, and a self-defined soldier in a self-declared military *jihad* against the West—the complete opposite of the quietist Sufi approach of the Barelwi, he also invokes as his central message the unity of the *umma*, when the core of Barelwi life is the restriction of attention and religious awareness to an extended family network which gathers around a particular spiritual guide or shrine.

An Obstacle To 7/7

Bin Laden's version of Wahhabism is the exact and total antithesis of the kind of Traditional Islam that Mohammad Sidique Khan, Shehzad Tanweer and Hasib Hussain were raised within. That Traditional Islam—as they were raised to understand it, and as it surrounded them in Beeston—did not and could not lead them to follow Osama bin Laden. The Islam the three bombers were raised within was actually an *obstacle*, blocking the road to 7/7.

11

In The Name Of God

The Language Of Religious Terrorism

Parity Of Esteem

Before we look at our topic in more detail, it may be useful to consider the idea of 'Islamic terrorism'. In this book, we will avoid this term, for the same reason that we will avoid the terms 'Christian terrorism' and 'Jewish terrorism'. It is certainly true that a Muslim can find quotations from Islam's scriptures, opinions from major Islamic thinkers, and precedents from Islamic history, to support the use of violence for politico-religious purposes. It is equally true that a Christian can find quotations from Christian scripture, opinions from major Christian thinkers, and precedents from Christian history, to support the use of violence for politico-religious purposes. Similarly, within Judaism. All these things could be called 'religious terrorism', substituting the relevant religion. However, in the West, we tend not to use the term 'Christian terrorism', despite its applicability, for example, to the Christians who have carried out an armed campaign against abortion clinics in the United States in recent years—for avowedly Christian reasons. We tend not to use the term 'Jewish terrorism', despite its applicability, for example, to Jews who have carried out an armed campaign against Palestinians in the Occupied Territories—for avowedly Jewish reasons.

The lawless military activity of the Lord's Resistance Army in Uganda is inspired by a certain reading of the Christian Bible, and directed to the establishment of the laws set down in part of the Christian Bible. The LRA could therefore be fairly described as a 'Christian terrorist movement'. There are other possible candidates for the term, apart from the killing of seven people (doctors, receptionists, police officers) between 1993 and 1998, in shootings and bombings by Christian anti-abortion/pro-life activists in the US.[1] For example, the bombing of the Oklahoma City Federal Building may have been connected to a grouping of fundamentalist churches named 'Christian Identity'. Timothy McVeigh, the lead bomber, phoned a Christian Identity camp named 'Elohim City' in the run-up to the bombing, and seems to have had close connections with the head of security there.[2] An FBI report on extremists and cults posing a threat to US national security describes Christian Identity in the following terms:

> Christian Identity is an ideology which asserts that the white Aryan race is God's chosen race and that whites comprise the ten lost tribes of Israel... Adherents refer to the Bible to justify their racist ideals. Interpreting the Book of Genesis, Christian Identity followers assert that Adam was preceded by other, lesser races, identified as "the beasts of the field" (Gen. 1:25). Eve was seduced by the snake (Satan) and gave birth to two seed lines: Cain, the direct descendent [sic] of Satan and Eve, and Abel, who was of good Aryan stock through Adam. Cain then became the progenitor of the Jews in his subsequent matings with the non-Adamic races. Christian Identity adherents believe the Jews are predisposed to carry on a conspiracy against the Adamic seed line and today have achieved almost complete control of the earth. This is referred to as the two-seedline doctrine, which provides Christian Identity followers with a biblical justification for hatred...
>
> Christian Identity also believes in the inevitability of the end of the world and the Second Coming of Christ. It is believed that these events are part of a cleansing process that is needed before Christ's kingdom can be established on earth. During this time, Jews and their allies will attempt to destroy the white race using any means available. The result will be a violent and bloody struggle—a war, in effect—between God's forces, the white race, and the forces of evil, the Jews and nonwhites...[3]

Based on this interpretation of the Christian Bible, some Christian Identity believers think there will be a 'race war' in which they are called upon to 'physically struggle with the forces of evil against sin and other violations of God's law (i.e., race-mixing and internationalism)', after which the surviving Aryans will finally be recognized as the one and true Israel. The Christian Identity theology provides a unifying belief system for a wide range of groups, especially white supremacists. Five years after the FBI report, in 2004, the Southern Poverty Law Center found 28 Christian Identity groups operating in 18 states in the USA.[4]

The phrase 'Jewish terrorism' was actually used by then Israeli Prime Minister Ariel Sharon, referring to the shooting of four Palestinians by Jewish settler Eden Natan-Zada in August 2005. His spokesperson said: 'Prime Minister Ariel Sharon takes seriously this act of Jewish terrorism targeting innocent Palestinians that was carried out with the depraved idea that it can stop disengagement' (from the Gaza Strip).[5] (Incidentally, despite the Prime Minister's explicit request, no terrorism-related compensation could be paid to relatives of the three Arab men, because under Israeli law, only attacks by 'enemies of Israel' are considered terrorism. Natan-Zada was not considered an 'enemy of Israel'.[6])

Casting A Shadow

Why do Westerners tend to avoid the terms 'Christian terrorism' and 'Jewish terrorism'? For a pointer in the right direction, let us refer to a European Commission report of September 2005 entitled 'Violent Radicalisation and Terrorism Recruitment'. This paper advised the European media to stop using the term 'Islamic terrorism', so that the vast majority of peaceful Muslims would no longer be portrayed as terrorist sympathisers:

> The commission believes there is no such thing as 'Islamic terrorism', nor 'Catholic', nor 'red' terrorism... The fact that some individuals unscrupulously attempt to justify their crimes in the name of a religion or ideology cannot be allowed in any way... to cast a shadow upon such a religion or ideology.'[7]

The position we are taking here, however, is that there may well be such things as 'Christian terrorism' or 'Jewish terrorism' or 'Islamic terrorism', but that using such terms tends to 'cast a shadow'—as the Commission warns—on a whole body of believers, in a way that should be avoided.

As we shall see shortly, the atrocities carried out in London on 7 July were carried out by four young Muslims in furtherance of their religious duty to their fellow Muslims—as they understood it. However, we will avoid the term 'Islamic terrorism', precisely as Westerners tend to avoid the terms 'Christian terrorism' or 'Jewish terrorism'. There should be parity of esteem, and equality of treatment, for Islam. If we read the Christian and Hebrew Bibles literally and selectively and with a view to violence, we can find divine precedents and justifications for brutality. (We have not referred to the apocalyptic Christian text of Revelation, whose genocidal[8] fantasies inspire some violent Christian fundamentalists.) It would be absurd to suggest, however, that most Christians or most Jews are in any way inclined to violence or terrorism because of what one can find with a selective and literal reading of their holy texts.

Muslim Attitudes

We began this discussion of Islam with an insight into British non-Muslim attitudes towards the British Muslim community. Let us finish with some evidence as to British Muslim attitudes to these questions. Responding to the statement 'Islam is incompatible with the values of British democracy', only 14 per cent of British Muslims told the polling agency MORI that they agreed; 52 per cent disagreed. Does the *Qur'an* justify suicide bombings? 2 per cent agreed, 91 per cent disagreed. (According to some readings of the *Qur'an*, verse 4:29 forbids suicide. In the *hadith*, Muhammad is unequivocal in condemning this sin.) 86 per cent felt they belonged to Britain.[9] In a separate poll carried out by the YouGov agency, 86 per cent of British Muslims said that the 7 July bombings were not justified; only 6 per cent said they were justified. The figures for possible future al-Qaeda atrocities were exactly the same. Only 16 per cent of British Muslims said they did not feel loyal towards Britain. 79 per cent said they did feel loyal (46 per cent said 'very loyal'). YouGov also found that only 1 per cent of British Muslims agreed with the sentiment that, 'Western society is decadent and immoral, and Muslims should seek to bring it to an end, if necessary by violence'. 31 per cent thought only nonviolent means should be used. (It is not clear what proportion of non-Muslims wish to bring about the end of Western decadence by nonviolent means.) 56 per cent thought that Muslims should live with Western society, 'and not seek to bring it to an end'.

The most troubling findings of the YouGov poll were that 24 per cent of British Muslims had some sympathy for the motives and feelings of the London bombers, and 26 per cent of British Muslims disagreed with the Prime Minister that the ideas behind the bombings were 'perverted' and 'poisonous'.[10] We have seen that only a tiny percentage of British Muslims think Western society should be brought to an end by violence, or that the *Qur'an* justifies suicide bombings, or that the London bombings were justified. A substantial proportion of the British Muslim population, however, shares the disaffection of the bombers. How has this come about?

12

9/11 Reverts

The Reaction To The Backlash

A Lack Of Cultural Alienation

A widely-held view in the aftermath of the bombings was that the bombers were disaffected because they had been brought up to be culturally detached from British society. Commentator Paul Vallely, less than a fortnight after the bombings, blamed 'alienation', which he called 'a cultural rather than an economic business.' Vallely cited examples of real or perceived Islamophobia, including protests by non-Muslims against *halal* slaughter, and against the proposed incitement to religious hatred law. 'Whatever the individual rights or wrongs of all that, cumulatively it constitutes what Muslims see as a culture of disdain for them and their faith.'[1] Was he seriously suggesting that four young men had blown themselves up on packed trains and buses, killing over fifty fellow citizens, simply because they felt their faith was 'disdained'?

When we look at the lives of the three Leeds bombers, what we find is that at least two of them grew up in a highly 'integrated' fashion. True, those who knew Hasib Hussain have pointed to the level of tension and conflict between Asians and whites at his school as a possible cause of his alienation, as we saw earlier. However, the other two Leeds bombers did not have such a troubled background, and all three men had highly Westernized youths.

A BBC Radio 4 investigation into the background of Mohammad Sidique Khan discovered that, as a teenager, Khan completely rejected his Pakistani-Muslim identity, and chose to present himself as an entirely Westernised young man, using the nickname 'Sid'. 'He seemed to have more white friends than Asian friends,' said one of his closest friends from school days, Rob Cardiss. 'He used to hang around with white lads playing football. And he was very English.

Some of the other Pakistani guys used to talk about Muslim suffering around the world but with Sidique you'd never really know what religion he was from.' The Radio 4 documentary also revealed Khan's teenage dreams of emigrating to the USA and becoming an American.[2] In contrast to Hasib Hussain, Khan refused to align himself with Asian gangs. He also refused to desert to the white 'side', apparently preferring to separate himself from the race/religion conflict entirely. Unlike other young Muslim tearaways, Khan was not forced to go to the mosque, and seemed entirely uninterested in religion.[3]

As for Shehzad Tanweer, there are no reports of anti-Asian or anti-Muslim racism during his earlier life. As we noted earlier, he is said to have had a fully-integrated life. At school, and then at Leeds Metropolitan University, where he studied sports science, Tanweer was apparently popular. We have heard his cousin Safina Ahmad's verdict already: 'He felt completely integrated and never showed any signs of disaffection'.[4]

Now it could be that these young men experienced discrimination of some kind later in their lives, which contributed to their turn towards al-Qaeda. Perhaps Khan's failure to secure a visa to emigrate to the United States had some effect on his attitudes to the West. There is no evidence, however, for either Tanweer or Khan that their move towards terrorism was due to deep-seated resentments or childhood experiences of discrimination or 'disdain'.

It may be that the three Leeds bombers were able to approach 7/7 only after breaking away from the popular Islam of their families, and by approaching another version of Islam *from outside of Islam*. The question is: having broken away from Islam, why were they drawn back at all? What pulled these three young men back, so that they again adopted a Muslim identity, and why was it an identity quite distinct from the one previously formed by their families and mosques?

Turning Points

All three Leeds bombers became 'more religious' a few years before the attacks. In 1997, as we have seen, Khan was not particularly religious.[5] Then, in 1999, an Islamic fundamentalist preacher visited Beeston. Some believe that it was around this time that Khan started to become sympathetic to armed jihadism.[6] (In 2003, the Jamaican-born cleric, Abdullah el-Faisal, was sentenced to nine years' imprisonment for urging violence and murder.[7]) We have heard that at some point during this time Khan began praying five times a day.[8] Some say that it was around the time of the Iraq invasion, in 2003, that he began to distance himself from old friends, and associate more and more with two of the teenagers he had been mentoring at his gym, Hasib Hussain and Shehzad Tanweer.[9]

As for Tanweer, is said to have become 'more Muslim' and 'started going to mosque a lot more' around 2001.[10] Hasib Hussain, on the other hand, is said to have become more devout in 2003, the year of the invasion of Iraq.

What can we deduce from all this? For Khan, the key moments seem to have been, on this sketchy information: (brief) contact with a radical preacher; possibly the 9/11 attacks and, presumably, the anti-Muslim backlash to those events; and the invasion of Iraq. For Tanweer, something seems to have happened around the time of the 9/11 atrocities. Hasib, on the other hand, made a dramatic 180 degree change of direction as the result of a period going 'off the rails', followed by a conversion (or 'reversion') experience, all in the same year as the invasion of Iraq.

It was claimed that the Leeds bombers were banned from their usual mosques. It seems this is inaccurate. They apparently did not provoke scenes such as the one described by Abd Samad Moussaoui in his book about his brother, the intended 9/11 pilot. Zacarias Moussaoui stood up in the Narbonne mosque at Friday prayers, and preached an anti-Sufi sermon. As the incident is recorded by his brother, the newly-converted Wahhabi was routed by the *imam*, who pointed out, among other things, that as Zacarias did not know Arabic, he could not quote with confidence from the *Qur'an*. There was an altercation, and the future would-be suicide bomber was ejected from the mosque.[11]

Horror At 9/11

Incidentally, Abdullah Jamal converted to Islam before the 2001 attacks. Jamal's mother said: 'after September 11, I was devastated, and so was Germaine [Jamal]... We cried for all the people who died and wondered how Muslims could do this.'[12] An anonymous friend of Shehzad Tanweer reported a similar experience: 'After 9/11, I can remember talking to Shehzad. He said that what had happened was wrong, that there was a place in heaven for everyone who believed in one God.'[13]

The 9/11 attacks seem to have had a profound impact on at least Tanweer: 'Shehzad definitely opened his eyes because of September 11th,' said one friend named 'Ashid': 'That's when many young people got back into Islam around here.'[14] Someone who 'goes back to Islam' is referred to as a 'revert'. This comment is not explained further by 'Ashid', but the pattern is explored in the

Channel 4 film *Yasmin*, researched and written by Simon Beaufoy. Yasmin, the central character, begins as a young woman with a dual identity—Westernized at work, and thoroughly traditional at home with her family. Subjected to an arranged marriage to ease the immigration status of a stranger from Pakistan, she is on the verge of a relationship with a white colleague. Then, after the 9/11 attacks, her house is raided and her husband is seized and detained indefinitely as a suspected terrorist. Encountering anti-Muslim discrimination at work, her relationships with her colleagues break down—including with her almost-boy-friend, and she commits herself to supporting her husband. Arrested herself, she turns to the only reading material she is officially permitted: the *Qur'an*. Having started the film eager to change into jeans on the way to work, she finishes as a less divided and more integrated personality, wearing the *hijab* in every area of her life, and becoming a more devout Muslim. Her brother, who begins the film as a drug-taking tearaway, leaves to join the armed *jihad* in another country. These kinds of transformations ('thought reforms') seem to be what is meant by 'having your eyes opened'.

Faiza Chaudhri, an NHS women's health development worker and part-time broadcaster of 'Islamic Hour' on Manchester community radio, is one of those who turned to Islam after 9/11: 'It was the accusing looks and inquisitive questions she received after 9/11, that made her want to assert her Muslim identity. "Because I had a brown face, people thought I must have some inside info. It made me read up on my religion and start making changes to myself, to stand out and be seen as a Muslim." ' She came to adopt the *hijab* head scarf.[15]

Yet, in the case of the Leeds bombers, at least, the decision to embark on suicide terrorism did not come for another four years. Something is still missing from the puzzle. No doubt deeper investigations will uncover more of the story of the bombers, and no doubt part of it will be found to lie in the post-9/11 anti-Muslim backlash. However, it seems undeniable that the gravitational pull that drew these men back to Islam, though to a drastically different quarter of Islam, was generated by the suffering of the *umma*.

13

Riot

Community Rage,
Community Violence

Deprivation And Poverty

It has been argued that one source of disaffection lies in the social, economic and political conditions of British Muslims. The British trade union movement responded to the 7/7 bombings by calling for government funding to tackle poverty and poor health in Pakistani and Bangladeshi heritage communities. Brendan Barber, head of the national Trade Union Council (TUC), said:

> Social deprivation and poverty is no excuse for criminality, but it can be a breeding ground for poisonous beliefs of all kinds. Even if there had been no bomb attacks, a civilised country should not tolerate such high levels of poverty and deprivation.
>
> We have had too many cheap calls for Muslims to integrate, some of which have come close to asking people to give up crucial parts of their identity. Building a tolerant liberal society where we are all free to express the different sides that make up anyone's identity will be that much harder when some groups suffer from such extreme levels of deprivation and poverty.[1]

The TUC report, 'Poverty, Exclusion and British People of Pakistani and Bangladeshi Origin',[2] showed that people of Pakistani and Bangladeshi origin (who are over 90 per cent Muslim) made up 22 per cent of the British ethnic minority community and 1.8 per cent of the entire British population. People of Pakistani and Bangladeshi origin make up 60 per cent of the British Muslim population. The TUC concentrated on this section of the British Muslim population because these groups are, overall, 'the poorest and most excluded ethnic group in Britain, and this makes their situation worth consideration, regardless of any other

Table 4. The ethnicity of British Muslims, Britain, April 2001			
Ethnic group		Number of Muslims	Proportion of Muslims from this ethnic group
Asian or Asian British		1,172,886	73.8%
	Pakistani	686,179	43.2%
	Bangladeshi	261,380	16.5%
	Indian	132,566	8.3%
	Other Asian	92,761	5.8%
Mixed		65,592	4.1%
White		182,510	11.5%
Black or Black British		107,431	6.8%
All ethnic groups		1,588,890	100%

Source: calculated from *Focus on Ethnicity and Identity*, ONS, 2005, table 6.3.

Table 5. Population of the most deprived wards, England, 2002/3	
Ethnic group	Proportion of that group living in the most deprived wards
White	12%
Indian	23%
Other or Mixed	30%
Black Caribbean	36%
Pakistani	46%
Bangladeshi	60%

Source: *Housing in England*, ONS and ODPM, 2004, p 64.

concerns.' The report contains a string of statistics on health, education, over-crowding, employment and wage rates which all paint the same picture of deprivation.

Mohammad Sidique Khan, Shehzad Tanweer and Hasib Hussain came from two rundown suburbs of Leeds Beeston and Holbeck. Leeds, once seen as a dour northern English town, is now a bustling metropolitan city crammed with students—in parts of the town. In Beeston and Holbeck, on the other hand, only 10% of young people go to university, compared with 44 per cent in more afflu-ent areas. 'Unemployment is high and misuse of drugs is widespread.'[3]

Could these conditions have created the rage that ignited in London on 7 July? We know that at least two of the Leeds bombers had achieved some kind of foothold in society, with Khan working as a teacher and volunteering as a local community worker, and Tanweer studying sports at college, until shortly before the bombings. Tanweer's father was a prosperous and respected local busi-nessman. Hasib Hussain, according to his father, was due to start at university in September 2005. If the London bombings have any relationship to the social and economic deprivation of Pakistani Muslims in Britain (and the Leeds bomb-ers were of Pakistani origin), that connection is neither straightforward nor immediate.

Table 6: Risk of being poor by ethnic group, Britain, 2002/3	
Ethnic group	Proportion who are poor
Pakistani/Bangladeshi	69%
Black Non-Caribbean	46%
Black Caribbean	32%
Chinese or Other Ethnic Group	32%
Mixed	31%
Indian	22%
All individuals	22%
White	20%

Source: *Households Below Average Income*, DWP, 2004, tables 3.5 & 3.6. Poverty is defined as living in a household with net equivalised income below 60 per cent of median. Calculated on an 'after housing costs' basis.

I Predict A Riot

There is another factor that we have not so far considered, which may have helped to radicalize these young men. 2001 was not only the year of the 11 September atrocities, it was also the year of riots in Burnley, Oldham and Bradford—all involving young Muslim men. There are unescapable parallels with the riots involving young Muslim men in France, Belgium, and Denmark in November 2005.

In France, these riots caused considerable soul-searching, and a sense that one cause lay in the deprivation and discrimination suffered by communities of North African origin. As the riots raged, French Prime Minister Dominic de Villepin acknowledged that racial discrimination was a fact of life, 'as reflected in the preference given to jobseekers with native French-sounding names.'[4] At the same moment, in contrast to his public stance, President Chirac privately confessed that France itself was to blame for the riots, because it had abandoned North African immigrants and their descendants to the ghettos, and 'had not done everything possible for these youths, supported them so they feel understood, heard and respected'.[5] *The Times* of London commented that other European nations could not afford to feel smug: 'many of the underlying tensions that have sustained the uprisings in the suburbs are common across Europe: high concentrations of ethnic minorities, very high unemployment—in some French ghettos up to 40 per cent—widespread grievances at discrimination and perceived racism, and the influence of criminal gangs, drug dealers and religious extremists.'[6] Despite this last reference, there is no evidence that

Table 7. Male average (median) hourly pay, employees, 18 & over, Britain, 2004	
Group	£ per hour
Pakistani/Bangladeshi	£6.25
Black	£7.00
Non-white	£7.54
Mixed/other	£7.60
White	£9.31
Indian	£9.56

Source: *National Minimum Wage*, Low Pay Commission Report 2005, table 4.6.

'religious extremists' played a significant role in the street violence. A *Financial Times* investigation found 'A revolt of youth without religious motivation', quoting Oliver Roy, a French expert in Islamic fundamentalism: 'there's no Middle Eastern connotation to the riots'. Roy pointed out that: 'The rioters aren't defining an identity, except that of their neighbourhoods. It's a revolt of youth, of young men, an anti-police and anti-society movement... an expression of a youth sub-culture, not tied to Islam. And not all the rioters are Muslims.'[7] Asked whether he felt French by the *Guardian*, an anonymous young French Algerian man in a riot-torn suburb responded: 'We hate France and France hates us. I don't know what I am. Here's not home; my gran's in Algeria. But in any case France is just fucking with us. We're like mad dogs, you know. We bite everything we see.'[8]

Abd Samad Moussaoui, brother of would-be 9/11 pilot Zacarias Moussaoui, writes movingly in his autobiography of his family's struggle with racism in France. His Algerian parents (who separated early in his life) both kept their heads down, working. Abd Samad and Zacarias both pursued education, became more fully French, and tried to assert themselves, but suffered in various ways from institutionalized racism — including within the state education system. Moussaoui is convinced that his family's experience of white racism in France was part of what drove his brother towards al-Qaeda and the 9/11 plot. Despite his qualifications, and despite the shortage of skilled workers in the field, whenever Zacarias Moussaoui applied for work as a sales technician in mechanical engineering and electrical engineering, it was always: 'Too late!' Abd Samad comments: 'All these accumulated frustrations were like so much fertiliser that would make my brother susceptible to an ideology that he would unfortunately come across very readily in England.'[9]

Abd Samad Moussaoui records an incident of police brutality which he experienced in July 1989. He was assaulted on the street by a white stranger, and ran to some police to seek protection, only to be teargassed in the face. The police station refused to lodge a complaint against either the assailant or the police officer. (The man who launched the initial attack was later fined. There were no proceedings against the police officer, so far as is known.) Moussaoui remembers his rage: 'The cop didn't just gas and insult me. It was worse than that. For him, quite obviously, when an Arab and a native Frenchman are involved, it's always the Arab who's guilty. That kind of thing can really fill a person's heart with hatred for a long time.'[10]

A North African rioter in Saint Denis, Ait Mochrane, pleaded guilty at his trial in November 2005, and expressed regret for setting fire to a pancake house and a cash dispenser. Mochrane, who had no previous convictions, said: 'The riot police spoke racist words to me during Ramadan.' One of the judges asked: 'So you burnt the pancake house in return? It was a form of vengeance?' Mochrane nodded.[11] There were many reports of police racism during the riots. In an estate in Sevran, north of Paris, the *Guardian* was told that the enemy was the police: 'They harass you, they hassle you, they insult you the whole time, ID checks now, scooter checks next. They call you nigger names.' Karim, 17, reported being harassed and told: 'Go back home, Arab. Screw your race.'[12] The trigger for the rioting was, of course, the deaths of two young French North African men, electrocuted in a power substation, while reportedly being chased by police (the French police deny this version of events).[13]

As in many previous cases of ghetto rebellion, there seems to have been an incendiary mix of segregation, exclusion, deprivation, racism, and police harassment, with a particularly outstanding act (real or perceived) of official violence serving as the ignition point for existing grievances.

2001 Riots

When we turn to the North of England, and the summer of 2001, we find a similar underlying picture, but with grassroots white racism rather than police violence triggering unrest.

In Burnley, according to the report, the immediate trigger for violence was a series of violent incidents (not all of them interracial, some of them disputes between drug dealers) linked to the belief amongst young Asians in the town that young whites were preparing to launch an assault on the Asian community.[14] One of the triggers for the riots in Oldham was the organising of far-right white racist groups such as the National Front. The official inquiry notes that some Asians believed that the police had effectively supported the far right by allowing them to march: 'This in turn resulted in increasing tension in the community causing young Asian men to go out into the streets in the belief that they were defending their community.'[15] In Bradford, the *Guardian* reported: 'The tinderbox atmosphere created by rumours of a National Front rally—which never materialised—was ignited by [an attack on a young Asian by white drunks], with Asian youths pouring on to the streets of Manningham to "defend" the community.'[16] A pattern is emerging—young British South Asians 'defending' their communities through offensive street violence.

While police violence does not seem to have triggered the riots, there are traces in the reports of hostility between Asian communities and the police. One extraordinary incident during the riots is suggestive. On 25 June 2001, Shahid Malik, then a member of the Labour Party's National Executive, and a Commissioner on the Commission for Racial Equality—now a Labour MP—was beaten to the ground by a line of riot police, while calling on Asian youth to maintain calm. Turning from the crowd of youth to the police and putting his hands up to say: 'There is no trouble here', Malik was smashed in the face with the edge of a riot shield, and then struck again when he was on the ground, by more than one police officer. He was briefly knocked unconscious. Malik said later: 'When I came round, I heard an officer saying: "Stop fucking acting and get up." I could see in their eyes all logic had gone.' Malik was arrested on suspicion of inciting violent disorder, and taken to hospital in handcuffs (and then released without charge). He said later: 'The riot shields were smashed in my face, causing four to five stitches above the eye, a black eye, lacerations to the arm, bruises on the back of the head, on the body, and on the legs.'[17]

'Defending' The Community

Criminologist Dr Colin Webster of Leeds Metropolitan University observes that many Pakistani and Bangladeshi men who migrated to Britain from the poorer rural areas of Punjab, Mirpur, Kashmir and Sylhet often lost their jobs after the collapse of the British textile industry between 1975 and 1985. Their children now experience 'the highest rates of joblessness, possess the lowest educational and training qualifications, and live in the worst housing' in Britain. They attend some of the worst schools among ethnic minority groups in Britain, and their parents generally possess low or non-existent qualifications and are often illiterate.

In Burnley, there are around 5,000 people of Asian origin living in a town of 90,000 people. They almost all live in one ward: Daneshouse. Daneshouse is the most deprived ward in the borough, and among the most deprived 1% of wards in England in terms of household income. Lord Tony Clarke, the chair of the Burnley Task Force, comments in the official report on the Burnley disturbances: 'it is clear that, whilst Burnley is not a city, it experiences all of the chronic problems associated with inner city deprivation.'[18] One can say something similar in the other areas which experienced street disturbances. Part of the problem, again, is employment discrimination. The official Home Office report into the disorders notes: 'We are concerned about the "typecasting" of certain groups in relation to employment opportunities and possible discrimination in some of the areas we visited. A number of notable private employers seemed to employ no visible minorities and "post code discrimination" was also referred to by several communities.'[19]

This deprivation, however, is not, in Colin Webster's view, the main explanation for the disorders of 2001. In the 1970s, Asian communities responded to racist violence by organising anti-racist movements with links into wider white society. Webster suggests that when the same racist violence, abuse and low-level harassment emerged against poor Pakistani and Bangladeshi communities in the 1980s and 1990s, on the other hand, the young people of these communities responded in a much less organized or open fashion: 'Unlike in the 1970s, a pattern was formed whereby territory was defended or extended using ad hoc, loosely organised self-defence groups that reacted to racist events and threats as they occurred.' Webster suggests that throughout the 1990s 'this increased confidence and solidarity on the street involved retaliation against known violent white racists, and some who were not.' In his view, the riots of 2001 'constitute[d] a search for respect and recognition from real and perceived adversaries, whether white young people or the police':

> In poor areas respect is won through the ability to stand your ground and fight. Ironically some young Asians have adopted and adapted a white working class street culture of violence and retaliation, and turned it around to defend themselves.[20]

In both Bradford and Oldham, residential and social segregation has been increasing, according to Webster, as whites leave areas and schools perceived as 'Asian'. The 'feelings of a separate "Asian" identity are a direct product of long-standing and widespread white hostility.'

Segregation

This process of segregation—but not its origin in white racism—was highlighted in the official Home Office report into the 2001 rebellions. The Cantle Report stressed the lack of 'community cohesion' in urban areas as the primary 'cause' of the violence, by which it meant the lack of *inter*-community bonds.[21] The Cantle Report observed that 'difficulties are more apparent when the separation is multi-faceted—eg when geographic, educational, cultural, social and religious divisions reinforce each other to the extent that there is little or no contact with other communities at any level.' However, the report did acknowledge that 'some minorities choose to live within their own communities', perhaps 'to ensure that there is a sufficient critical mass to support facilities such as shops and places of worship', or, crucially, 'to try to ensure safety of community members.'[22]

The Race Review in Bradford, led by Sir Herman Ouseley, observed that 'many white people feel that their needs are neglected because they regard the minority ethnic communities as being prioritised for more favourable public assistance', while 'Asian communities, particularly the Muslim community, are concerned that racism and Islamaphobia continue to blight their lives resulting in harassment, discrimination and exclusion'.[23] These conflicting views create a situation where 'different ethnic groups are increasingly segregating themselves from each other and retreating into "comfort zones" made up of people like themselves. They only connect with each other on those occasions when they cannot avoid each other, such as in shops, on the streets, at work, when travelling and, perversely, in Asian-owned restaurants by choice.'[24]

We have already noted the emphasis within Barelwi communities on the cohesion of the extended family network or *biradari*, on *biradari*-oriented mosques and *tariqas*, and a theology of self-segregation. This tendency towards seclusion and self-segregation has apparently been reinforced by the conditions affecting many British Pakistani communities. The question is how younger members of these communities react to these circumstances. With the riots in Europe, the question is a larger one, with a wider significance.

Community Violence

It might be useful at this point to draw a distinction between 'political violence' (terrorism) and 'community violence' (vigilantism or neighbourhood self-defence). Community violence of the kind seen in Burnley, Oldham and Bradford is a group effort on the streets, a 'defence' of threatened neighbours by a physical confrontation with those who might attack. It might be 'pre-emptive' (as seems to have been in the case of Burnley) or in some sense 'reactive' (as in Bradford), but it is a case of the young people—young men—of a community going onto the streets to meet a challenge to the community head-on and face-to-face. The purpose is not to kill, or necessarily to cause serious injury. It is to deter and defend against a (real or imagined) imminent assault.

Political violence of the kind we are considering, is, on the other hand, intended quite deliberately to kill, and it is indiscriminate, and aimed at individuals who are not posing a threat to any British community. It is not 'defensive' in the way that 'community violence' (as defined here) might be.

One can see how 'community violence' of the kind that occurred in the summer of 2001 flows out of the social, economic and cultural conditions of many South Asian communities. Political violence, particularly in the form of suicide terrorism, on the other hand, does not flow naturally out of these conditions.

In other words, the young British Muslims who were involved in the 2001 street disturbances have the same relation to the 7/7 bombers as rowdy white football fans have to David Copeland, the young white racist nail bomber who killed three people in a London gay pub in 1999.[25] These are different kinds of violence, with different origins and existing in different moral worlds.[26] That is not to say that the Northern riots of 2001 might not have had a radicalizing impact on the four 7/7 bombers, but it is to argue that the social, economic and cultural conditions of the Muslim communities in Leeds were, and remain, far from sufficient to explain the kind of cold rage that fired the Leeds bombers.

14

The Mullah Crew

Inside The Muslim Generation Gap

Generational Friction

Part of the story leading up to 7/7 is the friction *within* British Muslim communities. One young French rioter said in November 2005: 'We have to do this. Our parents, they should understand. They did nothing, they suffered in silence. We don't have a choice. We're sinking in shit, and France is standing on our heads.'[1] As we have seen, in British Pakistani communities, the Barelwi tradition teaches that Muslims should form an isolated 'island' within non-Muslim society.[2] This seems, roughly speaking, to be the stance of first-generation Muslims in France and of immigrants in many countries. The rioting in France was famously inflamed by the remarks of Nicolas Sarkozy, the Interior Minister, who described urban vandals as *'racaille'* or 'rabble'.[3] Oueinat Mouloud, a local Muslim councillor in the Saint-Denis municipality, said: 'When the interior minister described the youths as "rabble," he was talking about the second and the third generations of immigrants, who are more integrated into society than their parents.'[4] Being 'more integrated' is, paradoxically, to be more in conflict with non-Muslim white society.

Dr Sean McLoughlin, an Islam expert at Leeds University, who has visited all the mosques in the Leeds area, observed after 7/7: 'An important point about mosques both in Leeds and elsewhere is that they were set up by first-generation Muslims, and although some of them are becoming a bit more dynamic and open to younger people, they are not that accessible to the young. Many are almost like old men's clubs.'[5] The *Telegraph* interviewed the older generation of Muslims in the Beeston area: 'Some blame the failure of the mosques for not being more vigilant about the radical clerics preaching on the pavements or recruiting in the universities. Others insist Britain's foreign entanglements in Iraq and Afghanistan are to blame.'[6] In the *Guardian*, the older generation was represented by Qurban Hussain, deputy leader of the borough council in Luton: 'This is another tragedy: the generation gap between young and old in the ethnic minorities is much greater than in the indigenous population. Our elder generation were law-abiding and hardworking. Where they failed was they put all their God-given hours into work and didn't spend time with their children. When these people are brainwashed, they are brainwashed to an extent that they don't talk to their parents.'[7]

It's Not Only Iraq

When these newspapers turned to younger Muslims, they found a rather different perspective on the generation gap. A 23-year-old man in Beeston, who gave his name as Asif, told the *Telegraph* that the elders in the community were happy to turn a blind eye to atrocities elsewhere in the world, while young men were not. He said: 'A lot of them came over when they were young and are just happy to keep their heads down. We were born in Britain and raised in a different political climate. We know what's been going on in Bosnia, in Afghanistan, and as Muslims it hurts us.'[8] The *Guardian* encountered a young Muslim in Leeds named Hashim Talbot who declared that the older generation were 'theologically aware but politically passive'; while younger people were 'theologically dumb but politically active.' Talbot said: 'It's not only Iraq. A lot of people have sympathy for the Palestinians, who we see as brothers. But young Muslims are not as educated in their religion so they go for radical ideas because with these they can see change happen quickly.' Moderate Muslims were too slow for the young generation: 'Any young person is vulnerable to any form of extremism.'[9]

From another angle, the *Independent on Sunday* interviewed 'Arif' and North Leeds community worker Mohammed Shafique. These two young Muslim men stated that 'many parents fail to give younger Muslims the freedom to openly express themselves or to take active political and religious roles in their communities'. This is where 'parallel lives become secret lives; where parents, friends and imams lose control and influence'. They suggested that this was why, in part, young men such as Hasib Hussain and Shehzad Tanweer 'feel an explosive sense of anger.'[10] On this analysis, part—presumably a tiny part—of the rage of the bombers is the rage of children against over-controlling parents, in South Asian cultures characterized by authoritarian patriarchy.

Dr Philip Lewis of Bradford University's School of Peace Studies, notes that one 'solution' to the tensions pulling on the younger generation is an adapted form of US ghetto gangsterism (as satirized by comedian Sacha Baron-Cohen in the figure of 'Ali G'). Lewis notes that as long ago as 1997, the Runnymede Trust report on 'Islamophobia' had detected trends amongst young British Muslims 'towards territoriality and gang formation, and towards anti-social conduct, including criminality'. There has been an increase in young Muslims in prison. There were in October 2000 over 4000 Muslim prisoners in the UK, or 9 per cent of the prison population—three times more than the proportion of Muslims in the country. 65 per cent were young men aged 18-30, and one in four had been convicted of drug offences.[11] This is somewhat misleading, however. If we compare 'working-class, deprived, urban Muslim communities' with the national crime rate for 'working-class, deprived, urban communities'—and factor in any racial and religious discrimination Asians and Muslims may suffer in conviction and sentencing rates—we may have a clearer and more accurate picture.

An Assertive Muslim Identity

Lewis draws some conclusions from the existing research into Muslim youth in London, Birmingham and Bradford. He suggests that a new 'assertive Muslim identity' has been growing among young British Muslims. This identity is distinct from membership of self-consciously Islamic groups, which range from 'quietist sufi groups' to 'strident radical groups'. This 'assertive Muslim identity' is not necessarily rooted in any religious belief or even understanding. Dr Yunas Samad (also of Bradford University) notes that, in the context of an already conservative Yorkshire macho male culture, Islam can play a role in the construction of masculinity. Young Muslims can project a 'hard' image by claiming membership of Hamas or *Hizb ut Tahrir*: 'Yet the same individuals were unaware who Shias were, and how they differed from Sunnis, and did not know what Hamas or Hizb-ut-Tahrir represent. Neither were they observant in their religious rituals.' Such young men were quite often in trouble with the police for petty crime and drugs. Daubing walls with the slogan 'Hamas Rules OK', or supporting anti-semitic, homophobic and misogynist organisations such as *Hizb ut Tahrir*, 'was more an act of rebellion and defiance rather than the rise of "fundamentalism".' These affiliations 'seemed to be linked with territory', with names such as Hamas, *Hizb ut Tahrir* or *Tablighi Jamaat* used to map and define territorial control.[12]

The control exercised is not merely territorial, against outsiders. It is also directed internally against the community, and focused in particular on the control of the women of the community. A study of Pakistani heritage Muslims in a London borough makes clear that while young men may take advantage of this assertive Muslim identity 'to be largely irreligious in behaviour but Muslims in name', young Muslim women 'may, in a sense become the targets of the assertive Muslim identity of their male peers, who find that a convenient way of emphasising their own "Muslim" credentials is to insist upon the virtuous conduct of their wives, sisters and daughters'. This has led apparently to an escalation of violence perpetrated by a section of young British Pakistani/Kashmiri males in Bradford, especially against women. One form of harassment is organised and structured through Pakistani networks ('the mobile phone mob') and is 'almost always targeted at Pakistani people'. It frequently involves the assertion of misdemeanour or offence on religious grounds and is focused on the honour of women or the community. 'A range of behaviours is involved, including the anonymous but persistent, telephoning of "liberal" parents to criticise them and their daughters; the sustained and aggressive pressure put on young women to force them to stay at home; the organisation of searches for young women who have run away from home.' Another type of violence 'is that which takes place in the private domain and is inflicted on women family members, whether wives or daughters.'[13] This, of course, includes the policing of 'forced marriages' (as opposed to consensual 'arranged marriages'). The number of (mainly Muslim) women fleeing from such marriages has grown exponentially from single figures in 1990 to almost 300 women a year seeking police help in Bradford alone by the end of the decade.

Forced marriage is also an intercontinental issue. The British High Commission in Islamabad has set up a special team to assist young British Muslim women forced into marriage in Pakistan to escape. In 2004, they rescued 105 young people. Most were between 18 and 24. The youngest was 14. Khalida Salimi, from the Pakistani organisation 'Struggle for Change' (Sach), which supports victims of forced marriage and domestic violence, says: 'This is a patriarchal society where women and children are considered as the possessions of males. They have no options, no say, no choices.'[14]

The Breakdown Of Conformity

We must remember that many British Muslim areas, and particularly the Barelwi communities of the kind the three Leeds bombers grew up in, are effectively extensions of rural Pakistani society, connected by common values, religious leadership, blood ties, and property relations. Many British Pakistani communities are effectively Pakistani enclaves, ruled by the same fiercely patriarchal values as their parent villages back home. One young woman rescued from a forced marriage in Pakistan by the British High Commission blamed her situation on her father, a North of England taxi driver: 'He's a bit old-fashioned. He didn't like English clothes; he burned my jeans once. He didn't like girls going out and about.'[15]

In such communities, young Muslim women may come under enormous pressure to conform. Young Muslim men, on the other hand, are less easy to control. One member of the older generation expressed widespread feelings of dismay about the Muslim youth: 'The children *vigre ge* (are spoilt). Here all they do is sell drugs and thieve.... It is the fault of parents that these boys are in such a bad state. They have no responsibility. They won't go to weddings or to *Mattam* (mourning rituals) unless forced.'[16]

The Myth Of Control

Ramindar Singh, formerly a Deputy Chairman of the Commission for Racial Equality, and a founder member of the Bradford Racial Equality Council, puts the matter forcefully in another appendix to the Bradford Race Review:

> In Bradford, outwardly 'close-knit' looking South Asian communities are internally quite heterogeneous in composition. All these communities have their community-wide known and respected personalities but they do not carry the traditional position of influence and social control, especially on the younger generation that quite often operates beyond their narrow social group boundaries. This was very clearly demonstrated when the so-called community leaders were shouted down and heckled when they tried to mediate between the Police and the Muslim youth involved in the Manningham riots in 1995. Justifiably, South Asian youngsters may feel no traditional obligation to or reverence for those leaders who they believe neither understand their problems nor have taken any positive steps to address their issues or concerns. Thus it is wrong to assume that the community leaders are losing control over the youth. The existence of any such control has been a myth.[17]

Singh suggests that young South Asians continue to respect their parents. It is not immediate family loyalties that have changed, but attitudes to the extended social networks based on caste, clan, and regional loyalty. Young South Asians aspire to achieve 'more freedom in the choice of education, careers, friends and marriage and political activities.' (Note this reference to politics.) Singh suggests that it is in this wider context, outside the family, that young South Asians see the broader ethnic social networks, including their parents, as 'obstructive barriers'. This is an analysis of generational friction across the South Asian communities, including young Muslims, Hindus, Sikhs and so on. Singh remarks: 'The co-operation among Asian youth across the religious boundaries has disappeared. The religious issues seem to have taken priority over more general but serious concerns about discrimination, deprivation and social justice.'[18]

The Tacit Contract

We may turn now to one final supplementary document attached to the Bradford Race Review, by the controversial former Principal Race Relations Officer to Bradford City Council. Setting aside Graham V. Mahony's accusation that Bradford Muslims have reversed the usual pattern of colonists becoming immigrants—an inappropriate slur—he nevertheless has some interesting insights to contribute on 'the apparent collapse of parental control over their young men'. Mahony refers to 'significant groups of young men who are heavily involved in drug dealing and abuse, gang activities and crime', who 'are often abusive and threatening to white people in their areas and appear in significant and intimidating groups in the town centre area'. Mahony points out that 'these same young men, for the most part, profess their belief in Islam, do not drink alcohol and the vast majority will accept the arranged marriage.' He suggests that while their parents claim to have no control over them, 'yet these young men do not kick against certain fundamentals', indicating a degree of parental control, based on 'a tacit agreement with their young men' which requires them to accept Islam, teetotalism, and arranged marriages—in return for a degree of freedom in other aspects of their lives. Mahony detects 'a parental fear, no doubt well-founded, that if they exert pressure in other areas then they will lose their sons' commitments in those three vital areas.'[19] While Mahony's language is unnecessarily negative, he does seem to identify some unspoken contract.

The Mullah Crew

What is the relevance of all this to the story of the 7/7 bombers? Well, it seems that the Leeds bombers were situated precisely in this zone of friction between the older and younger generations, in an organized street gang that occasionally defended the community's turf against white gangs, but that had a much wider agenda. (Recall the concern expressed by Hasib Hussain's brother about the 'gang' he became involved in.) However, this gang, apparently known as the 'Mullah Crew', was a force for rehabilitation and rectitude rather than drug-dealing and criminality. It could therefore be classed as highly-organized and grounded form of the 'assertive Muslim identity' detected by Philip Lewis, one that had a solid grasp of Islam, rather than the empty, macho posturing described above.

Ian Herbert and Kim Sengupta of the *Independent* discovered that Mohammad Sidique Khan worked closely with fellow 7/7 bomber Shehzad Tanweer in creating a 15-strong vigilante group which carried out strong arm social work, with a measure of community approval.[20] The group met in the Iqra Islamic bookshop (which sold the videos which have been discussed above), and a gym beneath Beeston's Hardy Street mosque. 'Their radicalism was so blatant that the gym became known as the "al-Qa'ida gym", according to Tanweer's associates.' (Khan also ran a gym at the *Hamara* community centre in Beeston.) Apparently, local people were prepared to overlook their extreme views because they were known to be able to energise many disenchanted young Muslim men 'whose heroin abuse was giving the Asian community a bad name.' Shehzad Tanweer was apparently 'integral' to the process: 'Lads would be taken by the group and put through cold turkey by locking them in a room for five days.' It is tempting to speculate that the Mullah Crew also carried out 'moral policing' of sexual morality and liberal parenting and so on, of the kind described above, and also performed some 'community defence' function in relation to white racist gangs.

The Crew also organized a regime of outdoor activities such as paintballing, climbing in the North Yorkshire Moors and canoeing in North Wales. Tanweer is remembered for a paintballing trip in which he excelled with the gun. 'He was approaching it like a proper soldier,' Herbert and Sengupta were told. However, only proper Muslims could become part of this process. 'To be invited on one of these outings you had to be a part of their religious set,' said another source. 'They would not take lads who had become too "Westernised" for their liking.'

This is reminiscent of the activities of the so-called 'Black Muslims', the 'Nation of Islam' championed for a time by Malcolm X, which focused its recruitment efforts on African-American drug addicts, gamblers, alcoholics, prostitutes and thieves in US ghettos—and in prisons. (The 'Nation of Islam' was based on a separate revelation to a man calling himself 'Elijah Muhammad', involving a set of beliefs quite unrelated to mainstream Islam.) The Nation of Islam effort also involved a programme of physical rehabilitation, military-style training, and outreach to street gangs to try to convert them into instruments of the church. One bait offered to street criminals was the prospects of martial arts training.[21]

Unlike the Nation of Islam, however, the Mullah Crew had no national ambitions. It had a purely local, small-scale focus—or so it seemed.

While four members of the Crew died on 7 July 2005, others survived. Their presence continued to intimidate local people even after the bombing, as we discover through a chance remark by a neighbour of Khan's, who asked the *Scotsman* not to publish his name, saying: 'I don't want Khan's crew coming for me.'[22] Apart from this glancing reference, the anonymous sources who discussed the Mullah Crew with the *Independent* are the only local people to have broken the silence about this extremely important aspect of the 7/7 cell's history. It will be interesting to see what, if anything, the British government's official 'narrative' of the road to 7/7 has to say about the Mullah Crew. For the moment, a wall of silence seems to have fallen around the Crew.

An editorial in the *Daily Mirror* commented, 'Places like Khan's gym do a lot to keep youngsters on the right side of the law and give them an alternative to fanaticism.'[23] That is how the parents of Beeston must have seen it before 7/7.

15

Umma

The Global Muslim Community

Solidarity

Journalists visited the mosque in Luton, recently brought under mainstream control after being a hotbed of Islamic fundamentalism, in the aftermath of 7/7. Myfit Lleshi, 23, who fled Albania eight years earlier after losing his family, told them he condemned suicide bombings, but understood why they did it—after watching television images of dead civilians in Afghanistan and Iraq. 'I think there will be 100 more suicide bombings in this country,' he warned. 'In Islam there is no nationality. I am first a Muslim. Muslims are one body. If one part of the body hurts the whole body suffers.'[2]

In the week after the bombings, the *Sunday Times* found the young Asian men of Beeston (few young Asian women were found on the streets) 'as interested in affairs in the Middle East as in their local neighbourhood.' One young man said that it 'hurt' to see 'our brothers being killed' in the Middle East. Pav Khan, a 20-year-old who knew one of the suicide bombers, said by way of explanation: 'If he did it, look at what's happening in Afghanistan, Iraq and Palestine.' 'It's all about the stance of Tony Blair and British policies,' said Mohammed, a young man in his twenties who said he had known Mohammad Sidique Khan; 'You've seen innocent citizens dying [in the London bombs], but then innocent citizens died in Iraq, Afghanistan, Palestine and even Algeria.'[3]

Friends of Shehzad Tanweer told reporters in the days after 7/7 that it was likely to have been the US-led war in Iraq that drove him to blow himself up on an Underground train. 'He was a Muslim and he had to fight for Islam. This is called *jihad*,' said Asif Iqbal, 20, who said he was Tanweer's childhood friend.

Another friend, Adnan Samir, 21, nodded in agreement. 'They're crying over 50 people while 100 people are dying every day in Iraq and Palestine,' said Iqbal. 'If they are indeed the ones who did it, it's because they believed it was right. They're in Heaven. Have you ever been inspired in life?' he asked. 'All Muslims are connected,' Iqbal said.[4]

Bin Laden Was His Hero

Reporters found relatives of Shehzad Tanweer in Pakistan—he visited the village of Kottan in Punjab twice. On his first visit to his uncle, before the Iraq war, he was not religious. On his second visit in late 2004, his cousin, Ashfaq Ahmed, found him to be a devout Muslim who prayed five times a day and who would fast from dawn to dusk on Friday and Saturday: 'If you woke up in the night, sometimes he would be praying on his mat.' Tanweer was keen to discuss religious issues and often railed against America and the West. 'He said bin Laden was his hero and everything he did was right,' said Ahmed. 'He believed that America had made Muslims suffer all over the world. He also used to say about Kashmir that India was committing great atrocities against the Muslims.' When his father sent money from England for Tanweer to buy himself clothes, he spent it instead on 'buying coats for those waging the *jihad* in Kashmir.'[5]

Tahir Pervez, Tanweer's uncle, recalled his nephew's admiration for Osama bin Laden: 'Osama bin Laden was Shehzad's ideal.'[6] Another cousin, Saleem, 20, said: 'Whatever he has done, if he has done it, then he has done right. He knew that excesses are being done to Muslims. Incidents like desecration of the Koran have always been in his mind.' This is a reference to the mistreatment of the *Qur'an* by US guards at Guantanamo Bay.[7] Saleem added: 'Whenever he would listen about sufferings of Muslims he would become very emotional and sentimental. He was a good Muslim... he used to tell us about *jihad*. He also wished to take part in *jihad* and lay down his life.'[8]

Back in Beeston, Jamil Ali, 17, told reporters: 'If they kill one in Afghanistan you feel like you want to kill 100. You don't do it because you don't want to leave your family, but it is like your brothers and sisters dying. That is what people need to understand.'[9] As we noticed earlier, another young man, 'Asif', criticised the older generation of Muslims for turning a blind eye to atrocities elsewhere in the world.[10]

At this point. It may be useful to recall a key paragraph from the Home Office/Foreign Office report on 'Young Muslims and Extremism', which encapsulates this phenomenon in the language of Whitehall:

It seems that a particularly strong cause of disillusionment amongst Muslims including young Muslims is a perceived 'double standard' in the foreign policy of western governments (and often those of Muslim governments), in particular Britain and the US. *This is particularly significant in terms of the concept of the "Ummah", i.e. that Believers are one "nation". This seems to have gained a significant prominence in how some Muslims view HMG's policies towards Muslim countries.*[11]

When the Prophet Muhammad began converting people in Makka and Madina to his new revelation, he dissolved the bonds that separated them into warring tribes to create a super-tribe, a transnational fellowship of believers, which he called the *umma*. The *umma* is the whole community of Muslims.

However, the *umma* has never been a homogeneous and entirely unified entity, even in the time of Muhammad and his Companions. Today, as we saw earlier, there are many major divisions, between Shia and Sunni, and within Sunnism and Shi'ism. In each of these traditions, there are varying degrees of orthodoxy and observance. Nevertheless, as Ron Geaves points out in a thoughtful discussion, despite these sometimes bitter divisions, 'there is a sense of belonging which is maintained through the unity of Islam's ritual or cultic practices': 'The *salat* [Muslim prayers said five times daily], *Hajj*, and Ramadan provide Muslims with a strong sense of religious communion that cannot be repeated in any other world faith community.' Geaves observes: 'if I was to be transported to any Muslim nation, I would know within minutes that I was in a Muslim environment', because of the cultural commonalities in these societies.[12]

No Crusade

It so happens that in many countries around the world, Muslims are being brutally oppressed either by non-Muslim governments, or by Muslim regimes funded and supported by non-Muslim governments. For many Muslims, this reality makes it plausible that the rich white Christian governments—the United States, in particular—are engaged in a war against Islam itself. This is the Muslim version of Samuel Huntington's *Clash of Civilizations* thesis.[13]

Unfortunately, space does not permit a proper survey of the *umma*, or of the varied forces repressing Muslim populations in places as different as Uzbekistan, Thailand, Chechnya, Iraq, Palestine, Egypt, Algeria, Afghanistan, and so on. The charge against the United States and Britain is that they are either turning a blind eye (Thailand), offering political support to the oppressor (Russia/Chechnya,

Uzbekistan), funding and supplying the oppressor (Egypt, Israel/Palestine, Algeria), or directly engaging in oppression (Iraq, Afghanistan). An honest investigation demonstrates the essential truth of this analysis.

What is not true is the claim that this constitutes a systematic and conscious campaign against Islam led by Washington. The most obvious counter-evidence is the long-standing and total commitment of the United States to the House of Saud, one of the most fundamentalist Islamic regimes ever seen. While the harsh Saudi version of Islam—Wahhabism—may be rejected by a majority of Muslims in the world, it is certainly recognized as part of Islam. Washington has never seriously challenged Saudi Arabia on its brutal and dictatorial internal policies. As author Robert Dreyfuss points out in his book *Devil's Game: How The United States Helped Unleash Fundamentalist Islam*, 'If forced to choose between regimes in Egypt and Saudi Arabia led by left-leaning Arab nationalists or right-leaning Islamists, Washington will pick the Islamists every time.'[14] Dreyfuss also asks why, if the United States is really opposed to the Islamic Right, it has invested so much time and energy undermining the governments of Iraq and Syria, and the authority of the PLO—which were all implacable opponents of Islamic fundamentalism.[15]

In the case of another famous Islamic fundamentalist regime, it turns out that '[b]etween 1994 and 1996, the USA supported the Taliban politically through its allies Pakistan and Saudi Arabia, essentially because Washington viewed the Taliban as anti-Iranian, anti-Shia, and pro-Western.'[16] A State Department official wrote: 'The Taliban will probably develop like the Saudis. There will be Aramco, pipelines, an emir, no parliament, and lots of sharia law. We can live with that.'[17] During this period of US-Taliban cooperation, the CIA funded 'educational' programmes in Pakistan and Afghanistan, run by a US academic named Thomas Gouttierre, that produced fundamentalist and jihadist propaganda including children's textbooks in which young Afghanis were taught how to count by enumerating dead Russian soldiers and adding up Kalashnikov rifles, 'all of it imbued with Islamic fundamentalist rhetoric.'[18]

Dreyfuss documents these and many other cases, over many decades, of US sponsorship—direct and indirect—of the Islamic Right.[19] The key issue is not whether a group or government is composed of Muslims or Christians, or whether they are Islamic fundamentalists or Islamic liberals. The key issue is whether they will subordinate their own goals to the goals of the United States, as the House of Saud has done consistently, and as the Taliban refused to do after the August 1998 missile attacks.

A View From Pakistan

One explanation for 7/7 has it that the Leeds bombers were 'brainwashed' and/
or trained in Pakistan, and that therefore Pakistan is the key to the whole affair.
Pakistan is, in this light, the source of the bombers' extremism. In Pakistan,
things are seen rather differently. Maulana Samiul Haq, the cleric who heads
Darul Uloom Haqqania, one of Pakistan's leading institutions of Islamic learning,
as well as being a Pakistani MP, told *The Times*:

> The bomb attacks in London are the reaction against the British Govern-
> ment's support for America's war against Muslims. The loss of innocent lives
> is regrettable, but the British Government should think why it all happened.
> It is time to review its policy on Iraq and Afghanistan.[20]

The Pakistani Government had a similar analysis, if in somewhat more restrained
language. Speaking to BBC Radio 4 ten days after the bombings, the Pakistani
ambassador to the UN, Munir Akram, pointed out that 'You cannot brainwash
somebody instantly, unless he is inclined to be brainwashed.' It was not the
months spent in Pakistan, but 'the years spent in Britain' that transformed these
young men:

> It is important not to pin blame on somebody else when the problem lies
> internally. Your policies in the Middle East, your policies in the Islamic world,
> that is the problem with your society and that is where the problem lies as far
> as this incident is concerned. It would be a grave mistake to point fingers at
> Pakistan or anybody outside your country.[21]

One of the particular accusations made against Pakistan was that the Leeds
bombers were brainwashed in Islamic schools or *madrasas*. There is little doubt
that many of these schools preach a militant form of Islamic fundamentalism.
However, as Pakistani journalist Arif Jamal, who has studied the *madrasa* phenomenon since 2000, points out: 'The fact that Shehzad Tanweer decided to go to
Pakistan to take up an Islamic education indicates that he had already decided
on which path he would take. Perhaps what he heard in Pakistan might have
reinforced those views, but ultimately the process of radicalisation and indoctrination must have begun at home.'[22]

The head of one school, Mullah Riaz Durrani, who is also the leading spokesperson for the *Jamiah Ulema Islam* (JUI), one of Pakistan's major opposition parties,

said: 'It is not speeches in *madrasas* that make these young men into suicide bombers. That job is done by the Americans and the British themselves, by Fox television and CNN, who broadcast the outrages of Abu Ghraib and Guantanamo Bay.'[23] This is an almost exact echo of the analysis of Shane Brighton, of the quasi-governmental RUSI Institute in London, quoted earlier.[24]

We have already noted that the 7/7 cell seems to have cohered not merely around the watching of mainstream news, but around jihadist atrocity videos and DVDs.[25] Recall that in the *Daily Mirror*'s account of one attempted recruitment (discussed earlier), the key video contained 'grotesque footage' of Chechen fighters being executed by Russian soldiers. 'Muhammed' was asked by the recruiters: 'You see what's happening to your brothers and sisters?'[26]

This was not an appeal on the basis of a theological argument, or a reference to the glories of the Golden Age of Islam. The recruiters did not attempt to play on any resentment or revulsion 'Muhammed' might feel towards the West's material power or cultural 'degeneracy'. 'Muhammed' was not approached on the basis of 'ideology'. He was approached on the basis of the reality of the suffering of much of the *umma*. A reality that the older generation of British Muslims, like most non-Muslim Britons, chose to ignore.

While the older generation of Barelwis mobilized over an insult to the Prophet, they have not had similarly strong feelings over the unity of the *umma*. The *Ahl as-Sunnat wa Jamaat* (Barelwi Sufi Sunni Islam) is parochial. This form of Islam defines, confirms, encapsulates and sacralizes a small ethnic, geographical and kinship grouping. According to the research cited earlier, the focus of many if not most such mosque congregations is the *biradari* extended family network of which it is, in a sense, a subset.

For a younger generation, on the other hand, Islam has become the doorway to a transnational fellowship of belief and a global community.

16

Jihad

Struggling In The Way Of God

The Lesser *Jihad*

The word *jihad* means 'striving in the way of God'. There is a famous *hadith* which relates that the Prophet, returning from the battle of Uhud, said: 'you have now returned from the lesser *jihad*; the greater *jihad* still remains as a duty for you.' The 'greater *jihad*' being the moral struggle against oneself. Iran's Ayatollah Khomeini went so far as to suggest that the lesser *jihad* (military action) is not only of no avail but is actually satanic unless the greater *jihad* (spiritual reform) has been fulfilled.[1]

Armed *jihadis* such as Osama bin Laden, however, set this reported saying of the Prophet aside, pointing out (correctly) that it is not included in the most authoritative *hadith* collections. Even so, unarmed forms of *jihad* are recognized within Islam. Gilles Kepel, the doyen of Islamic fundamentalism, points out that the campaign to reconstruct Iran after the ravages of the Iraq-Iran war was directed by the *jahad-e sazandegui* or 'reconstruction crusade' organization.[2]

Just as Islamic fundamentalists claim to represent the essence of Islam, and therefore take the name 'Islamists' (by analogy with 'communists' and so on), the military *jihadis* claim to represent the true meaning of the word *jihad*, and therefore call themselves *jihadis*. With reluctance, we will adopt their terminology from this point, using the word to refer to armed *jihad*, unless otherwise specified.

Engagement in military *jihad* has, for British Muslims, generally meant travelling to foreign lands in which Muslim populations are under attack, and putting oneself in harm's way. Sometimes this has happened under the cover of humanitarian aid work. Thus on 17 September 1992, a 44-year-old British Muslim aid volunteer Gulam Jilani Soobiah was killed in an artillery attack near Mostar during the war in Bosnia. He was supposedly on a humanitarian mission carrying medicine, blankets and food. According to the only survivor of his group, Soobiah was actually smuggling rifles, grenades and other weapons to Bosnian Muslim fighters.[3]

Travelling to another country to help an oppressed people fight back is not by itself a sign of fundamentalism, nor necessarily an act to be condemned. The foreign volunteers who travelled to Spain to help in the fight against Fascism during the Spanish Civil War are now widely respected figures. What matters is what the cause is, and how the volunteer behaves. Travelling to another country to fight alongside an oppressed minority is not, in and of itself, morally objectionable, except from an absolute pacifist point of view.

Solidarity *Jihad*

Many of those now taking on the *jihadi* identity in fact began in this non-ideological fashion. Fawaz Gerges, author of an important study of al-Qaeda, observes: 'Thousands of young Muslims, who were genuinely moved by the plight of their co-religionists and who had no previous links to militants, left their secure homes and families and traveled the world to fight for what they perceived to be a just cause.' In interviews, they declared that 'they felt enraged by the suffering of Muslims worldwide, which they watched on their television screens, and this motivated them to leave everything behind and migrate to defend fellow believers.' Having made this ultimate commitment, Gerges comments, 'many of these zealous young men were transformed by the baptism of blood and fire and the comradeship of arms with other activist Muslims and *jihadis* alike.' They developed a new consciousness and a new sensibility that 'made them vulnerable to radical calls by militants like bin Laden.'[4]

Nasir Ahmad Nasir Abduallah al-Bahri (known as Abu Jandal), who spent several years as one of Osama bin Laden's senior bodyguards, has written about this process in his memoirs. One radicalizing moment for al-Bahri came from the Israel-Palestine conflict: 'I recall a picture that is still printed in my mind to this day. It is of a Jewish soldier breaking the limbs of a Palestinian child with a stone, in front of the eyes of the world. No one moved for his sake. I cried at that sight.' Gerges comments: 'A similar version of al-Bahri's story is often told by religious activists, who, time and again, list injustices inflicted on Muslims worldwide as a contributing factor behind their decision to join in *jihad*.'[5]

In 1995, al-Bahri 'was watching the tragedies of Muslims in Bosnia; the slaughtering of children, women, and old people; the violation of honor and mass rape of girls; and the huge number of widows and orphans left by the war': 'Therefore I decided to go to *jihad* as a young man who was raised on religious principles and chivalry and who is full of zeal about religion and care for Muslims.' Al-Bahri notes: 'My journey for *jihad* at that time was not organized; it was an emotional trip to wage *jihad*.'[6] We may call this emotional commitment: 'solidarity *jihad*'.

Gerges points out that 'there is more to al-Bahri and his generation's story than the simple emotional reaction to social and political upheaval in distant Muslim lands'. There was a 'fertile religious environment', made up of Friday sermons, tape cassettes of speeches, magazines covering such events, and other media. There was a global call to solidarity *jihad* within the Muslim world, which had begun in earnest—with official sponsorship and Western patronage—in relation to the Soviet invasion of Afghanistan.[7]

Al-Bahri ran away from home without the permission of his family at the age of 21. At that point, al-Bahri says, 'I used to consider *jihad* and carrying arms a kind of voluntary work. I did not view *jihad* as a religious duty prescribed to every individual (*fard 'ayn*, or a personal obligation) [as *jihadis* do], but a collective duty (*fard kifaya*), i.e., if it is carried out by some, then others are exempt from it, albeit with their parents' consent.' By the time he left Bosnia, al-Bahri was a changed man. Among other things, he had adopted the belief that *jihad* was a fundamental Muslim obligation, on a par with the five recognized 'pillars' of Islam (the profession of faith, the daily *salat* prayers, fasting during Ramadan, the giving of *zakat* alms, and the *Hajj* pilgrimage to Makka). In this view, armed *jihad* is the sixth pillar, as argued in a key *jihadi* text entitled *al-Farida al-Ghaiba* ('The Absent Duty').[8] With the adoption of this doctrine (and others), al-Bahri had moved on from 'solidarity *jihad*' to 'jihadism'. Another key part of the *jihadi* outlook is pan-Islamism, described by al-Bahri in relation to his time in Bosnia:

> We began to have real contact with the other trends, the enemies of the *ummah*, and the ideology of the *ummah* began to evolve in our minds. We realized we were a nation [*umma*] that had a distinguished place among nations. Otherwise, what would make me leave Saudi Arabia—and I am of Yemeni origin—to go and fight in Bosnia? The issue of [secular] nationalism was put out of our minds, and we acquired a wider view than that, namely, the issue of the *ummah*. Although the issue was very simple at the start, yet it was a motive and an incentive for *jihad*.[9]

The 'ideology of the *umma*'. The 'issue of the *umma*'. The 'enemies of the *umma*'. Starting with a simple desire to help defend fellow believers under attack, many young Muslims came to adopt an enveloping militarist ideology.

The Far Enemy

There was one major division in this armed *jihad* ideology. For most *jihadis* over the last quarter century, the focus has been the local oppressor: usually an oppressive—avowedly Muslim—government (supported by outside powers). This, in *jihadi* terminology, is known as the 'near enemy'. In *Al Farida al Ghaiba*, Egyptian activist Mohammed Abd al-Salam Faraj argued that Muslim governments which did not apply sharia law, and which took unbelievers as their allies, had thereby forsaken their religion, and such rulers—though they might *pretend* to be Muslims—were actually apostates who deserved to die. They were the 'near enemy', and the struggle against this near enemy should be the first priority, above even the liberation of Jerusalem.[10]

The alternative strategy, now associated with Osama bin Laden and his close colleague Ayman al-Zawahiri, was to prioritize taking on the 'far enemy': the United States (and its allies, especially Israel). The far enemy is the power behind the near enemy. Unless the far enemy is dealt with, argue bin Laden and Zawahiri, the local struggles will be fruitless. While there is a certain logic to this analysis, the method chosen to 'deal with' the United States (the 9/11 attacks) quite apart from being immoral and barbaric in themselves, actually undermined local *jihadi* struggles against the near enemy—until the invasion of Iraq.[11]

We should be clear, however, that al-Qaeda is not simply anti-Western. Theodore Gabriel, an Indian anthropologist, notes that al-Qaeda and other militant organisations also operate against perceived Hindu oppression of Muslims in Kashmir, and against Eastern European nations such as Russia and Serbia: 'These instances invalidate the thesis of a general and innate opposition by Islamic faith communities to the West on political grounds. It would rather seem that opposition exists wherever and from whosoever oppression of Muslim people is perceived.'

Gabriel observes: 'The sanctions and subsequently unjustified war and conquest of Iraq, the high-handedness of Indian paramilitaries against the people of Kashmir, Russian excesses against Chechnya, and Israeli atrocities against Palestinians are legitimate causes from which attention can be diverted by characterising people seeking justice as terrorists, and these incidents as symptoms of a general Islamic antipathy to the West or to non-Muslim faiths.'[12]

Defense, Revolution And The 'Great Satan'

Fawaz Gerges, author of *The Far Enemy*, the first major English-language work focussed on the divisions within the *jihadi* movement, observes that not only have most *jihadis* prioritized the near enemy, they have also criticized the bin Laden strategy. Gerges presents a picture of recent history which contradicts much of what is assumed about al-Qaeda in Western circles:

> from the early 1970s until the mid-1990s, the far enemy, as represented by America and Israel, was not an operational priority for Sunni-oriented *jihadis*. The shift to globalism occurred much later, long after the end of the Afghan war around the mid-1990s, and reflected monstrous mutations within the jihadist movement itself. However, since the mid-1990s, a small minority of *jihadis*, transnationalists led by Al Qaeda, a network composed of several tiny militant groups, launched a systemic onslaught to hijack the whole jihadist movement and strategically change its direction and destination.... Although transnationalist *jihadis*, like Al Qaeda, were a tiny minority within the jihadist movement, their actions plunged the whole movement into an existential crisis.[13]

Gerges distinguishes between struggles against outsider oppressors such as Chechnya and Palestine—which he calls 'irredentist jihadism', local *jihad* against the near enemy—which he calls 'religious nationalism', and al-Qaeda-style *jihad* against the far enemy—which he calls 'transnational *jihad*'. I would like to offer a slightly different terminology.

The Islamic fundamentalist element of the struggle in Chechnya does not seem to be motivated primarily by the idea that Chechnya is part of some historic 'Islamic world', and should therefore be liberated from Russian rule. It seems to be motivated primarily by the fact that the Muslim population of Chechnya is being assaulted by a non-Muslim power (as part of what *jihadis* believe is a global onslaught on Islam). Therefore the label 'irredentist' seems inappropriate. Perhaps a more useful term might be 'defensive *jihad*'.

In countries like Egypt or Algeria, many *jihadis* who prioritise the near enemy are aiming (eventually) for a non-national 'solution' to their problems—by recreating the old Islamic empire or Caliphate—so that 'religious nationalism' seems an awkward fit. 'Nationalist' *jihadis* also often have to organise their activities across international boundaries. Indeed, it is thought that the major jihadist group in Algeria, the GIA, disintegrated into unstructured violence in September 1997 largely because Abu Hamza, the London cleric, ceased publication of a

GIA bulletin (he believed they had abandoned *salafi* doctrine), demonstrating the importance of transnational organizing for national struggles.[14] It may be that the description 'revolutionary *jihad*' is a more useful term—to indicate that the priority is to replace the government of a particular country.

As for the last category of *jihad*, it is important to capture the fact that al-Qaeda is not merely practising terrorism across national borders, but is focused on the United States in particular (as well as key US clients). Perhaps it might be useful to draw on Ayatollah Khomeini's demonizing description of the United States and refer to what Gerges calls 'transnational *jihad*' as 'Great Satan *jihad*'. (This, of course, is not to endorse the characterization of the United States or any other country as a 'Great Satan'.)

Three Responses

The United States does indeed support governments that kill Muslims in considerable numbers (in Palestine and Chechnya, for example) or that oppress them brutally (in Algeria and Egypt, for example), and it is engaged directly in wars against Muslim populations (in Afghanistan and Iraq). The solidarity *jihad* response to the first and third situations is to go to the country concerned and to lend a fighting hand to the Muslims who are being attacked. This may or may not be morally acceptable, depending on the way in which the battle is fought (the record in Bosnia is rather ugly). The revolutionary *jihad* solution to the second situation—of oppression—is to take up arms to overthrow the local government. A moral judgement depends, again, on the objectives and the methods applied.

The Great Satan *jihad* answer to all three situations is to inflict brutalities on the general populations of the United States and its allies.

While much remains to be examined, we may say at the moment that the 7/7 bombings fall into the category of what we are calling here 'Great Satan' rather than revolutionary or solidarity *jihad*. It may also be that there was virtually no 'transnational' element to the plot, and that the tragedy was entirely home-grown.

17

Fundamentalism

Defending The Faith

Origins

We have identified a two-stage process of conversion to 'Great Satan *jihad*', as exemplified by bin Laden bodyguard Nasir al-Bahri. Al-Bahri moved from a religious but relatively non-ideological Muslim moral outrage, to the 'ideology of the *umma*'—a particular kind of armed Islamic fundamentalism.[1]

As many commentators have pointed out, there are pitfalls in using the term 'fundamentalism' in relation to Islam. The word began life in Christianity, with the listing by some US Presbyterians of what they considered 'fundamental' Christian criteria. The first list, published in 1910, included: the 'inerrancy' (literal truth) of Scripture; the virgin birth of Jesus; the death of Jesus on the cross as a substitutionary atonement for original sin; the bodily resurrection of Jesus; and the authenticity of miracles. Later groups drew up their own lists. Volumes containing these various lists were then published as *The Fundamentals*, giving rise to the word 'fundamentalist' by 1920.[2] The term quickly acquired a wider meaning than this narrowly-defined 'theological fundamentalism', growing to include 'cultural fundamentalism', and then 'political fundamentalism'—the demand that the state impose a particular religiously-inspired kind of social order—which is now the key meaning of the word.[3]

The Reverend Canon Professor Martyn Percy, principal of Ripon [theological] College Cuddesdon, Oxford, suggests that there are certain hallmarks of fundamentalism. He refers to Christian fundamentalism in particular, but his remarks have a wider application. The conventional view is that early Christian fundamentalism was an attempt to counter new forms of historical and literary criticism of the Bible (which demonstrated, for example, that the first four books of the Old Testament were not written by a single author, Moses), and to repel Darwinian ideas (which undermined the Bible story of human origins). For Percy, 'a doctrine of inerrancy helps constitute a habit of mind, viable perceptions of reality, in short, a whole world', not simply to fend off modern ideas.[4] Fundamentalists see theological doctrine as complete, rigorously defined and 'as a controlling mechanism for the establishment of order in the Church', whereas non-fundamentalists acknowledge the incompleteness of their knowledge and faith, and tolerate pluralism.[5] Percy argues that fundamentalism 'exists in relation to and opposition to trends in society that it perceives as modernist (i.e. where the authority of the existing tradition is challenged), pluralist (i.e. where beliefs and moral, religious values have to compete for attention), or compromised.' '[F]undamentalism refuses to engage in dialogue. It has nothing to receive from the world, since the world must receive it first, wholesale.'

Percy argues that fundamentalism is a tendency, a habit of mind, rather than a single movement. It involves 'a hostile reaction to the mixed offerings of modernity, and to combat it, a set of "fundamentals", such as a "core doctrine", an absolute source of authority, a specific programme that is to be imposed rather than shared, clear patterns for mediating authority and power, and authenticating procedures (e.g. "Have you been born again?") that validate and recognize existing members and potential recruits.'

In his most important contribution, Percy argues that what distinguishes fundamentalism from other faith perspectives, is its opposition to theological and ethical liberalism. Percy argues that 'where opposition to liberalism is lacking, I hold that one cannot speak of true fundamentalism, but only of a close relative.'

Percy refers to the views of noted church historian Martin Marty, who has suggested that fundamentalism appeals to a particular class and personality type. Marty argues, noting that Catholic, Jewish, Christian and Islamic fundamentalists all share the same mindset, that theological issues are 'merely tools, excuses or alibis for the fundamentalist mindset. Without the mindset, the doctrines wither.'[6]

Defending Traditional Patterns Of Authority

What is this mindset, and why does it arise? Cultural fundamentalism generally involves adherence to what are described as 'traditional norms', centred around obedience and respect for traditional family and religious authority. This moral authority system tends to have strict attitudes to the use of alcohol and pornography, to gay rights, to 'pro-family' and 'decency' issues, and to issues around women's reproductive rights. In fact, male domination of gender relations, and control of women's sexuality and reproductive rights generally form central elements of cultural fundamentalism. 'Cultural fundamentalism' is very nearly synonymous with 'patriarchy', organized around both age and gender.[7]

Cultural fundamentalism can also include racial supremacism. In fact, fundamentalism and racism have many similarities, as they are both collective, authoritarian, 'consolidating' responses to perceived threats to 'the community'. Recall the significance of 'Christian Identity' fundamentalism to armed racist groups in the US.[8] Protestant supremacism in Northern Ireland is, in many ways, a disguised form of racial supremacism by the descendants of the Anglo-Scottish colonists.[9]

Fundamentalism has been described as a 'reaction to modernity', in particular 'a communally organized response to modernity', in which the 'traditions' that fundamentalists appeal to 'are no more self-evident and uncontested than their scriptures'.[10] From a fundamentalist perspective, 'tradition is not what the mainstream believes or does. Rather, it is that set of beliefs and practices that fundamentalists identify for themselves as hallowed by the past and from which they try to construct safe havens in a fallen world.'[11] 'Safe havens' are needed because the familiar order is under threat from changing circumstances and changing ideas.

Parity Of Esteem

In passing, we should note that one problem with applying the term 'fundamentalism' to any strand within Islam is that the literal truth of the *Qur'an* is a mainstream tenet of the faith. A literalist approach to scripture, which is a minority theme in modern Christianity, is the dominant theme in (at least) High Sunni Islam.[12] Another problem is that 'cultural fundamentalism' as sketched out above is also a mainstream phenomenon in Islam, within the Sufi Sunni community as much as within their Deobandi rivals. Which is another way of saying that attitudes in the Western Muslim mainstream early in this new century resemble those in the non-Muslim Western mainstream fifty years earlier.

One argument for retaining the word 'fundamentalism' despite these problems is that it offers parity of esteem. 'Christian fundamentalism' and 'Jewish fundamentalism' are understood and used widely to mean a harsh implementation of a selective, literal reading of scripture. The phrases 'Islamism' or 'political

Islam', as has already been pointed out, suggest instead that this harsh, reactionary and selective interpretation is merely the 'pure' form of the religion. An alternative to the word 'fundamentalism', again maintaining parity of esteem, would be to refer to the 'Islamic Right',[13] as we already refer to the Christian Right. It is clear from this formulation, both that we are referring to a right-wing interpretation of scripture, and, secondly, that there are other, equally valid interpretations.

The Disruptive Moment

For people in many faiths, the unsettling effects of 'modernity'—where science and rationality undermine 'traditional' (right-wing) beliefs, pluralism and liberalism undermine 'traditional' (right-wing) morality, and social liberation movements undermine 'traditional' (right-wing) patterns of authority—are associated with the social dislocation of urbanization, commercialization and industrialization. Nineteenth-century German sociologist Ferdinand Tönnies distinguished between *gemeinschaft* (an organic community bound together by tradition, blood, and a common mind, where authority is based on age) and *gesellschaft* (a selfish society of individuals based on the exchange of commodities).[14] The moral and social disruption caused by the shift from rural *gemeinschaft* to urban *gesellschaft* typically brings out a defensive response.

Robert A. Denemark remarks that for the newly-urbanized, struggling to survive in a new ruthless environment, one defensive response is 'to strive to invent new social contexts within which mutuality and justice of the old-fashioned sort may still prevail.' Religious groups can, in these circumstances, 'affirm truth, morality and justice amid the corruptions of an urbanized world, bring like-minded people together so they may support one another, and may even aspire to punish unrighteousness and reform society as a whole.'[15] The fundamentalist 'mindset', in this light, can be an attempt to preserve what is seen as a proper, decent human society. Liberalism and dialogue can be seen as forms of corruption, undermining faith and decency and authority and certainty.

One can see how such factors could plausibly give rise to Islamic fundamentalism in the newly-urbanizing societies of the Middle East (and Christian fundamentalism in the increasingly atomized societies of the West). Denemark points out that: 'Just as rural-to-urban migration creates fundamentalist propensities, so, too, does international migration.'[16] For the Barelwi communities we have been discussing, the older generation has insulated itself from the moral vertigo of urbanization by reproducing *gemeinschaft* within Muslim ghettos. It is the younger generations which experience the existential disorientation of entering *gesellschaft*.

A New Form Of Citizenship

For young Muslims experiencing these cultural tensions, there has been the further shock of being rejected and condemned as Muslims by the backlash since the 11 September attacks. Ron Geaves comments that many young British Muslims 'feel let down by both the culture of their birth and the culture of their parents'. The latter they perceive as 'riddled by traditional attitudes and beliefs that have no bearing on their own situation'. The wider culture demands assimilation, but offers discrimination.[17] Sophie Gilliat-Ray observes that due to the level of racism embedded in parts of British society, young Muslims' feelings of belonging to Britain 'may be insecure', while at the same time 'they do not feel that an identity based upon being of Pakistani origin offers a viable identity in this country'.[18] Fundamentalism attracts young Muslims, observes Geaves, 'because it is quintessentially modern; that is to say, it constitutes a response to events and conditions in the present.' This is how, for young Muslims in Britain and elsewhere, the *umma* can become of central importance. 'In Britain, it links many British-born Muslims to an identity which transcends both their allegiance to nationality and the culture of their parents.' The concept of the *umma* can also be 'used as a challenge to that overriding secular view of the world they find in the indigenous culture which is so often unaccepting of their presence.'[19]

Writing of the equivalent generation of young Muslims in France, Jocelyne Cesari comments that, 'the more their Islamic and Arab origins are despised, the stronger their identification with them'. This identification with the Muslim or Arab world does not mean that they *live* as Muslims or Arabs; 'it is a more symbolic allegiance.' Extending beyond their parent's country of origin, is a new, 'very emotional and passionate' identification with the whole *umma*, 'especially involving solidarity with an interest in struggles such as the Palestinian cause and conflicts in Bosnia and Chechnya.'[20] Cesari suggests that for such young Muslims, 'Islam is a credible alternative to the prospect of unemployment, drugs, alcohol or delinquency.' Islam allows them to 'recover some personal dignity and to project a better image of themselves.' They find in this revivalist Islam a 'new form of citizenship'.[21]

They tend to reject the traditional, folk Islam of their parents for a more austere and more personally demanding version of High Islam. Islamic fundamentalism can be a form of rebellion against the authority of the older generation while apparently submitting to the older generation's command to follow tradition.

Re-Reading The Book

Islamic fundamentalism, like Christian fundamentalism, invites converts to undertake their own personal, literal reading of holy texts. As many scholars have noted, 'fundamentalists are rebels against their religious establishments'. Previous authorities, theologians, and clerics can be set aside, and what is claimed to be a 'pure' version of the faith can be directly gleaned from the Holy Book. However, the 'traditions' that fundamentalists appeal to 'are no more self-evident and uncontested than their scriptures'.[22]

For example, a key text for *jihadis* is the *Qur'anic* verse: 'Fight them until there is no persecution and the religion is God's [entirely]' (*Qur'an* 2:193, 8:39). Rudolph Peters observes that: 'The modernists emphasize the first part of this verse and point out that, in this case, fighting is lawful as a defence against persecution, whereas the fundamentalists stress the second part and read this verse as a command to fight against the unbelievers with the aim of establishing a universal Islamic order.'[23] But there is more to verse 2:193. There is the typical *Qur'anic* qualification: 'but if they cease, Let there be no hostility except to those who practise oppression' (Yusuf Ali translation[24]).

We should remember that it is possible to interpret this verse, as with any verse in the *Qur'an*, as an instruction concerned with the particular historical circumstances within which the revelation was received.[25] Again, the decision to treat the verse as either context-bound or a universally-applicable and eternal law is not derived from the text itself.

In the same way the interpretation of the sayings of Jesus is often morally- and politically-flavoured rather than simply literal. Most modern Christians have their own interpretation of those passages where Jesus explicitly endorses ancient Jewish law and the acts of the Jewish prophets, or where he appears to exult in his followers' power to create discord and family division.[26]

Fundamentalism Is Not Terrorism

The Christian Right is a growing phenomenon in the United States. There are no doubt many reasons for this. Mary Ann Tétreault observes that: 'Even those whose life situations appear comfortable may feel alienated in a world where "all that is solid melts into air," especially if they find themselves unable to control their spouses, communicate with their children, or exercise what they regard as their rightful authority over both.'[27] Noam Chomsky points out that normally the level of religious fanaticism in a country tends to decline as industrialization increases—apart from Canada, which has rather more fanaticism than one would expect, and the United States, which has a level of religious fanaticism one might expect in a devastated peasant society such as Bangladesh. He suggests that part of the answer is that the US has 'an unusually weak labor movement' and 'an unusually narrow political system', and has experienced recently the 'virtual collapse of civil society'.[28]

One popular manifestation of the US Christian Right is apocalyptic fundamentalism in the form of the *Left Behind* novels by Hal Lindsey and Tim LaHaye, which look forward to the end of time, when God will pluck true believers off the earth, and condemn the unworthy to appalling deaths. Aeroplanes full of unbelievers will fall from the sky as Christian pilots are lifted up, and so on. Online columnist Joe Bageant observes:

> If a Muslim were to write an Islamic version of last book in the *Left Behind* series, *Glorious Appearing*, and publish it across the Middle East, Americans would go beserk. Yet tens of millions of Christians eagerly await and celebrate an End Time when everyone who disagrees with them will be murdered in ways that make Islamic beheading look like a bridal shower. Jesus—who apparently has a much nastier streak than we have been led to believe—merely speaks and 'the bodies of the enemy are ripped wide open down the middle.' In the book Christians have to drive carefully to avoid 'hitting splayed and filleted corpses of men and women and horses'... This may be some of the bloodiest hate fiction ever published, but it is also what tens of millions of Americans believe is God's will. It is approximately what everyone in the congregation sitting around me last Sunday at my brother's church believes. Or some version of it.[29]

The *Left Behind* series of books has sold 65 million copies in the United States.

Quite clearly, the overwhelming majority of those buying these books are not engaged in politico-religious violence. Fundamentalism, even apocalyptic fundamentalism, is not equivalent to terrorism. Similarly, the majority of Muslim fundamentalists are not involved in violence. The fundamentalist group *Hizb ut Tahrir*, which the British government has threatened to ban, has an outlook which is similar in many ways to that of Osama bin Laden, but avoids violence.[30] Similarly, the Muslim Brotherhood movement, which is the largest and oldest organized Islamic fundamentalist grouping in the world, also avoids involvement in armed *jihad* (though of course there are violent factions within the broad movement).

Gilles Kepel notes that there are two forms of Islamic 'separatism' that are likely to arise among European Muslims: armed *jihadism*, and nonviolent *salafi* segregationism—which will be 'more numerous'. The British government's leaked 'Young Muslims and Extremism' report concurs, stating that '[m]ost' Islamic extremist groups 'do not advocate violence'.[31] Kepel observes that the segregationists will form authoritarian closed communities: 'Opposed to violence—which they combat relentlessly with *Quranic* verses, Prophetic sayings, and rulings of apostasy—these salafists nevertheless adhere to a version of Islam that imposes complete cultural separation from the West.'[32] This form of fundamentalism often prioritizes such issues as the *hijab* or veil (which is not specifically commanded in the *Qur'an*, but incorporated into Muslim practice from Persia and the conquered Christian Byzantine culture[33]). Kepel notes that the arrival of a *salafi*-style fundamentalist preacher in a European Muslim ghetto tends to 'galvanize young male zealots, who reinforce his influence by applying social pressure on the young women in their neighborhood'.[34] The 'assertive Muslim identity' engaged in religious vigilantism.

What often unites violent and reclusive forms of Islamic fundamentalism is the belief that Islam is under attack (from a Christian-Jewish 'crusade' of annihilation). Such a basic worldview lies at the heart of fundamentalism in different religions—the sense of being besieged by outside forces, as Karen Armstrong demonstrates in her survey of Christian, Jewish and Islamic fundamentalisms, *The Battle for God*. The choice then becomes one between a retreat from wider society (which is seen as a threat), or a campaign against wider society (which is seen as a mortal enemy). That campaign can be nonviolent, or it may be an armed struggle.

The invasion of Iraq may not have caused the bombings in any simple linear causality but when they chose to attack the US, London, Madrid, Australia—the allies—it's symbolic. These are not the acts of mindless murderers but strategic symbolic acts.

It is absolutely no coincidence that what happened in London happened at the time of G8.

Far more than feeling angry with the bombers or angry about what has happened to me, I feel angry with the political leaders.

Professor John Tulloch,
who was severely injured on the Edgware Road train.
(Taken from a news report.[1])

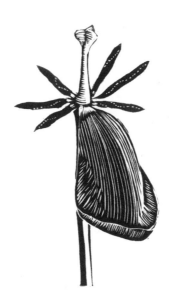

18

Through The Bombers' Eyes

What They Say About What They Did

The Other Bombers

There had been British suicide bombers before 7 July 2005. It is just that their attacks, and attempted attacks, took place outside the United Kingdom. The first well-known attempted British suicide bombing in December 2001, with Richard Reid the 'shoe bomber'. Reid, a 28-year-old Londoner of Jamaican and white English parentage who converted to Islam in prison, failed to blow up an American Airlines flight from Paris to Miami with a bomb hidden in his shoe because the fuse had got damp on the way to the airport.[1] British Pakistani Saajid Badat (whose family moved to Gloucester in the UK from Malawi), trained at the same al-Qaeda camp in Afghanistan as Reid, and was meant to carry out a similar attack on another aircraft in the same month. He withdrew at the last minute. When the explosives were found in his house, Badat pleaded guilty and received a 13 year sentence.[2] These were not the first attempted British suicide attacks, however. A year before Reid, in December 2000, Birmingham-born Mohammed Bilal, 24, blew himself up in a car bomb outside an Indian army barracks in Srinagar, in Indian Kashmir, killing six Indian soldiers and three Kashmiris.[3] This was a suicide bombing aimed at a military target. (The term 'suicide bombing' has become associated with attacks on civilians.) Reid is therefore the first British person known to have attempted a suicide attack on civilians.

Then in April 2003, Asif Mohammed Hanif, 21, and Omar Khan Sharif, 27, became the first entirely foreign suicide bombers in Israel, and the first known British suicide bombers to attack a civilian target. Sharif's bomb failed to explode, and he was later found drowned in the sea. Hanif's bomb killed a waitress and two musicians at 'Mike's Place', a seafront club in Tel Aviv.[4] 60 people were injured. A barmaid lost her arm in the explosion.

Motives

What motivated these earlier suicide bombing attempts? Richard Reid told his US judge before he was sentenced to 110 years imprisonment: 'Basically, yeah, I intended to damage the plane. I am a follower of Osama bin Laden. I am an enemy of your country and I don't care... Your government has sponsored the torture of Muslims in Iraq and Turkey and Jordan and Syria with their money and weapons.' Reid's lawyers said his actions had been motivated by his desire to defend Islam, which he said had saved him from a life of crime and drugs.[5]

The two British suicide bombers in Israel, unlike Reid, had no history of petty crime or prison, and were well-respected members of their communities. Hanif's brother Taz said: 'He was just a big teddy bear, that's what people said about him.' Neighbours described him as gentle and polite. His friend Asif said: 'Our name for him was huggy bear.' Far from advocating violence in the pursuit of Islamic causes, Hanif had at one time opposed to it: 'This is why we're all pulling our hair out, this is totally out of character. He hated movements like *al-Muhajiroun* and *Hizb-ut-Tahrir*.' Omar Khan Sharif's late father, Mohammed Sharif, was an entrepreneur who owned a kebab shop, a laundrette and amusement arcades. Sharif attended an expensive private 'prep school' for a time. A neighbour recalled Mr Sharif as a polite child who would cross the road to open the gate for her when she drove home from work. As with the 7 July Leeds bombers, there was a foreign connection of some sort. Hanif had travelled to Morocco and Damascus to study, in search of a greater understanding of his faith. Sharif dropped out of an undergraduate degree in multimedia information systems at Kingston University, London, travelled and returned to Britain with a wife. The couple had two daughters, believed to be aged seven and three. The chairman of the Hounslow mosque, Suleman Chachia, said: 'It makes you wonder why a 21-year-old man living in the western world who has got everything to live for goes out to another country and does this kind of thing.'[6]

The two men revealed their thinking in a videotape released posthumously by Hamas, the Islamic fundamentalist movement that organized their suicide attack. Sharif says: 'We will take revenge and we will get the Jews and the Crusaders out of the land of Islam. Fellow Muslims, we left Britain to look for martyrdom.' Hanif castigates Muslims living in the West for their lack of solidarity: 'You Muslims are sitting in your houses, watching whatever is happening here to your Muslim brothers in Palestine. We want to be martyrs for Allah and we want you to be martyrs for Allah as well. OK, even if you're not going to fight with us, please at least look into the facts.' Israeli Jews 'are raping our women, killing our children' every day, he claims.[7] 'Our' meaning 'part of the *umma*'.[8]

In yet another parallel with the 7/7 conspiracy, it emerged later that the two suicide bombers were 'known to MI5', as a *Guardian* headline put it.[9] In secret from their families and friends, both men were actually connected to *al-Muhajiroun*, a *jihadi*-linked Islamic fundamentalist group. 'At what point did they [the two men] decide to become suicide bombers? We don't know,' a security source told the *Guardian*. 'We are not thought police,' added a well-placed source.

What about Saajid Badat, the shoe bomber who withdrew from the al-Qaeda plot at the last minute? When he pleaded guilty to a conspiracy charge, Deputy Assistant Police Commissioner Peter Clarke, head of the Anti-Terrorist Branch, said: 'We must ask how a young British man was transformed from an intelligent, articulate person who was well respected, into a person who has pleaded guilty to one of the most serious crimes that you can think of.'[10]

A friend of Badat's family described him as an 'intelligent boy who always spoke out if something was wrong, a walking angel.' His head teacher at school said he was a 'punctual, cheerful and polite' student who worked with 'maturity and commitment'. When he was arrested, a neighbour said Badat 'always seemed a quiet, ordinary young man'.[11] Another neighbour, Mary Flanagan, said: 'My main feeling is one of pity and sorrow for his dad, Mohammad Badat, who is a lovely, lovely man.'[12] How many parallels with 7/7 can there be?

Though Gloucester is reportedly one of the most integrated Muslim communities in Britain, journalists were told that there were other intelligent local youngsters who sympathised with the idea of violence: 'There are small pockets of young people in the community who would be pro-Saajid... [thinking] that something needs to be done to correct the injustice, that they should do things to challenge what is going on.'[13]

Badat's defence lawyer Michael Mansfield, QC, said that the story of how a 'conscientious, hardworking student' came to consider mass murder 'is a story of our times.' Badat's Muslim faith 'in one sense took him to the brink, the very brink of disaster, and at the same time it was same faith that pulled him back,' Mansfield said.[14] When Badat was a teenager he felt 'increasingly concerned for the plight of Muslims being persecuted around the world, and wanted to fight their cause'. But by 2001, Badat became caught up in the 'cauldron of concern and activity' in Afghanistan and faced a 'moral dilemma' fighting for his Muslim brothers.[15] The dilemma had been resolved at the very last moment in favour of life and justice rather than death and revenge.

The underlying motivation that brought Badat to that point was his concern for the suffering of the *umma*, as with all the other known British citizens involved in suicide bomb plots.

The 7/7 Claim Of Responsibility

What information do we have about the intentions and motivations of the 7/7 bombers? So far we have heard from friends, employers and associates, and assessed the general cultural background from which they emerged. Do we have any direct communications from the bombers themselves? There are two pieces of information. The first is the claim of responsibility posted on the internet within hours of the attacks, which has been regarded as plausibly linked to the 7/7 conspiracy. The second is the video statement recorded by suspected lead bomber Mohammad Sidique Khan, which was released in two stages. We will examine both these pieces of evidence.

The statement of responsibility from the previously unknown 'Secret Organization Group of al-Qaeda of *Jihad* Organization in Europe'[16] was posted on the *jihadi* website '*Al-Qal'ah*' ('The Castle') by someone calling themselves 'Nur al-Iman', and identifying as a 'new guest', within hours of the attacks. The BBC was able to access the website and make a translation available by 1.27pm, less than five hours after the first explosions. The website was then unavailable — it may have been brought down by a Western intelligence operation, or it may have been withdrawn by its sponsors.[17]

Professor Juan Cole, lecturer in Middle East studies, observed in the immediate aftermath of the bombings that the statement was plausible as it showed no signs of being hurriedly written: 'That suggests it was carefully composed before the fact.' He dismissed rumours that the statement had errors in the Arabic, or the quotation from the *Qur'an*. Cole had some interesting remarks to make on the language of the statement. It was written in Arabic, he noted, whereas all previous British Muslim participants in al-Qaeda-style terrorism were non-Arabs: 'None of them probably even knew Arabic well or could compose a statement in it.' He also noted that: 'The statement celebrated Arabness or *'urubah* along with Islam'. (Notice that it hails the 'Nation of Islam' and the 'Arab nation' — *'urubah*.) No British Bangladeshi or Pakistani would write such a text, declared Cole: 'The statement was probably not written by a second-generation Arab Briton or even by a long-term, integrated Arab Briton resident.'

After a keyword search in OCLC Worldcat, an electronic database with 40 million volumes, for 'urubah and Islam, Cole found that virtually all of the references came from Egyptian Muslim thinkers publishing in Cairo and Giza during the past 30 years, 'roughly in a Muslim Brotherhood tradition'. Cole wrote in his highly-respected blog *Informed Comment*: 'My guess is that the author of the statement is Egyptian or Sudanese, with some sort of intellectual genealogy in the radical fringes of the Muslim Brotherhood, perhaps al-Zawahiri's *al-Jihad al-Islami*.'[18] Given this linguistic analysis, it is extremely intriguing that when a 7/7 bomber video statement surfaced, it was paired with a video statement by precisely the man identified by Cole: Ayman al-Zawahiri, the second most senior commander in al-Qaeda. Cole's own conclusion after the video was released? 'Little did I realize at the time that it was probably written by Ayman al-Zawahiri himself.'[19]

On the other hand, it has been suggested to me that the more internationalized a *jihadi* group, the more likely it would be to be able to draw up such a document in Arabic, with intonation and vocabulary absorbed from the existing *jihadi* canon.[20] Curiously, this seems to be Cole's stance in his *Salon* article on the bombings (written before the video was released). Noting that 'urubah, or Arabism, is a secular nationalist ideal, Cole wrote: 'The diction suggests that the bombers are from a younger generation of activists who have not lived in non-Arab Muslim countries such as Pakistan and Afghanistan, and think of Arabism and Islam as overlapping rather than alternatives to one another.'[21] This analysis is perhaps strengthened by the fact that the claim of responsibility in the name of al-Qaeda was apparently rejected on 9 July as a 'fake' by Saif al-Islam al-Athari, a noted and well-informed al-Qaeda supporter.[22]

The BBC's translation of the statement seems to be generally accepted[23]:

In the name of God, the merciful, the compassionate, may peace be upon the cheerful one and undaunted fighter, Prophet Muhammad, God's peace be upon him.

Nation of Islam and Arab nation: Rejoice for it is time to take revenge against the British Zionist Crusader government in retaliation for the massacres Britain is committing in Iraq and Afghanistan. The heroic *mujahideen* have carried out a blessed raid in London. Britain is now burning with fear, terror and panic in its northern, southern, eastern, and western quarters.

We have repeatedly warned the British government and people. We have fulfilled our promise and carried out our blessed military raid in Britain after our *mujahideen* exerted strenuous efforts over a long period of time to ensure the success of the raid.

We continue to warn the governments of Denmark and Italy and all the Crusader governments that they will be punished in the same way if they do not withdraw their troops from Iraq and Afghanistan. He who warns is excused.

God says: 'You who believe: If ye will aid (the cause of) Allah, He will aid you, and plant your feet firmly.'[24]

Another factor increasing the credibility of this claim of responsibility is the reference to Britain 'burning' at all four points of the compass. It is now clear that the intention of the bombers was to travel north, south, east and west from King's Cross station before exploding their devices. It was only Hasib Hussain's as-yet-unexplained departure from the plan which resulted in the last explosion occurring so long after the others, and in quite a different direction. At the time the statement was written, the intended pattern of attack would not have been apparent from media reports.

Having assessed the validity of the statement, which has not been challenged by the police or security services, we may turn to the actual contents of the statement. It clearly links the bombings to the wars in Iraq and Afghanistan. There are two references. The first link is the description of the atrocities as 'retaliation for the massacres Britain is committing in Iraq and Afghanistan'. The second comes when the group says that it 'continue[s] to warn the governments of Denmark and Italy and all the Crusader governments that they will be punished in the same way if they do not withdraw their troops from Iraq and Afghanistan'. This is a form of negotiating, a conditionality which contradicts the usual picture of al-Qaeda as fanatically unworldly and immovably violent.

Mohammad Sidique Khan Speaks

The man who is believed to have led the 7/7 cell, Mohammad Sidique Khan, the exemplary teaching assistant and social worker, spoke from beyond the grave on 1 September 2005, when al-Jazeera broadcast a video from al-Qaeda featuring the suicide bomber and al-Qaeda leader Ayman al-Zawahiri. The video featured two excerpts from Khan's statement. The second section of Khan's statement was difficult to understand, apparently for technical reasons.

The full text of both parts of his statement, as first transmitted, runs as follows:

I'm going to keep this short and to the point because it's all been said before by far more eloquent people than me. And our words have no impact upon you, therefore I'm going to talk to you in a language that you understand. Our words are dead until we give them life with our blood.

I'm sure by now the media's painted a suitable picture of me, this predictable propaganda machine will naturally try to put a spin on things to suit the government and to scare the masses into conforming to their power and wealth-obsessed agendas.

I and thousands like me are forsaking everything for what we believe. Our driving motivation doesn't come from tangible commodities that this world has to offer. Our religion is Islam—obedience to the one true God, Allah, and following the footsteps of the final prophet and messenger Muhammad... This is how our ethical stances are dictated.

Your democratically-elected governments continuously perpetuate atrocities against my people all over the world. And your support of them makes you directly responsible, just as I am directly responsible for protecting and avenging my Muslim brothers and sisters.

Until we feel security, you will be our targets. And until you stop the bombing, gassing, imprisonment and torture of my people we will not stop this fight.

We are at war and I am a soldier.

Now you too will taste the reality of this situation...

I myself, I myself, I make *dua* (pray) to Allah... to raise me amongst those whom I love like the prophets, the messengers, the martyrs and today's heroes like our beloved Sheikh Osama Bin Laden, Dr Ayman al-Zawahiri and Abu Musab al-Zarqawi and all the other brothers and sisters that are fighting in the [unclear] of this cause.

With this I leave you to make up your own minds and I ask you to make *dua* to Allah almighty to accept the work from me and my brothers and enter us into gardens of paradise.[25]

Al-Qaeda expert Jason Burke commented that Khan's words were directed at Muslims in the West. Khan spoke in clear English 'devoid of religious rhetoric, reference to the Koran or Islamic history'. He explained why civilians are targets, saying that in a democracy everyone bears responsibility for the government's actions—its participation in atrocities against Muslims around the world. Burke pointed out that Khan rejected national identity in favour of the *umma*, the global community of believers, 'explaining that the violence will continue as long as the government continues to "perpetuate atrocities" against "his Muslim brothers and sisters".' Burke wrote:

> He also makes an important theological point often overlooked by Western observers but deeply relevant to activists who might be considering violence. He says bombs are justified because the *ummah* is under attack, violent resistance is an obligation on all believers and 'collateral damage' in the form of the death of innocents is thus acceptable.[26]

Incidentally, Khan's reference to 'tasting reality' is likely to be an echo of Osama bin Laden's words after 9/11, when he said: 'What America is tasting today is but a fraction of what we have tasted for decades.'[27]

The full 27-minute tape of Khan's statement was released in mid-November 2005.[28] The central argument remained the same: two wrongs can make a right—an eye for an eye can make the whole world see.

19

Revolutionary Suicide

Powerlessness, Rage
And The Ideology Of Despair

Operation Contest: Managing Discontent

The government's leaked report, 'Young Muslims and Extremism' observed that disillusionment with British foreign policy contributes to 'a sense of helplessness' in relation to the situation of the *umma*, with 'a lack of any tangible "pressure valves", in order to vent frustrations, anger or dissent'. This can lead, said the report (as we saw earlier), to 'a desire for a simple "Islamic" solution' to the oppression suffered by the *umma* in Palestine, Iraq, Chechnya, Kashmir and Afghanistan.[1] Why should young British Muslims feel 'helpless'? Because British foreign policy, as exemplified by the unpopular, illegitimate and illegal invasion of Iraq, is so immovable. It is typical of the State to think in terms of providing a 'pressure valve' that can 'vent' the rage of British Muslims, rather than a 'political lever' that can be used to alter British foreign policy when it violates international law and causes human suffering.

The central objective of the government's 'Operation Contest' is the management of discontent at least political cost. This is to be done by strengthening the hand of 'moderate student and youth organisations (such as the UMS [Union of Muslim Students] and FOSIS [Federation of Student Islamic Societies])', and, in particular, 'of moderates within such organisations'. The report also proposed engaging with and recognizing 'moderate scholars with followings amongst young Muslims, such as Imam Hamza Yusuf and Imam Suhaib Webb'; strengthening 'moderate Muslim media organisations... e.g. by giving them stories and interviews'; and 'promoting Muslim representation in public life'.

The Home Office and Foreign Office noted that: 'Any feeling that Muslim voices are not heard in places of influence is helpful to extremism.'[2]

The purpose is manipulative: to give the *appearance* of influence. The only recommendation that mentions foreign policy is the suggestion that the Foreign Office expands its dialogue with young Muslims on 'non-traditional foreign policy areas' of concern to Muslims, such as development, globalisation, and human rights. On the key issue of the 'global war on terror', including the wars in Iraq and Afghanistan, there is no suggestion of dialogue or negotiation. Foreign policy fundamentalism.

The 'Young Muslims and Extremism' report acknowledges that: 'Some young Muslims are disillusioned with mainstream Muslim organisations that are perceived as pedestrian, ineffective and in many cases, as "sell-outs" to HMG.'[3] Co-opting more 'moderates' will simply increase this disillusionment.

Moderation

There are several possible meanings to the term 'moderate Muslim'. One might be: 'a Muslim who rejects the use of inhumane punishments, the subjugation of women, and so on, as laid down in scripture.' In other words, a liberal Muslim. This would include those Muslims who argue that a proper reading of the *Qur'an* produces liberal values.[4] It would also include Muslims who simply set aside the text of holy scriptures where this conflicts with our present understanding of humanity. Just as many liberal Christians simply set aside, for example, injunctions regarding the position of women in the New Testament. Paul wrote in an Epistle that: 'women should be silent in the churches. For they are not permitted to speak, but should be subordinate... For it is shameful for a woman to speak in church.' (1 Corinthians 14:33-35, RSV) He also wrote that women should have their heads covered when praying in church—as a symbol of their subservience to male authority. (1 Corinthians 11:3-10 RSV)

Another meaning of the term 'moderate Muslim' might be: 'a Muslim who rejects the use of violence for political purposes'. There is a closely related possible definition: a 'moderate Muslim' might be: 'a Muslim who stands in the midstream of world opinion regarding international affairs'. In other words, someone who is outraged by terrorist atrocities in New York and Madrid and London, but who is also outraged by US/UK state terror in Afghanistan and Iraq, by Russian state terror in Chechnya, by Israeli state terror against Palestinians, and so on. This moderate strand of opinion was well-articulated by former President Nelson Mandela in the run-up to the Iraq war: 'I criticise most leaders all over the world for keeping quiet when one country wants to bully the world.'[5] This kind of 'moderate Muslim' could also be called an 'angry Muslim'.

What the British government means by the term 'moderate Muslim', on the other hand, is 'a Muslim who rejects the use of violence for political purposes—unless that purpose accords with the wishes of the United States and Britain.' Someone who will not condemn the political violence of the British and US governments in Iraq and Afghanistan, but who will condemn the political violence of official enemies. This kind of 'moderate Muslim' could also be called a 'collaborator Muslim'.

It is right and proper to be outraged by the brutality and violence of al-Qaeda. The fact remains, however, that political 'moderation' in mainstream Western society means 'service to power', even when that power is used for immoderate ends, and by immoderate means, as in Iraq. Noam Chomsky notes that Hitler was regarded as a 'moderate' by US policymakers for many years: 'As late as 1937, the State Department was describing Hitler as a moderate standing between the extremes of right and left, who we must support, or else the masses of the population might take power and move in a leftist direction.'[6]

So we must distinguish between political 'moderation' in the propaganda sense, which means 'obedience to US and British power', and in a more neutral sense of being in the mainstream of global opinion or aligned with liberal, humanistic values. (Chomsky observes that the term 'radical' tends to mean 'disobedient'. 'Radicalization' thus means 'growing more and more hostile to US and British policies'.) Using these definitions, it is possible to be a liberal Muslim, an angry Muslim and a radical Muslim (in the sense just mentioned) all at the same time. Or a liberal Muslim and a collaborator Muslim at the same time. It is possible to be angry in private and a collaborator in public.

Political Suicide

The collaboration of influential Muslims contributes to the despair of alienated Muslims. It is likely that the personal crisis of the potential Muslim suicide bomber is a multiple crisis. Anger mounts with, on the one hand, the growing realisation of the scale and depth of suffering in the Muslim world, and, on the other, the complicity and active participation of the British government in causing much of this suffering. Despair sets in, however, with the 'sense of helplessness' in the face of this suffering, and the belief that no human action can actually reverse US/UK foreign policy. (This despair may, of course, be unconscious.) One possible response is to leave matters in God's hands—to withdraw, and focus on the creation of 'pure' fundamentalist 'islands' within wider society. The potential suicide bomber, however, is someone who, despite despair, is unable to hand over to God their perceived responsibility for their brothers and sisters in the *umma*. The final element in the existential crisis of the potential suicide bomber, then, is the very human desire to feel effective in the world; to feel that one has made a significant contribution to the welfare of one's community—in this case, the *umma*. (Recall the earlier comments regarding the 'impatience' of younger Muslims.) The suicide bomber is in this sense 'over-responsible'.

Hopelessness

One study of suicide 'clearly showed that patients who ultimately commit suicide are among those who have the least hope', and that 'hopelessness is more predictive of suicide than is depression'. Hopelessness includes 'cognitive inflexibility, which includes difficulty in believing that there are non-suicidal alternatives to life problems.' In this case, hopelessness means 'a sense of helplessness' in relation to the *umma* and an inability to see non-suicidal solutions. Furthermore, 'Most people likely to commit suicide require an aggressive catalyst to do so.' In the generally-understood model of suicide, it is proposed that every person has a pain threshold beyond which they cannot function: 'Just before a suicidal act the individual's adaptive threshold is breached and they may resolve their pain by committing suicide.'[7] It may be that the war in Iraq constituted just such an 'aggressive catalyst' for the 7/7 bombers.

The Canadian Psychological Association sets out psychological aspects which appear to be key in moving into a suicidal state:

> *Unbearable Psychological Pain.* The common trigger for suicide is unbearable pain, a deep anguish, in which the person feels especially hopeless and helpless.
> *Narrow Thinking.* Tunnel vision, or rigid thinking, is common and one of the deadliest aspects of the suicidal state. The individual sees suicide as the one and only solution for their current difficulties. They think everything is hopeless and things will never be better.
> *Ambivalence.* The suicidal person is deeply ambivalent—he or she wants both to live and to die.
> *Mental illness.* About 90% of suicidal people have a psychiatric disorder, the most common being depression or psychosis. Suicidality is not a mental illness, but suicidal people are often suffering from a mental illness.

Sense of vulnerability. The suicidal person often feels very vulnerable, even fragile, and lacks a positive view of themselves and a sense of personal strength.

Problem Relationships. The suicidal person often feels alone and cut off from others. They may have experienced conflict and rejection from others. They may think they have been dishonourable or failed family, friends, society, etc.

Loss. An experience of loss, or concern about anticipated loss (for example, spouse leaving, fired from a job, ill health, social embarrassment or humiliation) is often a trigger for suicide. Research suggests that those who react with anger or aggression may be more at risk for suicide.

Escape. Suicide is seen as an escape from what feels hopeless and unbearable.[8]

Most of these factors seem to be relevant to the 7/7 bombers in relation to the 'ideology of the *umma*'. However, 'mental illness' seems not to be an issue for the London bombers—or for Palestinian suicide bombers. A survey of studies in suicide terrorism by Dr Scott Atran in *Science* magazine observes: 'Contemporary suicide terrorists from the Middle East are publicly deemed crazed cowards bent on senseless destruction who thrive in poverty and ignorance. Recent research indicates they have no appreciable psychopathology and are as educated and economically well-off as surrounding populations.'[9] Having said this, it is true that media reports have Mohammad Sidique Khan suffering from depression.[10] The *Independent on Sunday* reports that 'Khan went on sick leave in September 2004, said to be suffering from depression', and finally resigned from the school he was working at on these grounds in December 2004.[11] His marriage is also said to have broken down at around this time, in large part due to his increasingly harsh interpretation of Islam, and his wife's more liberal stance. There is therefore a 'problem relationship' risk factor in Khan's background of exactly the kind identified in the suicide literature.

Were the problem relationship and the depression *causes* of the turn towards suicide terrorism, or were they *consequences* of that deepening radicalization and alienation? (Of course they may have been concurrent, mutually-reinforcing phenomena.)

Stairway To Heaven

Professor Fathali M. Moghaddam, professor of psychology at Georgetown University, has proposed a 'staircase' metaphor for the development of a terrorist activist.[12] The stairs represent the narrowing path that an individual follows toward a life of terrorism - with the terrorist act being the uppermost and final step. Most people never leave the ground floor, despite frequent bouts of adversity. For Moghaddam, it is feelings of inadequacy and discontent that drive individuals up the staircase: 'Individuals begin their ascent to ease a sense of personal and collective deprivation and improve personal situations.' If these initial and seemingly tangible goals are not met, individuals continue from floor to floor where they have the potential to displace feelings of aggression on an 'enemy' figure. 'The staircase leads to higher and higher floors, and whether someone remains on a particular floor depends on the doors and spaces that person imagines to be open to her or him on that floor,' Moghaddam writes. 'The fundamentally important feature of the situation is not only the actual number of floors, stairs, rooms, and so on, but *how people perceive the building and the doors they think are open to them.*'[13] Moghaddam suggests a focus on persuading people on lower levels not to go higher.

Earlier we suggested that there was, roughly speaking, a two-stage process of radicalization in the creation of a Muslim activist willing to carry out a suicide bombing against Western civilians. The first stage involves a burning concern for the suffering of Muslims either directly oppressed by Western governments or abused by states supported by Western governments. The second stage of radicalization involves adopting and developing a fanatical theory of oppression and liberation, where everyone who opposes you or (in its most extreme form) everyone who refuses to support you is an unbeliever or an apostate, deserving of death. The first stage is centred on Muslim human beings, in living communities. In the second stage, this concern is fused with a focus on a particular vision of Islam as a religion. (No doubt the actual process of radicalization is not so clear-cut or linear.)[14]

This is not the place to explore the origins and thinking of al-Qaeda. It will suffice here to note that in the second stage of radicalization, the fight is no longer simply one against 'those who persecute Muslims; it is now against *kufr*, unbelief. The battle is no longer one of humans against humans, but one of belief against unbelief. With this larger framework, the psychological burden of finding an effective means of relieving the suffering of the *umma* is lifted. Gilles Kepel remarks: 'Convinced that their death will trigger a cataclysm which can save the community of believers and that they will be transported immediately to Paradise, [*jihadis*] eagerly volunteer for suicide operations.'[15] There is no clear idea of how sacrifice and cataclysm might result in any human benefit, at least in *jihad* against the far enemy.[16]

7/7: The London Bombings, Islam and the Iraq War

Misleading Precedents

For the potential suicide bomber, it is easy to be misled by the success of Lebanon's Islamic resistance in its defensive *jihad*. One massive suicide attack on 23 October 1983, which killed 146 US soldiers, led directly to the US Marines withdrawing from Lebanon four months later. Suicide attacks against Israeli occupation forces in Lebanon started in November 1982—they were part of the pressure that forced Israel to withdraw in May 2000. (Note that these were against military targets.) In October 1993, US forces in Somalia suffered 18 deaths in the course of a battle in which they killed perhaps 1,000 Somali fighters and civilians. Five months later, the US withdrew from Somalia.

From these incidents, Great Satan *jihadis* have formed an entirely unrealistic picture of the weakness of US foreign policy. The Provisional IRA began with a similarly unrealistic understanding of British staying power. According to Maria McGuire, who was close to IRA Army Council circles in the 1970s, the Provisionals studied British participation in recent conflicts such as those in Palestine, Cyprus, and Aden. She claims that the Army Council, the highest body in the Provisional IRA, set an initial target to kill 36 British soldiers because this was the number of troops believed to have been killed in Aden (now part of Yemen), leading to British withdrawal in 1967.[17]

In the real world, suicide atrocities against Western civilians (immoral in themselves), whether in Bali, New York, Madrid or London, have worsened the condition of the *umma*. Could George W. Bush have brought the people of the United States to acquiesce in the full-scale invasions of Afghanistan and Iraq, if not for the atrocities of 9/11? Could Tony Blair have secured the (reluctant) acquiescence of so many of his people and so much of his party to the invasions of Afghanistan and Iraq, if not for 9/11? Could Russia have won increased freedom of action in Chechnya and throughout its domains, if not for the destruction of the World Trade Center?

These are rational arguments, which have little impact on potential bombers who have ascended the staircase of terror. In their pre-suicidal state of mind, real-world considerations fall away, and the world of the *umma* and of *kufr* looms ever larger. The tunnel vision of the suicidal becomes impervious to fact and logic and humanity, even for the 'nicest' of men. It is the next world that becomes luminous and real. This world is just a shadow of reality. Now the bomber has resolved his (or her) existential crisis. The bomber is experiencing suicidal 'ambivalence': simultaneously in complete despair as to the unrelieved agony of the *umma*, and completely at peace with the coming victory of the *umma*. The suicide-homicide is an offering and a sacrifice. It is, on the one hand, a lethal blow to unbelief, paving the way for the victory of the believers, and, on the other, a gesture of hopelessness, a bitter farewell to an uncaring world, and an escape from the guilt and shame of powerlessness in the face of suffering.

When we look at the known British suicide bombers—the four London bombers and their predecessors—we find a wide range of personality types and class and social backgrounds. What seems to have united them was a need to assert their own dignity, and the dignity of all Muslims, and to reverse the humiliation and powerlessness of the *umma*.

It may be that the most important word in this book is 'humiliation'. The sense of humiliation and powerlessness felt by the suicide bombers in the face of Muslim suffering may have been the most important factor in pushing these four young men towards this tragedy. Acts of terrorism have been described as 'symbolic statements aimed at providing a sense of empowerment to desperate communities'.[18] Jessica Stern, after interviewing religious militants on several continents, concluded:

> My interviews suggest that people join religious terrorist groups partly to transform themselves and to simplify life. They start out feeling humiliated, enraged that they are viewed by some Other as second class. They take on new identities as martyrs on behalf of a purported spiritual cause. The spiritually perplexed learn to focus on action. The weak become strong. The selfish become altruists, ready to make the ultimate sacrifice of their lives in the belief that their deaths will serve the public good. Rage turns to conviction. What seems to happen is that they enter a kind of trance, where the world is divided neatly between good and evil, victim and oppressor. Uncertainty and ambivalence, always painful to experience, are banished. There is no room for the other side's point of view. Because they believe their cause is just, and because the population they hope to protect is so deprived, abused, and helpless, they persuade themselves that any action—even a heinous crime—is justified. They know they are right, not just politically, but morally. They believe that God is on their side.[19]

The bombers saw no way of regaining their honour other than massive indiscriminate violence. They had adopted a particular kind of thinking which matched their anger and despair and hatred, which led them to 'assert their dignity' in the most destructive, cruel and shameful fashion possible.

Revolutionary Suicide

Earlier we noted some parallels between the Khan-Tanweer Mullah Crew and the African-American 'Nation of Islam'. It may also be useful to draw a parallel between the 7/7 cell and the African-American 'Black Panthers'. The co-founder of the Black Panther Party, Huey P. Newton, set out a theory of 'revolutionary suicide' in a book of that name in 1973. Newton was troubled by the high and increasing rates of suicide among young African-American men. He described this phenomenon, in rather Maoist terminology, as 'reactionary suicide': 'the reaction of a man who takes his own life in response to social conditions that overwhelm him and condemn him to helplessness.' Deprived of dignity and crushed by oppressive forces, Black people committed physical suicide and also, in their millions, spiritual suicide:

> This death is found everywhere today in the United States. Its victims have ceased to fight the forms of oppression that drink their blood. The common attitude has long been: What's the use? If a man rises up against a power as great as the United States, he will not survive. Believing this, many Blacks have been driven to a death of the spirit rather than of the flesh, lapsing into lives of quiet desperation.[20]

'Revolutionary suicide', in Newton's terms, involved engaging in an armed struggle for revolutionary social change in which death was not actively sought, but armed confrontation with the forces of the state was welcomed: 'We have such a strong desire to live with hope and human dignity that existence without them is impossible. When reactionary forces crush us, we must move against these forces, even at the risk of death.... Other so-called revolutionaries cling to an illusion that they might have their revolution and die of old age. That cannot be,' said Newton.

The militarism and machismo of the Black Panthers undermined their ability to fulfil their ambitions—they were also targeted by the United States government in a major counter-insurgency operation[21] and riven by internal divisions—and finally the movement collapsed. Perhaps with the rise of a home-grown al-Qaeda, a distorted and religious reflection of African-American armed militancy is surfacing in Europe.

For Newton (one wonders how many of his followers in the Black Panthers were interested in such abstract theorizing) 'revolutionary suicide' meant re-directing the despair and desperation and loss of inhibition of the victim of racial oppression, someone who has in some sense been written off by society, and who cannot but feel the pain of that judgement. It could also refer to someone feeling intense pain at the suffering of others in the global community. For the 7/7 bombers, the pain was both personal and political. 'Revolutionary suicide', Newton argued, meant taking this kind of socially-created detachment from life and channelling it into a high-risk confrontation with authority, an intense mobilization within a disciplined political campaign for justice.

There is no reason why this kind of re-channelling cannot be a life-affirming form of nonviolent struggle. After interviewing religious terrorists on several continents, Jessica Stern comments: 'The same variables (political, religious, social, or all of the above) that seem to have caused one person to become a terrorist might cause another to become a saint'.[22] In the volunteers of the Christian Peacemaker Teams, Peace Brigades International, Voices in the Wilderness, the Ploughshares movement, and many other elements of the global peace movement, we find perhaps the same willingness to make a life-commitment as deep as that of the *jihadi*—or the Western soldier.

In Britain, no Muslim community has suffered deprivation and oppression on the scale that affected African-American ghettos in the United States in the 1970s. However, as we have seen, racist harassment has led to some form of disorganized 'community violence'. For the 7/7 bombers, however, the primary source of what suicide researchers refer to as 'unbearable psychological pain' seems to lie in the Muslim diaspora, and in the continuing assault on Iraq, in particular.

Mohammad Sidique Khan, for one, was known to be an extremely passionate opponent of the US/UK invasion of Iraq in 2003. After the July bombings in London, Arshad Chaudhry, head of the Leeds Muslim Forum, an umbrella group of local Islamic leaders, recalled Khan's rage: 'You could not carry out a civilized conversation with him on Iraq.'[23]

20

Timing

The Penalty, The Truce, The Elections

The Penalty

The timing of the 7 July bombings at 8:50am, seems to have been chosen to mark a particularly harsh passage from the *Qur'an*.[1] *Sura* 8, *ayat* 50 says:

> If thou couldst see, when the angels take the souls of the Unbelievers (at death), (How) they smite their faces and their backs, (saying): 'Taste the penalty of the blazing Fire'.
>
> (Yusuf Ali translation[2])

The Truce

7/7 also seems to have been chosen to mark an al-Qaeda anniversary.[3] In his statement accompanying the first Khan video, Ayman al-Zawahiri said: 'Didn't the lion of Islam, the Mujahid, the sheikh Osama bin Laden, offer you a truce? ... Look what your arrogance has produced.'[4] On 15 April 2004, bin Laden offered Europe a truce, arguing that the leaders of Europe were acting against the interests of the peoples of the Muslim world and the peoples of Europe:

> I also offer a reconciliation initiative to them, whose essence is our commitment to stopping operations against every country that commits itself to not attacking Muslims or interfering in their affairs—including the US conspiracy on the greater Muslim world. The reconciliation will start with the departure

of its last soldier from our country. The door of reconciliation is open for three months of the date of announcing this statement.[5]

The truce offer ran out on 15 July 2004. The anniversary of its expiry was 15 July 2005, almost exactly between the two attacks on 7 July and 21 July 2005.

Less than a week after the London bombings, Saad al-Faqih, a London-based Saudi dissident who has been linked to al-Qaeda, said he expected either bin Laden to reintroduce the truce offer, 'or otherwise I would expect maybe another attack [as in fact happened on 21 July] to prove that this offer is not the offer of a weak person or a weak organization. This offer has to be taken seriously. Otherwise, Europe has to take the consequences.'[6]

The Elections

It is perhaps also pertinent that the bombings in London came after the British General Election on 5 May 2005. Khan said in his video: 'Your *democratically-elected* governments continuously perpetuate atrocities against my people all over the world.'[7] Police believe it was in early June that the pace of the bomb plot began to pick up', when a friend of the bombers rented a flat in Leeds used by them as a bomb factory.[8]

In Spain, of course, the 11 March 2004 Madrid bombings took place just before a General Election. It may be that for many alienated British Muslims the 2005 General Election was an opportunity for British democracy to show that it really worked. The invasion of Iraq had been opposed by the majority of people in Britain. Would that majority manifest itself in the elections and vote out the government that had inflicted this disaster on Iraq? In the end, the electoral system returned Tony Blair to power, albeit with fewer votes for the Labour Party than in any postwar election bar 1983, and with the smallest proportion of the votes cast than for any winning party in any General Election.[9] The British people had endorsed Tony Blair—however reluctantly—by giving his party more votes than any other party, and they had endorsed his war by giving over twice as many votes to the two main pro-war parties (18.5 million) as they did to the 'anti-war' Liberal Democrats (6m) and to the other anti-war candidates from the Greens, the Scottish Nationalists, Plaid Cymru, Respect and the independent anti-war candidates (1m altogether).

There may be a connection between this democratic decision by the electorate, appearing to endorse the war, and the activation by the suicide bombers a few weeks later of their plans.[10]

21

Iraq

Humiliating The Muslim Taskforce

9/11–1991

One of Tony Blair's staple arguments was that 9/11 came before Iraq, 'proving' there is no connection between Iraq and al-Qaeda terrorism. However, there *is* a connection between 9/11 and the invasion of Iraq—the invasion of Iraq in 1991 by Britain, the United States and France. The French participant in the 9/11 conspiracy, Zacarias Moussaoui, was certainly affected by that war, according to his brother: 'That war crystallized feelings against American imperialism, be it political or economic'. Abd Samad Moussaoui observes: 'I think it was at that particular moment that Zacarias started to feel that he belonged to the "Blacks", whereas people of French extraction were "Whites". It was also at that time that he became convinced that the French are racists.'[1]

The Iraq War 2003—The Expert Consensus

Days after the 7 July bombings, a report from the authoritative Royal Institute for International Affairs, also known as 'Chatham House', stated that Britain was at 'particular risk' from al-Qaeda because it was 'the closest ally of the United States', and had deployed armed forces 'in Afghanistan and in Iraq.' The situation over Iraq 'has imposed particular difficulties for the UK', said Chatham House, with 'damage caused to the counter-terrorism campaign.' A 'key problem' for this campaign was that Britain had accepted a position as a pillion passenger 'compelled to leave the steering to the ally in the driving seat.'[2]

On 25 July, former CIA bin Laden expert Michael Scheuer made some telling remarks in a television documentary:

I think the Islamists are winning the war hands down, at least in terms of the United States. Our politicians—either because they're ignorant or they're not willing to tell the truth—continue to tell the American people that this war is aimed at our liberties and our freedoms and our election system and our quest for gender equality, when that has really almost nothing to do with it.

Until the American people are squared with, and our President—whether Democrat or Republican—says, 'They're mad at our policies in the Islamic world, and the impact those policies have', you have to say America is losing, simply because we haven't taken the measure of our enemy.[3]

Another former CIA officer, Robert Baer, was then asked, in connection with a documentary he had made on *The Cult of the Suicide Bomber*: 'If we want to stop being attacked, what do our governments have to do?' He responded:

The first thing is get out of Iraq. To pretend this has nothing to do with Iraq is idiocy. I mean, I don't know if it's in the back of these people's minds or if they think about it all day long, but what they see is that we attack Muslims, we provoke the killing of Muslims, Shia or Sunni, we provoke what they call 'fitna', which is chaos among the Muslims. They see it as neo-colonialism, hate for Muslims.[4]

One of the most respected British commentators on foreign affairs, Professor Lawrence Freedman, observed in the *Financial Times*: 'The role of Iraq [in turning Britain into a terrorist target] is difficult to refute, even while acknowledging that the roots of Jihadist extremism go far deeper and were evident long before the war.'[5] Freedman was joined by his colleague at King's College, Professor Michael Clarke, who predicted further terrorist attacks: 'The rationale of the attacks would be UK involvement in Afghanistan and Iraq.'[6]

Realism In The Media

BBC Correspondent Frank Gardner has since 2002 specialized in covering the 'war on terror'. In June 2004, he was shot and left for dead by an al-Qaeda gunman in a Saudi street.[7] Weeks after 7/7, Gardner suggested that Western leaders needed to 'take the trouble to really understand what on earth it is that al-Qaeda actually wants.' And the truth is 'al-Qaeda's leadership has never given a stuff how Americans behave in their own country. What they object to most is the presence of Western forces in Muslim lands.' Al-Qaeda's attacks do not come out of nowhere: 'They stem from a desire both for revenge for perceived injustices and to warn off the West from "interfering" in Muslim countries.' They have made their demands clear 'in their own pedantic and lecturing way'. These demands are: 'the withdrawal of all Western forces from Muslim lands, especially Iraq, the withdrawal of support for Israel, and of support for "apostate" governments, specifically in Egypt, Saudi Arabia and Pakistan.'

Gardner immediately interjected: 'I am not for one minute suggesting that the West must do al-Qaeda's bidding, but it is easy to see how the first of these demands [withdrawal from Iraq and Afghanistan] currently carries most weight amongst al-Qaeda's followers.' Some al-Qaeda ideologists yearn for a revived global Islamic empire, but such ideas have 'little popular appeal on the Muslim street'. Gardner observed:

By contrast, the invasion of Iraq and—to a lesser extent—the denial of a viable Palestinian homeland are two burning, emotive issues for many, many Muslims. If these can be resolved then the extremist ideologues risk being left as rebels without a cause. If they are left to fester then al-Qaeda and its associations will never be short of recruits.[8]

Presenter John Ware from BBC's *Panorama* programme noted: 'Of course Iraq and Palestine fuel violent extremism'.[9]

The respected columnist Geoffrey Wheatcroft declared in the *FT* that the al-Qaeda's immediate goals in Iraq are 'perfectly comprehensible, negotiable and indeed achievable': 'Just as Gerry Adams wants to drive British troops out of Northern Ireland, Mr Zarqawi wants—*as did the London suicide bombers*—to drive US and British troops out of Iraq.'[10] *Guardian* columnist Polly Toynbee commented: 'Iraq is a shockingly brutal error that has multiplied worldwide terrorism, for which Tony Blair has somehow escaped paying the price.'[11] History professor Joanna Bourke, author of *Fear: A Cultural History*, observed in the *Guardian*: 'What happened in New York, Washington, Bali, Madrid and London should not happen anywhere—including Basra, Kabul and Palestine. Indeed, ensuring it does not happen *there* will help prevent it happening *here*.'[12]

Labour Party Realism

There was also plenty of realism about the connection with Iraq inside the Labour Party. On 15 July, Shahid Malik, Labour MP and one of four Muslim MPs in the House of Commons, wrote in the *FT*:

We know what drives these young men: the feelings of isolation and disaffection, the political anger at what they see as the double standards of the west in relation to international Muslim areas of conflict, whether that be Palestine, Kashmir, Afghanistan, Iraq or Chechnya, and the hatred propagated by domestic extremists such as the BNP.[13]

A few days later, Clare Short, the former International Development Secretary under Tony Blair, said she had 'no doubt' that the war in Iraq was a factor in the London atrocities, and suggested that 'a good half' of Labour MPs agreed with her.[14] John Denham, the Labour chair of the Commons Home Affairs Select Committee, said Britain needed to change the 'emphasis' of its foreign policy if it was to gain British Muslim support in the fight against terrorism. 'It is no exaggeration to say that Israeli policy in the occupied territories is not simply a matter of foreign policy—it is a matter for British domestic security policy too,' he told the *Spectator*.[15]

Conservative Party Realism

Earlier we noticed outbreaks of realism in the senior ranks of the Conservative Party.[16] There were other breaches in the dam. Former Tory Prime Minister John Major said that the Iraq War had 'possibly' made the threat of terrorism 'more potent and more immediate': the 'events of the Middle East' had brought the terrorist threat 'forward' and 'brought it into focus.'[17] Three days later, former Conservative Foreign Secretary Douglas Hurd described the political and media self-censorship of the connection between Iraq and the London bombings as an 'unnatural taboo'. His remarks are worth quoting at length:

No sane person is making excuses for the London bombers. No one is saying that the al-Qa'ida brand of terrorism started because of the invasion of Iraq... The point being made is obvious and true, however unwelcome to ministers. The likelihood of young Muslims, whether in Britain or elsewhere, being attracted to terrorism was increased by our action in Iraq.

We attacked a Muslim country on grounds which turned out to be empty. We broke international law. We faced no serious threat from Saddam Hussein and received no authority from the Security Council. We brought about the deaths of thousands of innocent Iraqis.

The Downing Street spokesman airily dismisses this by saying that nowadays Muslims in Iraq were killing Muslims. Yes, indeed, as a direct result of our invasion and the situation which we created. We removed a cruel and wicked dictator and substituted the scene of carnage and anarchy in parts of Iraq today. We created in Iraq a new base for terrorism, and the world, including Britain, is less safe because of that.[18]

There were other remarks from the Conservative front bench, including from Shadow Foreign Secretary, Liam Fox.[19]

Muslim Opinion

On 2 August, Conservative Shadow Attorney-General Dominic Grieve was breathtakingly honest:

> I have to say, I find the suicide bombing totally explicable in terms of the level of anger which many members of the Muslim community seem to have about a large number of things. And I don't know quite how we are going to tackle that. I don't actually think that simply by going round and visiting community leaders we're going to get to some of these underlying issues.... I'm sure that something like the Iraq war contributes to it, because after all the Iraq war is about the intervention of Western countries in a state that is seen as being essentially Muslim.[20]

We have already sampled British Muslim opinion at the grassroots. A representative opinion was given by Imran Khan, a British Muslim documentary filmmaker: if you ask a moderate Muslim whether they want the US military out of Muslim lands, 'the answer would be the same as bin Laden's'. He adds: 'If you were to ask moderate Muslims whether they consider Egypt's Hosni Mubarak a dictator, their answer would also be exactly the same as bin Laden's. The beef we've got is exactly the same. The only way we differ is methodology.' *Newsweek* magazine observes that, 'Understanding that anger—and listening, even while cracking down on criminals killing in its name—is crucial. Get it wrong, and you could have a new generation of homegrown jihadists.'[21]

A late August poll by the Federation of Student Islamic Societies (FOSIS) found two-thirds of Muslim students thought British foreign policy towards the Middle East contributed to the bombings.[22] Curiously, this is the same result as in the *Guardian*'s national poll (64 per cent), and considerably less than the *Daily Mirror*'s national poll (85 per cent). On this evidence, British Muslim students may be more generous to the Prime Minister than the British public as a whole.

Humiliating The Muslim Taskforce

The Prime Minister 'engaged' with the Muslim community in the aftermath of the bombings by forming a 'Muslim taskforce' on 19 July. Seven working groups were appointed to deal with: the role of imams and mosques; ways of engaging women and young people; how communities could help tackle 'extremism'; issues around security, including Islamophobia; education; and community policing. '[Q]uestions were immediately asked about whether a gathering dominated by MPs, peers, knights of the realm and ageing businessmen would have any influence over the young people vulnerable to indoctrination by hardliners.'[23] The Muslim Council of Britain (MCB) pressed for the taskforce to be given a wider remit. Sir Iqbal Sacranie, MCB secretary-general, wrote to Hazel Blears, Home Office minister, at the end of August 2005, asking for two more working groups to be formed—one on the role of the media, and one on the effects of UK foreign policy on Muslims.[24]

These requests were denied.

Within weeks, it was clear that the seven working groups 'all [felt] that British foreign policy, especially Mr Blair's support for the Iraq war', had 'fuelled resentment.' They suggested a two-stage Royal Commission. The first stage would be to examine the bombings themselves. Then there would be 'an exploration of wider issues, such as the role of foreign policy in radicalising the terrorists, and whether victims of the bombings received speedy and adequate financial compensation and support.'[25]

This request was denied.

As part of the 'Tackling Extremism Together' process, Hazel Blears and Paul Goggins, Home Office ministers, toured Muslim communities, holding public meetings. A Home Office official said: 'Strong feelings were expressed about foreign policy, including Iraq. It was a running theme.'[26]

Having failed to secure a Royal Commission, the taskforce aimed lower, for a public inquiry. Lord Ahmed, another leading member of the taskforce, warned that any attempt by the government to reduce radicalism in the community would 'fail' unless it agreed to a wide-ranging public inquiry into the London bombings 'headed by an independent judge.' Strong words. Lord Ahmed—a Labour peer—declared: 'The inquiry would need to include an examination of the extent to which the government's foreign policy has radicalised Muslim youth. Without such an inquiry, the government is not going to win the confidence of the Muslim community.' He was supported by Ahmed Versi, the editor of *Muslim News*, who stated that a public inquiry along the lines being demanded by Lord Ahmed was 'the key to confidence building' in the Muslim community, without which extremism could not be tackled.[27] The demand for a public inquiry was supported by relatives of some of those who died in the four 7/7 bombings, and by survivors.[28] Muslim representatives accepted that an inquiry would expose fundamentalism and extremism in their community to public scrutiny. But they believed that it would draw government policy in Iraq and the Middle East into the spotlight, and that this was a necessary step forward in diminishing 'extremism'.[29]

At the launch of the taskforce reports on 22 September 2005, Home Secretary Charles Clarke appeared to give ground, saying that there would be an inquiry but that it might be held in secret: 'We have not ruled out a public inquiry.'[30]

Two and a half months later, Clarke ruled out a public inquiry.[31]

Madeleine Bunting commented in the *Guardian* that Paul Goggins, the Home Office minister on faith and community cohesion had asked Muslims to speak with a more 'united voice', because the factionalism of Muslim community politics was so confusing. 'The irony of course is that when Muslims do speak with one voice—on British foreign policy—Goggins and his government colleagues refuse to listen.'[32] The taskforce's 'Tackling Extremism and Radicalization' working group reported:

'British foreign policy—especially in the Middle East—cannot be left unconsidered as a factor in the motivations of criminal radical extremists. We believe it is a key contributory factor.'

Public Inquiry.
Most members of the working group felt that an inquiry into the events of July 7 and July 21 should be held. This would help place facts as opposed to speculation—informed or otherwise—into the public domain about the process by which some British Muslims are being radicalised.

What is the impact of UK Foreign policy on communities?
a. The government should learn from the impact of its foreign policies on its electors.
b. The radical impulse among some in the Muslim community is often emotionally triggered by perceptions (sometimes true, sometimes false, sometimes exaggerated) of injustices inherent in Western foreign policies

that impact on the Muslim world. The government should better explain Britain's role in the world, and highlight avenues of legitimate dissent. Criticism of some British foreign policies should not be assumed to be disloyal. Peaceful disagreement is a sign of a healthy democracy. Dissent should not be conflated with 'terrorism', 'violence' or deemed inimical to British values.[33]

These conclusions have been dismissed with barely a mention in either the press or the political system. Instead of a public inquiry into the causes of the war, the government announced an 'inter-faith advisory commission on integration and cohesion'—chaired by a minister—on the presumption that the problem is an inadequate sense of 'Britishness' amongst Muslims.

Does the fate of the Muslim Taskforce—and the humiliation of its members—diminish or increase the disillusionment and alienation of young British Muslims? In order to protect his government from criticism over its foreign policy, Tony Blair deliberately contributed to greater anger and despair in the Muslim community. National security is not the priority here.

Iraq

The Saudi government has been arresting young Saudis as they attempt to cross over into Iraq to fight as *jihadis*. According to one survey, 85 per cent of those interviewed were not on any government 'watch list' of recognized extremists or militants—nor were they known members of al-Qaeda. Saudi investigators also approached the families of men named on militant websites as 'martyrs' who had died fighting in Iraq. The bulk of these Saudi 'martyrs' turned out to have been driven to extremism by the war itself.[34] Most of them were apparently motivated by revulsion at the idea of an Arab land being occupied by a non-Arab country. These feelings were intensified by the images of the occupation they had seen on television and the Internet. The catalyst most often cited by intercepted would-be *jihadis* was the Abu Ghraib torture scandal, though images from Guantanamo Bay were also mentioned.

The war in Iraq has inflamed young Muslims around the world. Perhaps we should be asking not why al-Qaeda bombers struck London in July 2005, but why they did not strike sooner, and why, given the nature of the US/UK occupation, there have not been more such atrocities.

22

How To Stop The Bombers

Repression Will Only Make Things Worse

Blair Changes The Conversation

At the end of July 2005, as he was being interviewed by BBC Radio 4's *Today* programme, Tony Blair conceded: 'I accept entirely that they [al-Qaeda] will use Iraq.' Interviewer John Humphries broke in: 'So we are less safe as the result of our attack?' Blair responded: 'No.' His explanation? 'Because... they use whatever cause they need to use.' Blair defended his policy of standing 'shoulder to shoulder with the United States'. Humphries asked: 'Even if it has made us a less secure nation?' Blair replied: 'But I don't believe, *at least in the long term*, that it will make us less secure.'[1] The Prime Minister was perilously close to having to concede that in the short- and medium-term Britain was going to be less secure, as a result of his decision to invade Iraq.

Blair needed an escape route. He held a private meeting in July with civil servants and politicians to discuss possible new anti-terror laws. 'Banging the table with a frustrated fist, as the Home Secretary and his two startled opposition counterparts looked on, the Prime Minister was demanding to know "why the fuck" it was so impossible to rewrite human rights legislation to allow decisive action against a terrorist threat.'[2] The officials resisted Blair's ideas, and suggested consultation over the August holidays. Instead, without warning, on the eve of his own departure for a foreign holiday, the Prime Minister launched an ambitious programme of emergency legislation on 5 August with the words 'the rules of the game are changing'.[3] The Home Office had not been consulted, and officials did not receive their media briefings on the proposals, usually prepared well before an announcement, 'until hours after it had been made.'[4]

Blair has a track record of springing unprepared proposals on the public,[5] but the timing of these proposals was exceptionally convenient for the Prime Minister. Blair was immediately off the hook regarding Iraq. There now followed a passionate public debate about anti-terrorism and human rights.

By the end of 2005, few of the twelve 'pledges' made by the Prime Minister had been fulfilled. No 'preachers of hate' had been expelled from Britain (compared to 20 imams deported from Germany, and four each in Italy, France and Spain). Detention of suspected terrorists for up to 90 days was rejected by Parliament. The proposed new crime of 'condoning or glorifying' terrorism has also been rejected by Parliament. The proposed power to close 'extremist' mosques and the 'British test' for foreign *imams* were both abandoned. Diplomats failed to secure 'no-torture' agreements with torture states such as Algeria to pave the way for political refugees to be deported. No maximum time limit was set on future extradition cases involving terror suspects. *Hizb ut Tahrir* and other 'extreme' Islamic organizations had not been banned by the end of the year.[6] The rules had not changed as much as the Prime Minister had said they were going to. While embarrassing for the Prime Minister, the process had still been worthwhile, in distracting attention from his Achilles' heel at a critical time.

Undermining National Security

There is, at the time of writing, no evidence that foreign militants resident in Britain were involved in the 7/7 plot. There is some evidence that providing a safe haven for foreign militants including *jihadis*—which is sneeringly referred to as permitting 'Londonistan'—has actually had a restraining influence on young British Muslims. In the case of 'radical preacher' Abu Qatada, at the time of writing held in detention as a terrorist suspect, it has been revealed that British intelligence assessed Abu Qatada and concluded he was an asset rather than a danger. Having interviewed him several times, they believed he would use his influence to keep hotheads off the streets of London.[7] Hassan Butt, formerly of the extremist groups *Hizb ut Tahrir* and of *al-Muhajiroun* (he rejected them as insufficiently militant), explained in an interview with *Prospect* magazine (before July 2005) why Britain had been immune from *jihadi* attacks. One reason was the *Qur'anic* 'covenant of security', by which Muslims seeking protection in a non-Muslim state are forbidden from launching attacks on their safe haven. Another reason was strategic necessity: 'It would be unwise to carry out military operations here.' Especially with Afghanistan 'gone', *jihadis* 'don't really have a place where they can come back to and regroup, have time to think and relax without the authorities breathing down your neck.' 'A bomb in Britain would be strategically damaging', said Butt, in a country housing 'more radical Muslims than anywhere in the Muslim world': 'A bomb would jeopardise everyone's position.' *Prospect* asked: 'You mean that different groups have agreed not to attack Britain for strategic reasons?' Butt answered: 'Oh yeah, definitely.'

Butt speculated—prophetically, as it turned out—'If someone was to attack Britain, they would be a completely and utterly loose cannon. It would be someone who wasn't involved in the network.... I mean the *jihad* network.'[8]

The man who invented the term 'Londonistan', Dominique Thomas, believes that the UK became a target for armed *jihadis* for two reasons: 'The first factor is the British government's change of attitude after 11 September: arrests, a change in legislation, a suppression of propaganda. This was considered the first act of aggression' against the '*jihad* network'. 'The second factor is British military involvement alongside the US in Iraq. This was considered the second act of aggression. A clear act of war.'[9]

Michael Clarke, head of Defence Studies at King's College, London, expressed the views of British intelligence clearly and forcefully:

Under the previous regime, foreign Muslim extremists were given shelter in the UK, and in return recognised a 'covenant of security' with the UK, pledging not to launch acts of violence within Britain itself... The covenant approach generally suits the police, who know that their effectiveness is ultimately dependent on the legitimacy officers have at local level. They can run zero-tolerance campaigns on antisocial behaviour or any number of specific issues, but only with the implicit consent of the majority. A light touch in general allows for a heavy hand on occasion; it does not work in reverse.

Not least, the 'covenant of security' is favoured by most of the security services—it encourages local communities to join the intelligence effort and allows interesting individuals to be monitored more easily. US authorities were exasperated at the way that Abu Hamza was allowed to preach to a large crowd of radical followers every Friday outside the Finsbury Park mosque. But for a British spook, this kind of weekly photo opportunity is worth its weight in gold, and probably far harder to find with Abu Hamza now in custody, pending extradition to the US.[10]

Blair's reckless and aggressive approach seems to have been halted to a considerable extent by resistance from front-line counter-terrorism officials.

Placebos

After the 7/7 attacks, Downing Street officials admitted that it was difficult to legislate against 'suicide bombers with no previous connection to terrorist groups or those unknown extremists who seem to pose no threat.' An official said: 'You have to announce these legislative measures because otherwise people will be afraid and say we're not doing anything, but to a certain extent they are placebos.'[11] The assault on human rights is primarily for public relations reasons. These 'placebos' also serve to channel public anger away from the government's foreign policy and towards demonized elements of a feared minority.

The Invisible Bombers

On 7 August, the police revealed their interim assessment of the 7/7 plot. There was no evidence linking the 7 July bombers to al-Qaeda or any other known terrorist organisation. They seem to have been 'unaffiliated terrorists' who were 'inspired rather than directed by Al-Qaeda.' A Special Branch report circulated to senior police commanders concluded there was 'no control' over the men 'from any known terrorist commander'. It appeared that the 7/7 group 'may have been "self-starters"; do-it-yourself groups of radicalised young men who decided to express their faith by plotting to blow themselves up, killing dozens of others in the process.' This has 'far-reaching implications for the ability of the security services to win the war on terror':

> In the campaign against the IRA, a key strategy was infiltration of the republican command structure. If the new terrorist enemy has no such structure, where does the fight begin? Indeed, who and where is the enemy? It is so atomised it is invisible.
>
> The new breed of unaffiliated terrorist is potentially far more dangerous than the IRA or even Al-Qaeda because he is almost impossible to identify. It also explains why the July 7 and July 21 attacks caught MI5 off guard, with none of the attackers on the intelligence radar. The gap—between what the security services know and what they need to know in order to prevent the next atrocity—has dramatically widened....[12]

If this is the nature of the problem, then the public, identifiable 'preachers of hatred' are irrelevant to the solution, and surveillance of the points at which potential bombers initially congregate (bookshops, mosques and the like) is unlikely to catch the private discussions of closed friendship groups.

7/7: The London Bombings, Islam and the Iraq War

At the end of December 2005, the police and intelligence services confirmed their interim assessment. *The Times* reported: 'Investigations into the backgrounds of the 7/7 London bombers have forced counter-terrorist chiefs to tear up their intelligence assessments of potential terrorists. None of the four young men from West Yorkshire who killed 52 bus and Tube passengers during the summer fitted the existing "threat profile".'[13] Both Khan and Tanweer were noticed by the security services on the fringes of anti-terror investigations, but were judged too peripheral to be worth further inquiry.[14]

The police confessed that one crucial part of 'the July jigsaw' was still missing: how Mohammad Sidique Khan was radicalized. He radicalized the younger men, but we don't know how he was radicalized: 'Khan's mentor, the possible mastermind of the 7/7 attack, has not been identified and the possibility remains that Khan was a self-taught bomber, learning his craft from sophisticated internet sites that carry bombmaking manuals alongside religious instructions.' A senior police investigator said: 'It would be quite a revelation if this group had no one running it at all. If that is so we really are in a mess.'[15] An observation of enormous significance.

How can the police possibly monitor all the self-starting small, closed friendship groups floating around the Muslim communities? Even with the 50 per cent increase in MI5 staffing to 3000 officers by 2007, this task is beyond human powers.[16] A bomb plot that costs a few hundred pounds[17] does not require money transfers from abroad that can be traced, or criminal 'fund-raising' that might bring the conspirators to the attention of the police. This is why the terror alert was down-graded by the security services the month before the attacks: the origins of the atrocities were hidden in the folds of a small affinity group on the outermost periphery of the known *jihad* network in Britain. Whatever the connection between the London bombers and Ayman al-Zawahiri, it seems there is no evidence of the al-Qaeda leadership instigating or controlling the 7/7 plot.

At the end of a 14-month investigation into the Madrid bombings, Jorge Dezcallar, the former head of CNL, the Spanish security service, said: 'This was a local sleeper cell. It may have been inspired by al-Qa'ida but it had no links with Osama bin Laden. Some of the bombers were thieves and petty criminals. They did not even have an Islamic past. They are almost impossible to detect.'[18] We noted earlier that police officers investigating the Hanif-Sharif suicide bombings in Israel confessed ignorance of when the duo decided to become suicide bombers with the words: 'We are not thought police.'[19] Only 'thought police', however, can totally prevent these kinds of conspiracies.

Earlier, we sketched out the publicly-known facts of the four bombers' lives. Much is yet to be discovered, and some details—including the operation of the 'Mullah Crew'—will probably never be disclosed by those involved. In one sense the biographical details of these young men are important, in enabling us to set aside faulty or inadequate explanations of the July tragedy—brainwashing, religion, cultural isolation, deprivation and so on. Nasreen Suleaman concluded her BBC Radio 4 investigation into the life of Mohammad Sidique Khan with these words:

> To become a radical Islamist and someone who hated the West, Khan never needed to go abroad. He didn't need a radical *imam*, or a separatist education, because he had neither. Some videos, a group of like-minded friends, and a spare front room in someone's house, was probably all it took.[20]

It is also true that the biographical details of the bombers reveal some of the features that made them more vulnerable to these ideas.

In a deeper sense, however, the details of the 7/7 bombers' lives are irrelevant. When we look at the range of British suicide bombers—from Richard Reid the petty-criminal prison convert to Saajid Badat, his middle-class training camp co-conspirator from the 'integrated' Gloucester Muslim community, to the part-privately-educated Omar Khan Sharif, to the teaching assistant Mohammad Sidique Khan, the reformed tearaway Hasib Hussain, the cricket fanatic Shehzad Tanweer and the young convert Abdullah Shaheed Jamal—we find no common factor one can use to identify or predict the next bomber.

Former CIA field agent Robert Baer observes: 'You are fighting an enemy within. An enemy that can spring up like a virus from nowhere without reference to any far-flung leader or foreign terrorist organisation. And all they need to get into the killing business is a list of instructions on how to make explosives from the internet and their own willingness to die.'[21]

Repression And Alienation

If Khan really was a self-started, self-brainwashed, self-radicalized—self-made—terrorist, using the resources of the internet and the radical *jihadi* communications system, then this kind of invisible conspiracy can grow up undetected again. Not only in Britain, but in any Western Muslim community.

Throughout Europe, the non-Muslim political and media establishment is turning against Muslim minorities. From a European Muslim point of view, this is merely an intensification of an already-existing experience of discrimination, fear and distrust. The Netherlands has changed the tone of discussion, requiring Muslims to prove that they are Dutch first and that other parts of their identity—their Muslim identity, or their racial heritage—come second. The German state of Baden-Württemberg is now leading the way in setting a questionnaire for Muslims to prove their loyalty to Germany before being allowed to become citizens. On top of the normal test for foreigners, Muslims—and only Muslims—are being asked about their attitudes to gay rights; the acceptability of western clothing for young women; whether husbands should be allowed to beat their wives; and how they stand on the 9/11 attacks. If someone answers 'correctly', but later acts against expected behaviour, by beating their wife, for example, they may have their citizenship removed.[22]

This kind of discrimination is wrong in itself—why should only wife-beaters who are immigrant Muslims have their citizenship stripped?—and it also reinforces the *jihadi* analysis that there is a war on Islam. In the aftermath of the killing of Dutch film-maker Theo van Gogh by Mohammed Bouyeri, an Islamic fundamentalist, *Financial Times* journalist Simon Kuper wrote:

> In theory the Dutch could expel all known Muslims, hunt down converts such as Bouyeri's associate Jason W. (son of a US soldier and a Dutchwoman), and stop anyone else converting. Short of doing this, they will have to accept there may be a few would-be terrorists among them. To use this as an excuse perennially to test the loyalty of all Muslim inhabitants is counterproductive. Nor should we exaggerate the risk: smoking still kills thousands of times more Dutch people than Islamic fundamentalism.[23]

Repression only intensifies the sense of grievance and humiliation that is part of the background to the London bombings.

The Road To 7/7

The 7/7 bombers were not brainwashed into bombing London; they were not driven to terrorism by cultural alienation, racism and poverty; they were not led to mass murder by the Islam they were brought up with. The South Asian reclusive *biradari*-oriented Sufi Sunni Islam the Leeds bombers were brought up with was the precise opposite of the Saudi-Egyptian politically-engaged, *umma*-oriented, High Islam of the al-Qaeda leadership. The religion they were brought up with was an *obstacle* to joining the Great Satan *jihad*.

Having said this, the self-segregation and cultural isolation of their particular Muslim community in Beeston may well have made the Leeds bombers more vulnerable to anti-Western fundamentalism. It is tempting to draw a parallel with the reluctance—or inability—of the 2001 rioters in Northern England to form an anti-racist movement with non-Asians and non-Muslims. Just as the new 'assertive Muslim identity' of the deprived South Asian inner city ghetto strikes out alone against the perceived threat, so too did the Leeds bombers strike out on their own, despairing of larger political movements, rejecting the assistance of non-Muslims. Let us not forget, however, that self-segregation and isolation is, in the present generation, to a considerable extent the result of white racism and Islamophobia, which almost certainly also contributed to the anti-Western sentiments of the bombers.

The bombers turned to an anti-Western form of fundamentalist Islam. However, we should be clear that the majority of these forms of fundamentalism are nonviolent. Furthermore, the majority of violent fundamentalist *jihadis* are focused on struggles within the Islamic world, as we have seen.

Why were these men vulnerable to the particular ideology of Osama bin Laden? Because Osama bin Laden, like the bombers, is determined not to turn away from, or shut his ears to, the suffering of his fellow Muslims around the world. Watching atrocity videos from Chechnya, Palestine and Iraq, however distasteful, was an engagement with reality. Part of their reason for turning to jihadism may well have been despair at nonviolent attempts to alter this reality. A massive nonviolent movement failed to prevent the Iraq war, and failed to prevent the re-election of the men who had led Britain and the US to war. These young men may also have felt there was no nonviolent movement around them that felt the same anger at the abuses being inflicted on the global Muslim family. They had no movement around them that they saw presenting a convincing picture of how these abuses could be stopped by nonviolent means. What they did have around them was a jihadist communication system which fed them an intensified and politicized rendition of global Muslim suffering, a theological justification and a strategic rationale for revenge attacks, and a fundamentalist worldview that removed all moral inhibitions. This philosophy made sense of the world, and gave them a way to make a difference.

Powerlessness

David Miliband, a rising star of the Blair cabinet, is responsible for promoting 'respect'. At the 2005 Labour Party Conference, Miliband said the government needed to act to prevent voters turning to extremism. Pointing to recent BNP successes in council elections in Burnley, Lancashire, he said: 'It's when people feel powerless, when they feel the system doesn't work for them, they don't just get apathetic, they get angry. When they turn to anger, they turn to extremism.' Miliband declared that: 'to stay in power we have to release power. We know that the new enemy is a sense of powerlessness.' He added: 'I think this sense of powerlessness is a very, very profound thing for us to come to terms with. Over the next 10 years the issue of power is going to be the core of politics.'[24]

While these remarks seem addressed mainly to the danger of 'white extremism', they apply equally to the position of British Muslims. Earlier we noted Dr Colin Webster's suggestion that the Asian riots of 2001 'constitute[d] a search for respect and recognition from real and perceived adversaries, whether white young people or the police'. It may be that in part, the 7/7 atrocities spring from a similar impulse, on a far wider scale, on a far larger canvas. Earlier we also noted the view of a young Muslim in Leeds, Hashim Talbot, who suggested that young Muslims 'go for radical ideas because with these they can see change happen quickly.'[25] There is a hunger, not only in the Muslim community, for a sense of personal effectiveness.

When we look into the roots of the London bombings, we find four fairly ordinary young men who wanted change to happen quickly. They seem to have been led by an unshakeable sense of 'powerlessness' towards mass murder and suicide. They seem to have been driven to a special kind of immoral fanaticism by an acute empathy with the suffering of the *umma* around the world, a highly developed sense of responsibility to their fellow Muslims, a profound religiosity, a fanatical and violent interpretation of Islam, and despair at the apparent immovability of British foreign policy. By general consent, the war in Iraq was a critical factor in their radicalization.

A person who commits suicide is often someone who has adopted (or been indoctrinated into accepting) absolute standards—of morality, beauty, wealth, power, popularity, honour, status—by which they judge themselves radically unacceptable. A person who commits murder is often someone who has adopted (or been indoctrinated into accepting) absolute standards by which they judge someone else radically unacceptable. A homicide-suicide is often committed by someone who kills, and then cannot live with themselves for having killed. It may be that suicide bombers such as the 7/7 bombers have their priorities around the other way. Perhaps they are people who cannot live with themselves for being unable to end the suffering around the world that they are so painfully aware of, and who are determined to take a goodly number of the rest of us (also guilty of doing too little for those who are suffering) with them.

A 'nice' person may often assume or believe that they are unacceptable, that they have to work hard to be 'good' (and therefore acceptable), and may feel guilty at how far short they fall of the standards they have inherited or accepted. A 'nice' person is often someone who assumes or believes that we live in a Just World where good is rewarded and evil defeated. Dorothy Rowe, an expert on depression, suggests that these two axioms amount to a failsafe recipe for depression. All that is required is a disaster of some kind that violates Assumption Two.[26] This model seems highly relevant to the case of the 7/7 bombers. The evidence of the Khan video statement, and of the bombers' friends and associates in Britain and in Pakistan, point to the relevant 'disaster' being a global rather than a personal event.

Suicide can occur in someone who is not suspected of harbouring such feelings in any way. At the time of writing, Britain is still pondering the case of a successful, attractive, wealthy, popular and outwardly happy lawyer, who leapt to her death from a fourth storey hotel window on 4 January 2006.[27] The four 7/7 bombers also hid their true emotional lives from their families and their friends. One thinks of Shehzad Tanweer, apparently carefree, playing sport in the park as usual on the evening before his suicide bombing. However, unlike most unexpected suicides, the focus of the inner lives of the bombers was not their personal circumstances, but the circumstances of the global *umma*. More precisely, their focus was almost certainly their painful inability to end the suffering of their fellow Muslims. This was their 'secret despair'.[28]

So a 'nice man' may commit appalling atrocities when he turns to an appalling and brutal ideology in despair at his ability to make things right, to make the world the way it should be. A 'nice man' may conclude that he himself does not deserve to live because of his inability to make a Just World for 'his' people, who are suffering extreme agony. He may conclude that those around him also do not deserve to live because of their inability or unwillingness to do something about, or deliberate ignorance of, the suffering of 'his' people.

Not Victims

It should be emphasized at this point that nothing that has been said so far in any way removes the moral responsibility of the bombers for their actions.

The bombers were not victims. They had choices other than atrocity. They had the choice to try to make an effective nonviolent politics here in Britain that

could shift brutal and unacceptable British and US policies. If they were irrevocably committed to taking up arms, they had the choice of going to a country
where Muslims were under armed attack, where they could have joined a legitimate military struggle against oppression under the laws of war (there are
Geneva Conventions to cover guerrilla warfare,[29] which contain limitations similar to those in the classical Islamic laws of war).

No one forced Mohammad Sidique Khan, Shehzad Tanweer, Hasib Hussain
and Abdullah Jamal to adopt a way of thinking that demonized and dehuman-
ized all the people of Britain—Muslim and non-Muslim—and made them all
'legitimate targets'. Osama bin Laden did not force them. Ayman al-Zawahiri
did not force them. Tony Blair did not force them. George W. Bush did not force
them.

Having said this, bin Laden and al-Zawahiri cannot escape their responsibility for promulgating a call to action that encourages young Muslims to carry out
such barbaric actions. The leaders of al-Qaeda share some responsibility for
the atrocity of 7/7. By the same token, Blair and Bush cannot escape their responsibility for deliberately, unnecessarily and dishonestly inflicting massive
suffering on the peoples of Afghanistan and Iraq, thereby inflaming the rage
and despair of young Muslims around the world, and making them more willing
to listen to al-Qaeda's message of hatred and revenge. Blair and Bush cannot
evade their responsibility for inculcating a 'sense of helplessness'—or 'powerlessness'—in young Muslims around the world.

Democracy And The War

According to Michael Scheuer, who headed the CIA's bin Laden unit from 1996
to 1999, the United States has to find a way to 'slow the growth in the Muslim
world of support for Osama bin Laden'. This has to start with an 'understanding
that the motivation for the people fighting us has to do with our policies.' The
United States must review those foreign policies 'in an open and democratic
way' to decide whether they still serve the interests of the United States—'the
military can't possibly win this war over the long term'. What is needed in the
US? 'My answer to that is, first of all, we need a shot of democracy inside the
United States.... The American people, I think, deserve to at least have a voice
in policies that have basically been on auto-pilot for 25 years, whether toward
Israel, energy policy, support for the Saudis and the Egyptians—all of that—I
think it deserves a debate.' Scheuer observes: 'I think it would make a difference
if there was some kind of change in our policy toward Israel.'

If, at the end of such a debate, the democratic process resulted in a decision to keep those policies as they are, Scheuer says: '[W]ell, I think that might be a mistake', but, 'if that's what the country would want, then at least the country would be going into the war against Islamic militancy with its eyes open, knowing that those policies, more than anything else, motivate our enemy.' Scheuer comments: 'We would go into it with our eyes open. We'd be expecting a very long war, and a very bloody and costly war.'[30]

At the very least, the people of Britain deserve such a democratic debate.

Iraq

At the end of August 2005, Foreign Secretary Jack Straw denied that the war in Iraq had led to Britain becoming a greater terrorist target. 'Would we have been safer had we not taken the military action in Iraq?' He answered himself: 'there is no guarantee whatsoever that we would have been safer had we not taken military action in Iraq.' He rejected any suggestion that if Britain had not invaded Iraq, it would have been 'immune' from this type of attack.[31]

Straw was accurate, but intentionally misleading. The question is not whether 'not invading Iraq' would have 'guaranteed' a reduced risk of terror, or whether it would have made Britain 'immune' from al-Qaeda-type terror. This was intended to distract attention from the real questions.

One of these questions is: did invading Iraq 'heighten' the risk of al-Qaeda-type terror, as the Joint Intelligence Committee (JIC) warned Tony Blair it would do before the invasion? The British public believe it did increase the risk of a 7/7-style attack, as we have seen. The fact that London was not bombed by al-Qaeda-type terrorists before the war, and has been bombed by such terrorists since the war, is *prima facie* evidence that they are right. Chatham House and the intelligence agencies cited earlier support this analysis.

Another key question: did the Prime Minister, and the British government, enter the war knowing that this 'heightened' risk of terrorism was the predictable consequence of their illegal and unpopular invasion? We have already established this by reference to the JIC warning.

Did the government deliberately mislead the British people about the connection between British foreign policy in general—and the war in Iraq in particular—and the 'heightened' risk of terrorism in Britain? We know what the government believed, from the 2004 Home Office/Foreign Office report 'Young Muslims and Extremists', if nothing else. We know what ministers have said since 7/7. They have concealed and distorted. They have lied.

Finally, the central issue is the question Jack Straw was wriggling away from at the end of August 2005, and that Tony Blair has been desperate to avoid throughout this crisis: whether a different course of action in the past—*or in the future*—would have resulted—*or would now result*—in a lessening of the risk of terrorism. The Foreign Secretary was desperate to keep the issue historical, and to frame it in terms of whether or not invading Iraq in March 2003 would have affected the risk of terrorism in Britain. Straw and Blair want this to remain an academic 'what if' exercise, when they knows full well that it was and remains one of the most politically-charged and burning questions in Britain today. The central question being posed in relation to all the leaked documents surveyed earlier is whether withdrawing from Iraq *now* would reduce the risk of terrorism in Britain *in the future.*

For the authentic anti-war movement, this question of self-interest is irrelevant. The occupation of Iraq is simply wrong, and should be ended as soon as possible, even if this would increase the risk of terrorism in Britain. For a large part of the British population, however, unenthusiastic and uncomfortable about the occupation, but equally uncomfortable at the idea of immediate withdrawal, the question of self-interest is extremely important. If the government were forced to admit that Britain's security is being damaged, and that British citizens are likely to go on dying in these kinds of atrocities for the foreseeable future—*because of the occupation of Iraq*—this might well tip the balance in favour of withdrawal.

The high probability that withdrawal from Iraq will reduce the risk of terror in Britain, is therefore of critical significance. This explains the government's desperate attempts to distract attention from this prospect, and to mislead the British people.

It should also be said that if that complete withdrawal were followed by the deployment of an independent international security force, perhaps headed by the UN, composed of nations which have not been involved in the occupation, this might allay concerns inside and outside Iraq about post-withdrawal chaos. Such a proposal has been made by an Iraqi clerical group close to the broad mass of the Sunni insurgency.[32]

Three weeks after the London bombings, Muslim newspaper columnist Yasmin Alibhai-Brown wrote:

> This outreach work is of no use if the government doggedly refuses to take seriously the anxieties and anger of Muslims who detest the war in Iraq and

our blind loyalty to the neo-cons in the US. How dare Tony Blair lecture Muslims on the dangers of fundamentalism while remaining blindly insistent on the special relationship with the US? If integration means having to consent to that fundamentalist foreign policy, I'll have none of it. If it requires of me acquiescence in human rights violations, you can count me out.[33]

Violent fundamentalist Islam is a danger to the world. So is violent fundamentalist Christianity, and violent fundamentalist Judaism. What British Muslims have been united in demanding since the July bombings is an end to denial and the beginnings of realism. What they have demanded is honesty from the British government about the part played in this disaster by Britain's violent and inflexible—'fundamentalist'—foreign policy.

Theologian Martyn Percy observed in the aftermath of 9/11 that terrorism is certainly evil, 'but it is also a demand to be heard'. Terrorism, he wrote, is invariably 'the messenger, not the message'. We need a wisdom to hear that message, however hard it may be:

> We would do well to remember that this is not, in spite of what politicians want to tell us, 'a war of good against evil', or 'of civilisation against terrorism'. It is not as simple as that. It was, is, and will continue to be, a war about contested land and sacred space, and a more complex dispute over the values that control our societies. Atta's accomplices did what they did for the children of Palestine, Iraq (as much as they did it for infamy and revenge), and those other places where 'civilisation' has been seen to act oppressively, or been deaf to Arab causes.
>
> Arguably, the most fitting memorial to the thousands of dead in New York is not only the rooting out of terrorism, but also a new kind of building. Not a physical one to replace the twin towers, but rather the building of a dynamic political, ethnic and religious consensus that robs this kind of terrorism of its root causes.[34]

This would also be a fitting memorial to the 52 victims of 7/7, and to the hundreds whose lives were damaged on that day.

I do not know how we can lay the foundations of this memorial without withdrawing from our war of occupation in Iraq, without offering a heartfelt apology for what we have done there, and without paying due restitution.

Notes

Rachel North

1 Rachel North, 'Rachel's story', *Sunday Times*, Review, 27 November 2005 <http://tinyurl.com/do5h2>.

Introduction

1 Rachel North, 'The July 7 questions that still haunt victims', *Sunday Times*, Review section, 18 December 2005 <http://tinyurl.com/dcan3>.
2 Ian Evans, 'No public inquiry into 7/7 bombings', *Times*, 14 December 2005 <http://tinyurl.com/d54of >.
3 Stephen Glover, 'A shameless suppression of the truth: The Government refuses an inquiry into 7/7 because it knows the truth will expose its mendacity', *Daily Mail*, 15 December 2005, p. 14.
4 Crispin Black, 'Contempt is the new sleaze', *Independent*, 18 December 2005 <http://tinyurl.com/7fp86 >.
5 Fergus Shanahan, 'Give us 7/7 answers', *Sun*, 16 December 2005, p. 11.
6 James Slack and Matthew Hickley, 'What do they have to hide?', *Daily Mail*, 15 December 2005, p. 1.
7 Chapter 2, pp. 15–17
8 *Joint Publication 1-02 DOD Dictionary of Military and Associated Terms*, US Department of Defense, 31 August 2005 <http://tinyurl.com/bglev>.
9 Noam Chomsky, *Pirates and Emperors: Old and New: International Terrorism in the Real World* (London: Pluto, 2002), p. 121.
10 Rachel North, 'The July 7 questions that still haunt victims', *Sunday Times*, Review section, 18 December 2005 <http://tinyurl.com/dcan3>.
11 Robert Fisk, 'How easily we have come to take the bombs and the deaths in Iraq for granted', *Independent*, 28 August 2005 <http://tinyurl.com/9f353>.
12 James Hider, 'Weekend of slaughter propels Iraq towards all-out civil war', *Times*, 18 July 2005 <tinyurl.com/7vs9o>; Iraq Body Count Database, July 2005 <tinyurl.com/dttl7>.
13 See my discussion of the *Lancet* study, with references, at <http://tinyurl.com/7ulxp>.

1: Near Consensus

1 Julian Glover, 'Two-thirds believe London bombings are linked to Iraq war', *Guardian*, 19 July 2005 <http://tinyurl.com/b58zz>. The poll itself is available as an Adobe Acrobat pdf file on the *Guardian* site at <http://tinyurl.com/73hke>, and (in full) on the ICM site at <http://tinyurl.com/8ndrm>.
2 Rosa Prince, 'Exclusive: 85% blame bombs on war in Iraq', *Daily Mirror*, 25 July 2005 <http://tinyurl.com/9mfaa>. The full results of the poll are obtainable as a pdf from the YouGov site at <http://tinyurl.com/76yc3>.
3 James Boxell, 'Business relaxed on terrorism threat before July bombs', *Financial Times*, 27 September 2005 <http://tinyurl.com/amukb>. The *FT* noted that this was below the 93 per cent figure found in 2004.

4 The entire poll can be found as a pdf on the GLA website at <http://tinyurl.com/8ykgg>. This part of the poll was not mentioned in the GLA's press release <tinyurl.com/aao5c>.

5 ' "1 in 3" want troops out of Iraq', BBC News Online, 12 October 2005 <tinyurl.com/9xfpc>.

6 'Kenneth Clarke: Speech in full', BBC News Online, 1 September 2005 <tinyurl.com/dn7wf>.

7 Andrew Grice, 'Electing Clarke would be Tories' "Clause IV moment" ', *Independent*, 5 September 2005, p. 9.

8 Norman Lamont, 'Ken hits the spot on war in Iraq', *Times*, 5 September 2005 <http://tinyurl.com/a5g4q>, emphasis added.

9 Matthew Parris, 'From a rural view, it is too easy to blame those with darker skins', *Times*, 11 July 2005 <http://tinyurl.com/b9z4o>.

10 'Galloway: Bombings price of Iraq', BBC News Online, 8 July 2005 <tinyurl.com/9ywa9>.

11 'Press Briefing: 1545 BST Tuesday 12 July 2005', Number 10 website <http://www.number-10.gov.uk/output/page7925.asp>.

12 'Statement to Parliament on the London bombings', 11 July 2005, Number 10 website <http://www.number-10.gov.uk/output/Page7903.asp>.

13 'Press conference with Tony Blair and Afghan president Hamid Karzai 19 July 2005', Number 10 website <http://tinyurl.com/do85b>.

14 'PM's Press Conference - 26 July 2005', Number 10 website <http://tinyurl.com/dfdk5>.

15 The Prime Minister's attempt to airbrush out all the suffering caused directly by the occupation forces was challenged by a journalist, who interjected: 'More civilians have been killed by the Americans and the British than have been killed by these attacks.' Blair disputed this claim, and went on to say: '[T]here is all the difference in the world in us taking action against these terrorists and as will happen when military action is taken innocent civilians get killed. We deeply regret every one of those lives. They don't regret the loss of innocent, civilian life. They rejoice in it, that is their purpose.' So there is no feeling of grievance in Britain as a result of the invasion and occupation of Iraq because British politicians regret the (allegedly) inadvertent loss of 'innocent civilian life' they have caused.

16 'PM's Press Conference—26 July 2005', Number 10 website <http://tinyurl.com/dfdk5>.

17 *Today* programme, BBC Radio 4, 29 September 2005, my own transcription.

18 'PM's Press Conference—26 July 2005', Number 10 website <http://tinyurl.com/dfdk5>.

19 'Full text: Blair speech on terror', BBC News Online, 16 July 2005 <tinyurl.com/dgpzl>.

20 'PM's Press Conference—26 July 2005', Number 10 website <http://tinyurl.com/dfdk5>.

21 *ibid*. This was not merely a slip of the tongue, he repeated the statement a moment later.

22 *ibid*.

23 *ibid*.

24 Toby Helm, 'Straw changes the line on link to Iraq war', *Telegraph*, 25 July 2005 <tinyurl.com/8y23f>.

2: Tony Blair Lied

1 Intelligence and Security Committee, 'Iraqi weapons of mass destruction—Intelligence and Assessments', 9 September 2003, p. 34, large pdf at <http://tinyurl.com/7df4m>. The Intelligence and Security Committee, which, unlike the House and Senate Select Committees on Intelligence in the US, is a creature of the British executive. It is based in the Cabinet Office attached to No. 10 Downing Street; its cross-party membership of nine (from both the Lords and the House of Commons) is appointed by the Prime Minister— after consultation with the Leader of the Opposition; and it reports to the Prime Minister. It is the Prime Minister who then presents sanitized ISC reports to Parliament.

2 The Prime Minister was questioned by the ISC—but mainly in relation to the possible spread of weapons of mass destruction to terrorists. There is no record in their report of

any discussion of the JIC warning regarding the 'heightening' of the risk of terrorism in general. Blair told the ISC: 'One of the most difficult aspects of this is that there was obviously a danger that in attacking Iraq you ended up provoking the very thing you were trying to avoid.' This is not how he put it to the British people at the time. He also told the ISC: 'this is my judgement and it remains my judgement and I suppose time will tell whether it's true or it's not true." ' ISC, 'Iraqi weapons of mass destruction—Intelligence and Assessments', <http://tinyurl.com/7df4m>, p. 35. But before the war, Blair told MPs that history would prove him right.

One of the members of the ISC was questioned on this point by the Australian Broadcasting Corporation television programme *Lateline* on 15 September 2003. (The transcript is at <http://tinyurl.com/9g9ut>.) Presenter Tony Jones asked Labour MP Kevin Barron, a member of the Intelligence and Security Committee, whether Tony Blair had explained why he hadn't told the British public about the JIC assessment. Barron said: 'I can't remember whether that question was put directly to him', but it wasn't particularly important—'it wasn't very high on our metre reading at the particular time'. Should the British public have been told that the war they were about to enter could actually make terrorism worse? In a typical politician's manoeuvre, Barron avoided the question, saying that we don't know whether it would have changed the public's opinion on the war. This is not an answer to the question. It also ignores the fact that until the bombs started falling the polls showed a majority opposed to the war.

3 Hansard, 18 March 2003 cols. 767-9, starting at <http://tinyurl.com/7hopk>.

4 For a range of opinion, see my *War Plan Iraq* (London: Verso, 2002).

5 Michael White, 'Kenneth Clarke: "Revolting regime is not a basis for war" ', *Guardian*, 27 February 2003 <http://tinyurl.com/ay2yk>, emphasis added.

6 For an example, see this article by BBC Political Correspondent Nick Assinder, 'London bombs: The Iraq question', BBC News Online, 12 July 2005 <http://news.bbc.co.uk/1/hi/uk_politics/4674913.stm>. The JIC warning is said to have warned that military action against Iraq '*might* "heighten", rather than reduce, the terrorist threat to western interests.' In fact, the JIC warned that the terrorist threat '*would* be heightened by military action against Iraq' (emphases added). The overall effect of the article is to de-emphasize these warnings and to accept the Prime Minister's propaganda constructions.

7 Michael Jay, Permanent Under-Secretary of State to the Foreign Office, 'Relations with the Muslim community', letter to Andrew Turnbull, Cabinet Secretary, 18 May 2004, emphases added, document available from the *Guardian* website from the accompanying story, Martin Bright, 'Leak shows Blair told of Iraq war terror link', *Observer*, 28 August 2005 <http://tinyurl.com/7cbyr>.

8 Ben Russell, 'Straw backed memo saying war would anger Muslims', *Independent*, 31 August 2005 <http://tinyurl.com/atnvx>.

9 FCO/Home Office paper, 'Young Muslims and Extremism', April 2004, p. 1, available from the *Sunday Times* website in four pdfs at <http://tinyurl.com/dmc77>. An HTML version is available from GlobalSecurity.org at <http://tinyurl.com/bttgc>. Note that 'arguing [or assuming] that it is not possible to be Muslim and British' is a staple of the debate around Islam in Britain. There are constant references in some form to being either 'Muslim' or 'British'.

10 FCO/Home Office paper, 'Summary: Young Muslims and Extremism', April 2004, p. 1, available from the *Sunday Times* website at <http://tinyurl.com/dmc77>.

11 FCO/Home Office paper, 'Young Muslims and Extremism', April 2004, pp. 4-5, available from the *Sunday Times* website at <http://tinyurl.com/aum6p>, emphasis added.

12 See pp. 10–12. 'Press conference with Tony Blair and Afghan president Hamid Karzai 19 July 2005', Number 10 website <http://tinyurl.com/do85b>; 'PM's Press Conference—26 July 2005', Number 10 website <http://tinyurl.com/dfdk5>.

13 Robert Winnett and David Leppard, 'Leaked No 10 dossier reveals Al-Qaeda's British recruits', *Sunday Times*, 10 July 2005, p. 1 <http://tinyurl.com/d62nw>.

14 The Select Committee on Home Affairs, which had been carrying out an investigation of 'Terrorism and Community Relations', was annoyed to discover the existence of the 'Young Muslims and Extremism' report from the press. Home Secretary Charles Clarke was forced to suggest that not of significance in terms of forming policy. John Gieve, head of the Home Office, suggested that one reason why the document was not released to the Select Committee was that, 'This was quite an unusual paper in that it was mainly setting the context and giving a diagnosis but without moving on very far into the policy options.' Which suggests that this was an extremely important document—of strategic significance across several departments. 'The Work of the Home Office: Rt Hon Charles Clarke and Sir John Gieve', Uncorrected transcript of oral evidence to be published as HC 604 - i: Minutes of Evidence Taken Before Home Affairs Committee, 25 October 2005' <http://tinyurl.com/a7hed>.

15 Robert Winnett and David Leppard, 'Britain's secret plans to win Muslim hearts and minds', *Sunday Times*, 30 May 2004 <http://tinyurl.com/blca7>.

16 Richard Norton-Taylor, Vikram Dodd, and Hugh Muir, 'Ministers warned of Iraq link to UK terror', *Guardian*, 20 July 2005 <http://tinyurl.com/7nocw>.

17 Vikram Dodd, Hugh Muir and Alan Travis, 'Islamist clerics face treason charges', *Guardian*, 8 August 2005 <http://tinyurl.com/d3ovm>.

18 Richard Norton-Taylor, 'There's no such thing as total security', *Guardian*, 19 August 2005 <http://tinyurl.com/dl2m3>.

19 I discussed these reports on the JNV website at <http://tinyurl.com/8epgu>.

20 MI5, 'Organisation', MI5 website <http://www.mi5.gov.uk/output/Page65.html>.

21 Elaine Sciolino and Don Van Natta Jr., 'June Report Led Britain to Lower Its Terror Alert', *New York Times*, 19 July 2005 <http://tinyurl.com/9tg52>.

22 Michael Evans, 'MI5 admits war in Iraq motivates bombers', *Times*, 28 July 2005, p. 8 <http://tinyurl.com/9rtgc>.

23 MI5, 'Threat to the UK from international terrorism', MI5 website <tinyurl.com/8lfz4>.

24 Edward Herman and Noam Chomsky, 'Propaganda Mill: The Media Churn Out the "Official Line" ', *The Progressive*, June 1988, p. 15; Noam Chomsky, *Towards a New Cold War* (London: Sinclair Browne, 1982) p. 14; Herman and Chomsky, 'Propaganda Mill', p. 15. This article summarizes their *Manufacturing Consent* (New York: Pantheon, 1988).

25 'Intelligence report forces Blair on to defensive', *FT*, 19 July 2005.

26 'PM's Press Conference—26 July 2005', Number 10 website <http://tinyurl.com/dfdk5>. This was not merely a slip of the tongue, as he repeated the statement a moment later.

3: Disbelief

1 'London bombings toll rises to 37', BBC News Online, 7 July 2005, 20:50 GMT <http://tinyurl.com/cqg9d>.

2 'Britain's enemy within', *Scotland on Sunday*, 17 July 2005 <http://tinyurl.com/bnydm>.

3 Jeremy Armstrong, 'My Hasib must have been brainwashed', Daily Mirror, 2 August 2005 <http://tinyurl.com/7s3o8>.

4 Simon Freeman, 'Controlled explosion at home raided by anti-terror police', *Times*, 12 July 2005 <http://tinyurl.com/bq9wu>.

5 Ben Macintyre, 'Hitchhikers to Heaven who created Hell on Earth', *Times*, 16 July 2005 <http://tinyurl.com/7o2fj>.

6 Jeremy Armstrong, 'My Hasib must have been brainwashed', *Daily Mirror*, 2 August 2005 <http://tinyurl.com/7s3o8>; Kate O'Hara, 'Suicide bomber "was a perfect son" ', *Yorkshire Post*, 3 August 2005 <http://tinyurl.com/77t3o>.

omb suspects identified', *Chicago Tribune*, 14 July 2005 <http:/

e Teenager', *Daily Mail*, 13 July 2005 <http://tinyurl.com/7drda>.
ing Suspects' Quiet Lives', CBS News, 13 July 2005 <http://

didn't stand out', *Guardian*, 14 July 2005 <http://tinyurl.com/dzc4n>.
ikers to Heaven who created Hell on Earth', *Times*, 16 July 2005
249e>.
erbert, 'Hasib Hussain: The boy who grew up to bomb the No 30
July 2005.
hikers to Heaven who created Hell on Earth', *Times*, 16 July 2005
9249e>.
'My Hasib must have been brainwashed', Daily Mirror, 2 August
rl.com/7s3o8>.
rt, 'Hasib Hussain', *Independent*, 14 July 2005.

within', *Scotland on Sunday*, 17 July 2005 <http://tinyurl.com/bnydm>.
ert, 'Hasib Hussain', *Independent*, 14 July 2005.
: Hasib Hussain', *Times*, 14 July 2005 <http://tinyurl.com/bzurg>.
y within', *Scotland on Sunday*, 17 July 2005 <http://tinyurl.com/bnydm>.
rbert, 'Hasib Hussain', *Independent*, 14 July 2005.
r profile: The Teenager', *Daily Mail*, 13 July 2005 <http://tinyurl.com/7drda>.

14, pp. 101–3.
'Hitchhikers to Heaven', *Times*, 16 July 2005 <http://tinyurl.com/9249e>.

Herbert, 'Hasib Hussain', *Independent*, 14 July 2005.
omber profile: The Teenager', *Daily Mail*, 13 July 2005 <http://tinyurl.com/7drda>.
rmstrong, 'My Hasib must have been brainwashed', *Daily Mirror*, 2 August
p://tinyurl.com/7s3o8>.

McGrory, 'Did the 7/7 bus bomber lose his nerve for train blast mission?', *Times*,
ust 2005 <http://tinyurl.com/bo6f5>.
cMahon and James Button, 'Faces in a peak-hour crowd', *Sydney Morning Herald*,
y 2005 <http://tinyurl.com/bz8ss>.

8: Self-Brainwashing

ide bomber profile: The cricketer', *Daily Mail*, 13 July 2005 <http://tinyurl.com/aaqab>.
rt J. Lifton, *Thought Reform and the Psychology of Totalism* (London: Pelican, 1967), p. 16.
, p. 478.
hleen Taylor, 'Thought crime: "Brainwashing" is routinely invoked to explain atrocities, but
nat does it really mean?', *Guardian*, 8 October 2005 <http://tinyurl.com/cjl9o>.
estern nations only carry out atrocities through morally-neutral 'error', it is assumed.
lga Craig, 'The path to mass murder', *Sunday Telegraph*, 17 July 2005 <tinyurl.com/b8dhh>.
Craig, 'The path to mass murder', *Sunday Telegraph*, 17 July 2005 <tinyurl.com/b8dhh>.
Robert J. Lifton, *Thought Reform* (London: Pelican, 1967), p. 516.
Matt Roper, 'They tried to make me a suicide bomber', *Daily Mirror*, 14 July 2005
<http://tinyurl.com/b6g5m>.
10 Robert J. Lifton, *Thought Reform* (London: Pelican, 1967), p. 478.
11 Robert Baer, 'This deadly virus', *Observer*, 7 August 2005 <http://tinyurl.com/7pb37>.

7 John Steele, 'Rucksack gang filmed at King's Cross "looked like the infantry going to war",' *Telegraph*, 13 July 2005, p. 4.
8 'Britain's enemy within', *Scotland on Sunday*, 17 July 2005 <http://tinyurl.com/bnydm>.
9 Jason Burke, Antony Barnett, Martin Bright, Mark Townsend, Tariq Panja and Tony Thompson, 'Three cities, four killers', *Observer*, 17 July 2005, <http://tinyurl.com/82xz7>.
10 *ibid*.
11 David Harrison, 'Were they suicide bombers or were they duped?', *Telegraph*, 17 July 2005 <http://tinyurl.com/9ltpf >
12 Jeff Edwards and Patrick Mulchrone, 'The Suicide Murderers: "He has gone to London with some friends" - what worried parents said when they called bomb helpline', *Daily Mirror*, 13 July 2005 <http://tinyurl.com/drgw2>
13 Ben Macintyre, 'Hitchhikers to Heaven who created Hell on Earth', *Times*, 16 July 2005 <http://tinyurl.com/9249e>.
14 J.F.O. McAllister, 'Hate Around The Corner', *Time* magazine, 25 July 2005 <tinyurl.com/8ze5m>.
15 'Sources: July 7 London Bomb Plot May Have Been Much Larger—London Investigators Find 16 Unexploded Devices in Attacker's Trunk, Sources Say', ABC News, 27 July 2005 <http://tinyurl.com/crctj>. If the bombs used on 7 July had also been made into nail bombs, they would have killed many more people.
16 'Britain's enemy within', *Scotland on Sunday*, 17 July 2005 <http://tinyurl.com/bnydm>.
17 Melanie Swan, 'Scarred by evil... now taunted by a killer's vile video', *News of the World*, 4 September 2005 <http://tinyurl.com/y361>.
18 Tom Hundley and Christine Spolar, '3 of 4 bomb suspects identified', *Chicago Tribune*, 14 July 2005 <http://tinyurl.com/994me>.
19 Carol Midgley, 'A suburb wakes up to the horror of having bombers in its midst', *Times*, 13 July 2005, p. 2 <http://tinyurl.com/8x6c9>.
20 'Suicide bomber profile: The cricketer', *Daily Mail*, 13 July 2005 <http://tinyurl.com/aaqab>.

4: Mohammad Sidique Khan

1 Daniel McGrory, Michael Evans and Dominic Kennedy, 'Killer in the classroom', *Times*, 14 July 2005 <http://tinyurl.com/9qkj9>; Sandra Laville and Dilpazier Aslam, *Guardian*, 14 July 2005, <http://tinyurl.com/8dgak>
2 'School "devastated" to learn teacher was bomber', *Telegraph*, 14 July 2005 <tinyurl.com/dymeh>.
3 'Suicide bombers' "ordinary" lives', BBC, 18 July 2005 <http://tinyurl.com/ary9k>; Mohammad Sadiq Khan: Teacher and father who led a double life', *Daily Mail*, 13 July 2005 <http://tinyurl.com/7ssem>; 'Britain's enemy within', *Scotland on Sunday*, 17 July 2005 <http://tinyurl.com/bnydm>.
4 Sandra Laville and Dilpazier Aslam, *Guardian*, 14 July 2005, <http://tinyurl.com/8dgak>
5 Associated Press, 'Friends: Iraq War Spurred Bombers', 15 July 2005 <tinyurl.com/bs4z9>.
6 Carrick Mollenkamp, 'How a teacher's aide evolved into a terrorist bomber', *Wall Street Journal*, 25 July 2005 <http://tinyurl.com/daqb7>.
7 'Suicide bombers' "ordinary" lives', BBC, 18 July 2005 <http://tinyurl.com/ary9k>.
8 *ibid*.
9 *ibid*.
10 *ibid*.
11 *ibid*.
12 'Mohammad Sadiq Khan: Teacher and father who led a double life', *Daily Mail*, 13 July 2005 <http://tinyurl.com/7ssem>.
13 'Suicide bombers' "ordinary" lives', BBC, 18 July 2005 <http://tinyurl.com/ary9k>.

14 'Mohammad Sidique Khan', *Times*, 14 July 2005, p. 5.
15 Ben Macintyre, 'Hitchhikers to Heaven who created Hell on Earth', *Times*, 16 July 2005 <http://tinyurl.com/9249e>.
16 Shenaz Kermalli, 'Feelings of denial and dismay emerge from bombers' hometowns', *Muslim News*, 29 July 2005, <http://tinyurl.com/clx2w>.
17 Sandra Laville, Audrey Gillan and Dilpazier Aslam, ' "Father figure" inspired young bombers', *Guardian*, 15 July 2005 <http://tinyurl.com/bro6p>.
18 'Suicide bombers' "ordinary" lives', BBC, 18 July 2005 <http://tinyurl.com/ary9k>.
19 'Mohammad Sadiq Khan', *Daily Mail*, 13 July 2005 <http://tinyurl.com/7ssem>.
20 Paul Stokes, 'Teacher used gyms to enlist disaffected Muslim youths', *Daily Telegraph*, 18 July 2005 <http://tinyurl.com/bdt4a>.
21 Ben Macintyre, 'Hitchhikers to Heaven who created Hell on Earth', *Times*, 16 July 2005 <http://tinyurl.com/9249e>.
22 Mark Hosenball, 'Bombers Next Door', *Newsweek*, 8 August 2005 <tinyurl.com/b8ko4>.
23 'Statements from bombers' families', BBC News Online, 17 July 2005 <tinyurl.com/98p3m>.

5: Shehzad Tanweer

1 Andrew Norfolk and Russell Jenkins, 'A laughing lad from the chippie and his wild mate', *Times*, 13 July 2005, p. 4 <http://tinyurl.com/b55xe>.
2 Sudarsan Raghavan, 'Friends Describe Bomber's Political, Religious Evolution', *Washington Post*, 29 July 2005, p. A16 <http://tinyurl.com/7tc28>.
3 Craig Whitlock, 'Trail From London to Leeds Yields Portraits of 3 Bombers', *Washington Post*, 15 July 2005 <http://tinyurl.com/7ukyw>.
4 Sudarsan Raghavan, 'Friends Describe Bomber's Political, Religious Evolution', *Washington Post*, 29 July 2005, p. A16 <http://tinyurl.com/7tc28>.
5 Kevin Cullen, 'Bombing suspects' identities shock Leeds: Acquaintances say they saw no signs', *Boston Globe*, 14 July 2005 <http://tinyurl.com/btk7p>.
6 Arifa Akbar, ' "He could not decide what he wanted to be",' *Independent*, 13 July 2005, p. 4.
7 Carol Midgley, 'Shehzad Tanweer', *Times*, 14 July 2005, p. 4.
8 'Bomber's uncle: " 'Forces' drove him to kill" ', *Daily Mail*, 13 July 2005 <http://tinyurl.com/cfqbq>.
9 Sudarsan Raghavan, 'Friends Describe Bomber's Political, Religious Evolution', *Washington Post*, 29 July 2005, p. A16 <http://tinyurl.com/7tc28>.
10 *ibid.*
11 'Suicide bomber profile: The cricketer', *Daily Mail*, 13 July 2005 <http://tinyurl.com/aaqab>.
12 Sudarsan Raghavan, 'Friends Describe Bomber's Political, Religious Evolution', *Washington Post*, 29 July 2005, p. A16 <http://tinyurl.com/7tc28>.
13 Jeff Edwards and Patrick Mulchrone, 'The Suicide Murderers: "He has gone to London with some friends"—what worried parents said when they called bomb helpline', *Daily Mirror*, 13 July 2005 <http://tinyurl.com/drgw2>.
14 Sudarsan Raghavan, 'Friends Describe Bomber's Political, Religious Evolution', *Washington Post*, 29 July 2005, p. A16 <http://tinyurl.com/7tc28>.
15 *ibid.*
16 The British Government defines one of the characteristics of 'Muslim extremism' (which is seen as a highly dangerous phenomenon) as the belief 'that it is not possible to be Muslim and British'. See the 'Young Muslims and Extremism' report, leaked to the *Sunday Times* on 10 July 2005 <http://tinyurl.com/b3ake>.
17 'Suicide bomber profile: The cricketer', *Daily Mail*, 13 July 2005 <http://tinyurl.com/aaqab>.
18 Sudarsan Raghavan, 'Friends Describe Bomber's Political, Religious Evolution', *Washington Post*, 29 July 2005, p. A16 <http://tinyurl.com/7tc28>.

19 *ibid.*
20 'Suicide bomber
21 Ben Macintyre, 'H <http://tinyurl.com
22 Sudarsan Raghavan, *ington Post*, 29 July 20
23 'The loving boy and m
24 Andrew Norfolk and Ru *Times*, 13 July 2005, p. 4
25 Paul Stokes and Nick Brit chip shop', *Telegraph*, 13 Ju
26 Sandra Laville and Ian Cob suspect', *Guardian*, 13 July 20
27 Andrew Norfolk and Russell Jen *Times*, 13 July 2005, p. 4 <http://
28 Kevin Cullen, 'Bombing suspects <tinyurl.com/btk7p>.
29 Henry Schuster, 'Who and why: Ne 15 July 2005, posted 7:26 a.m. EDT (
30 Sudarsan Raghavan, 'Friends Describe *ington Post*, 29 July 2005, p. A16 <http:/
31 'The loving boy and murderous terrorist', (

6: Abdulla

1 Lizette Alvarez, 'New Muslim at 15, a bombi 2005 <http://tinyurl.com/cc8w3>.
2 Alvarez, 'New Muslim at 15', *New York Times*, 1
3 *ibid.*
4 *ibid.*; David Sapsted and Duncan Gardham, 'Lost ye *Telegraph*, 16 July 2005 <http://tinyurl.com/7n4ro>.
5 Sapsted and Gardham, 'Lost years of the "nice boy" w
6 *ibid.*
7 Alvarez, 'New Muslim at 15', *New York Times*, 19 July 2
8 *ibid.*
9 Roya Nikkhah and Tariq Tahir, 'He cut all contact with *Telegraph*, 17 July 2005 <http://tinyurl.com/9snts>.
10 Alvarez, 'New Muslim at 15', *New York Times*, 19 July 2005
11 *ibid.*
12 'Widow of bomber "abhors" attack', BBC News Online, 23 Septe 82c76>.
13 'Suicide bombers' "ordinary" lives', BBC News Online, 18 July 2005,
14 *ibid.*

7: Hasib Hussain

1 Jeremy Armstrong, 'My Hasib must have been brainwashed', *Daily M 2005 <http://tinyurl.com/7s3o8>.
2 Paul Stokes, 'The teenager', *Telegraph*, 14 July 2005 <http://tinyurl.com Tighe, 'London terror—the bombers: Hasib Hussain', *Financial Times*, <http://tinyurl.com/9jdfe>; Tom Hundley and Christine Spolar, '3 of 4 bom identified', *Chicago Tribune*, 14 July 2005 <http://tinyurl.com/994me>; Tom Hu

12 Olga Craig, 'The path to mass murder', *Sunday Telegraph*, 17 July 2005 <tinyurl.com/b8dhh>.
13 Nasreen Suleaman, '7 July bomber's motives examined', BBC News Online, 17 November 2005 <http://tinyurl.com/ccoxj>.
14 'Could it really happen again?', *Independent on Sunday*, 7 August 2005 <tinyurl.com/72r89>.
15 Jason Burke, 'Seven ways to stop the terror', *Observer*, 7 August 2005 <tinyurl.com/7pkgh>.
16 Right-wing US historian Richard Landes wrote: 'Orwell thought that you needed a Big Brother in order to be brainwashed, but in fact, people will brainwash themselves. They will go just to the sites that tell them the things they want to hear.' <tinyurl.com/93rsz> *Telegraph* journalist Damian Thompson contracted this idea into 'self-brainwashing' at <tinyurl.com/c3aj9>.
17 J.F.O. McAllister, 'Terror Next Door', *Time* Magazine, 31 July 2005 <tinyurl.com/agwn4>.

Danny Biddle

1 Ann McFerran, 'The Survivors', *Sunday Times* magazine, 4 December 2005 <tinyurl.com/b7mcp>.

9: Islam Is Not To Blame

1 YouGov poll, 1800 respondents, *Telegraph*, 9 July 2005 <http://tinyurl.com/96l7n>. Anthony King, 'Britons will never give in to terrorists', *Telegraph*, 9 July 2005 <tinyurl.com/7aht4>.
2 David Blair, 'I killed so many I lost count, says boy, 11', *Telegraph*, 3 August 2005 <http://tinyurl.com/csump>.
3 Martin Plaut, BBC Africa analyst, 'Profile: Uganda's LRA rebels', BBC News Online, 6 February 2004 <http://tinyurl.com/cpgs4>.
4 Simon Carr, 'The Sketch: These are atrocities that are producing civilities', *Independent*, 14 July <http://tinyurl.com/b7zzv>.
5 Karen Armstrong, 'The label of Catholic terror was never used about the IRA', *Guardian*, 11 July 2005 <http://tinyurl.com/awcmm>.
6 Matthew 24:34-39, RSV <http://tinyurl.com/ap2x8>.
7 Luke 12:49-53, RSV <http://tinyurl.com/97uyu>.
8 Luke 9:54, RSV <http://tinyurl.com/dlkqt>.
9 See Matthew 16:28; Matthew 23:36; Matthew 24:29-35; Mark 9:1; Mark 13:30-31; and Luke 21:25-32. For a pithy example: 'But I tell you truly, there are some standing here who will not taste death before they see the kingdom of God' (Luke 9:27 RSV).
10 *Sura* 9:4-5, *Qur'an*, Arberry translation <http://tinyurl.com/dk3w9>.
11 Juan Cole, 'The Koran and Fighting Unbelievers', 7 January 2003 <//tinyurl.com/bgwnh>.
12 Michael Cook, *The Koran: A Very Short Introduction* (Oxford: Oxford University Press, 2000), p. 34.
13 The *Qur'an* explicitly recognises Jews and Christians as 'People of the Book', who believe in the one God (see Sura 5:82), which was the basis for the considerable religious tolerance afforded to these groups in Islamic empires and nations. It is true, appallingly, that the men of a whole Jewish tribe were killed on Muhammad's orders, but this was not anti-semitism. The men were killed, and the women and children sold into slavery, not for being Jewish, but for having broken their alliance with the Muslims, and aided the Makkans during the Makkan-Muslim war. Other Jewish tribes who remained loyal to the Muslims continued to be honoured as part of the Muslim alliance. Karen Armstrong, *Muhammad: A Biography of the Prophet* (London: Phoenix, 2001), pp. 204-9.
14 Juan Cole, 'The Koran and Fighting Unbelievers', 7 January 2003 <tinyurl.com/bgwnh>.
15 Cook, *The Koran* (Oxford: Oxford University Press, 2000), p. 34.
16 Karen Armstrong, *Muhammad* (London: Phoenix Press, 1991), p. 131.
17 *Qur'an* 16:126, Arberry <http://tinyurl.com/8f6xg>.
18 Armstrong, *Muhammad* (London: Phoenix Press, 1991), pp. 134-5.

19 *ibid.*, p. 198.
20 *ibid.*, pp. 214-223.
21 Michael Northcott, *An Angel Directs The Storm: Apocalyptic Religion and the American Empire* (London: I.B. Tauris, 2004), p. 150.
22 A useful map of Moses' campaign of conquest is contained in Martin Gilbert, *Jewish History Atlas* (London: Weidenfeld and Nicolson, 1969), p. 3.
23 Karen Armstrong, 'The label of Catholic terror was never used about the IRA', *Guardian*, 11 July <http://tinyurl.com/awcmm>.
24 See Anonymous (Michael Scheuer), *Imperial Hubris: Why The West Is Losing The War On Terror* (Dulles: Brassey's, 2004) pp. 6-8, 131-138. The authoritative treatment is Rudolph Peters, *Jihad in Classical and Modern Islam* (Princeton: Marcus Wiener Publishers 1996).

10: Living Islam

1 Ziauddin Sardar presents a sceptical but not unfriendly view from within Islam, based on his own experiences, in his *Desperately Seeking Paradise: Journeys of a Sceptical Muslim* (London: Granta Books, 2004), Chapter 4.
2 Abd Samad Moussaoui with Florence Bouquillat, *Zacarias Moussaoui: The Making of a Terrorist* (London: Serpent's Tail, 2003), p. 109.
3 *ibid.*, p. 109.
4 Ron Geaves, *The Sufis of Britain: An Exploration of Muslim Identity* (Cardiff: Cardiff Academic Press, 2000), p. 188.
5 See Bill Musk, *The Unseen Face of Islam: Sharing the Gospel with Ordinary Muslims* (Eastbourne: MARC, 1989). Musk is a Christian evangelist seeking to identify entry points for Christian missionaries. His treatment of Muslim beliefs is nevertheless valuable.
6 Geaves, *The Sufis of Britain* (Cardiff: Cardiff Academic Press, 2000), p. 1.
7 We follow the distinction between *shaykh* and *pir* suggested by Usha Sanyal in *Devotional Islam and Politics in British India: Ahmad Riza Khan Barelwi and his Movement, 1870-1920* (Delhi: OUP, 1996), though 'the two terms are generally used interchangeably' by Sufis (p. 128 n1).
8 Geaves, *The Sufis of Britain* (Cardiff: Cardiff Academic Press, 2000), p. 67.
9 *ibid.*, p. 82.
10 TUC, 'Poverty, Exclusion and British people of Pakistani and Bangladeshi Origin', 7 October 2005 <http://tinyurl.com/bnt4z>.
11 'Corrections and Clarifications', *Guardian*, 19 July 2005 <http://tinyurl.com/a4ewh>.
12 Madeleine Bunting, 'Orphans of Islam', *Guardian*, 18 July 2005 <tinyurl.com/a4ewh>.
13 Geaves, *The Sufis of Britain* (Cardiff: Cardiff Academic Press, 2000), p. 77.
14 *ibid.*, p. 97.
15 A.D.J. Overall, M. Ahmad, M.G. Thomas and R.A. Nichols, 'An Analysis of Consanguinity and Social Structure Within the UK Asian Population Using Microsatellite Data', *Ann. Hum. Genet.*, November 2003, 67 (Pt 6), pp. 525-37 <http://tinyurl.com/87r36>.
16 Dr Muhammad Haroon, *The World Importance of Imam Ahmed Raza Khan Barelvi* (Stockport: Raza Academy, 1994), p. 22.
17 Ahmad Y. Andrews, *Imam Ahmad Raza and British Converts to Islam* (Lahore: Vision Islamic Publications, 1993, in affiliation with Stockport: Raza Academy), p. 13.
18 Francis Robinson, 'Varieties of South Asian Islam', Centre for Research in Ethnic Relations (Coventry: University of Warwick, September 1988), pp. 6-7.
19 Robinson, 'Varieties of South Asian Islam' (University of Warwick), p. 8.
20 Geaves, *The Sufis of Britain* (Cardiff: Cardiff Academic Press, 2000), p. 81.
21 'Salafism' means veneration for the *salaf*, the ancestors who pioneered Islam. The companions of the Prophet and the two generations that followed are considered to be

the proper model for Muslims today. Now the term is generally used to signify another form of Islamic fundamentalism or revivalism, closely related to Wahhabism.

22 Geaves, *The Sufis of Britain* (Cardiff: Cardiff Academic Press, 2000), p. 59.

23 Dr Haroon, *The World Importance of Imam Ahmed Raza Khan Barelvi*, p. 20.

24 Robinson, 'Varieties of South Asian Islam' (University of Warwick), p. 9.

25 Geaves, *The Sufis of Britain* (Cardiff: Cardiff Academic Press, 2000), p. 77.

26 Tariq Modood, 'Muslims, Race and Equality in Britain: Some Post-Rushdie Affair Reflections' (Birmingham: Centre for the Study of Islam and Christian-Muslim Relations, June 1990), pp. 5-6, emphasis added.

27 Geaves, *The Sufis of Britain* (Cardiff: Cardiff Academic Press, 2000), pp. 69-70.

28 *ibid.*, p. 78.

29 Bruce Lawrence ed., *Messages to the World: The statements of Osama bin Laden* (London: Verso, 2005), p. 272.

11: In The Name Of God

1 Associated Press, 'Recent cases of abortion-related violence', 1998, <tinyurl.com/ameyj>.

2 There is a summary of the story by the Anti-Defamation League at <tinyurl.com/8lurn>. Jon Ronson's intriguing investigation for the *Guardian* is at <tinyurl.com/9yfjy>.

3 FBI, 'Project Megiddo', 1999, reproduced on the website of the Center for the Study of New Religions at <http://tinyurl.com/bwfd6>. You can also find the report as a pdf on the PBS Frontline website at <http://tinyurl.com/9vma5>.

4 See this map on the Southern Poverty Law Center website <tinyurl.com/ap3u9>.

5 'Sharon slams "Jewish terrorism" ', News24, 17 August 2005 <http://tinyurl.com/cdu4z>.

6 'Arabs lose Israeli terror stipend', BBC News Online, 30 August 2005 <tinyurl.com/b3rco>.

7 Nicholas Watt and Leo Cendrowicz, 'Brussels calls for media code to avoid aiding terrorists', *Guardian*, 21 September 2005 <http://tinyurl.com/djh8k>.

8 'And I saw, and behold, a pale horse, and its rider's name was Death, and Hades followed him; and they were given power *over a fourth of the earth*, to kill with sword and with famine and with pestilence and by wild beasts of the earth.' (Revelation 6:8, emphasis added)

9 282 interviews were conducted on-street and in-home among British Muslims aged 16+ 21-22 July 2005. 'Attitudes of British Muslims: 23 July 2005', MORI <tinyurl.com/cy9kp>.

10 YouGov interviewed 526 Muslim adults across Great Britain online, 15-22 July 2005 <tinyurl.com/bzjr2>. An analytical article by Anthony King is at <tinyurl.com/a68gk>.

12: 9/11 Reverts

1 Paul Vallely, 'Bridging the cultures', *Independent*, 16 July 2005, p. 9 <tinyurl.com/7ub4y>.

2 Nasreen Suleaman, '7 July bomber's motives examined', BBC News Online, 17 November 2005 <http://tinyurl.com/ccoxj>.

3 Nasreen Suleaman, 'Biography Of A Bomber', BBC Radio 4, 16 November 2005.

4 Sudarsan Raghavan, 'Friends Describe Bomber's Political, Religious Evolution', *Washington Post*, 29 July 2005, p. A16 <http://tinyurl.com/7tc28>.

5 'Suicide bombers' "ordinary" lives', BBC, 18 July 2005 <http://tinyurl.com/ary9k>.

6 Mark Hosenball, 'Bombers Next Door', *Newsweek*, 8 August 2005 <tinyurl.com/b8ko4>.

7 'Suicide bombers' "ordinary" lives', BBC, 18 July 2005 <http://tinyurl.com/ary9k>.

8 *ibid.*

9 Mark Hosenball, 'Bombers Next Door', *Newsweek*, 8 August 2005 <tinyurl.com/b8ko4>.

10 Sudarsan Raghavan, 'Friends Describe Bomber's Political, Religious Evolution', *Washington Post*, 29 July 2005, p. A16 <http://tinyurl.com/7tc28>.

11 Abd Samad Moussaoui with Florence Bouquillat, *Zacarias Moussaoui: The Making of a Terrorist* (London: Serpent's Tail, 2003), pp. 112-3.

12 Lizette Alvarez, 'New Muslim at 15, a bombing suspect at 19', *New York Times*, 19 July 2005 <http://tinyurl.com/cc8w3>.

13 Andrew Norfolk and Russell Jenkins, 'A laughing lad from the chippie and his wild mate', *Times*, 13 July 2005, p. 4 <http://tinyurl.com/b55xe>.

14 Sudarsan Raghavan, 'Friends Describe Bomber's Political, Religious Evolution', *Washington Post*, 29 July 2005, p. A16 <http://tinyurl.com/7tc28>.

15 Alison Benjamin, 'Hour of need', *Guardian: Society Guardian*, 7 December 2005, p. 3.

13: Riot

1 Lucy Ward, 'TUC urges action on Muslim plight', *Guardian*, 24 August 2005 <http://tinyurl.com/a25oc>.

2 TUC, 'Poverty, Exclusion and British people of Pakistani and Bangladeshi Origin', 7 October 2005 <http://tinyurl.com/bnt4z>.

3 'Britain's enemy within', *Scotland on Sunday*, 17 July 2005 <http://tinyurl.com/bnydm>.

4 Charles Bremner, 'Riot emergency brings back curfew laws of the colonial age', *Times*, 9 November 2005, p. 35.

5 Charles Bremner, 'Social divide and unrest: an epitaph for Chirac's presidency', *Times*, 9 November 2005, p. 36. Ten years earlier, Chirac secured the presidency in part by condemning the 'social fracture' in France which was excluding a generation through high unemployment and racial and religious prejudice.

6 Editorial, 'Dousing the flames', *Times*, 9 November 2005, p. 19.

7 Roula Khalaf and Martin Arnold, 'A revolt of youth without religious motivation', *Financial Times*, 9 November 2005, p. 6.

8 Jon Henley, ' "We hate France and France hates us" ', *Guardian*, 9 November 2005, p. 17.

9 Abd Samad Moussaoui with Florence Bouquillat, *Zacarias Moussaoui: The Making of a Terrorist* (London: Serpent's Tail, 2003), p. 86.

10 *ibid.*, p. 66.

11 Adam Sage, 'No mercy in conveyor-belt justice', *Times*, 9 November 2005, p. 36.

12 Jon Henley, ' "We hate France and France hates us" ', *Guardian*, 9 November 2005, p. 17.

13 'Paris riots prompt extra security', BBC News Online, 1 November 2005 <http://tinyurl.com/7dmh2>.

14 'The Burnley Task Force', available from <http://tinyurl.com/8m38k>, p. 35-36.

15 'Oldham Independent Review', December 2001, available from the Oldham Independent Review website at <http://www.oldhamir.org.uk>, p. 79.

16 Martin Wainwright, 'Riot-torn city voices dismay at "lawless idiots"', *Guardian*, 10 July 2001 <http://tinyurl.com/8e5s6>.

17 Angelique Chrisafis, 'CRE man to sue police for assault', *Guardian*, 27 June 2001 <http://tinyurl.com/8vro9>; 'Labour activist "hurt by riot police"', BBC News Online, 26 June 2001 <http://tinyurl.com/8fe3r>.

18 'The Burnley Task Force', available from <http://tinyurl.com/8m38k>, pp. 7-8.

19 Home Office, 'Community Cohesion: A Report of the Independent Review Team Chaired by Ted Cantle', December 2001, hereafter 'Cantle Report'; available from the *Guardian* at <tinyurl.com/dpogf> p. 41.

20 'Riots and the search for respect', BBC News Online, 2 July 2001 <tinyurl.com/9pogj>.

21 Cantle Report. See note 19.

22 *ibid.*, p. 29.

23 Sir Herman Ouseley, 'Community pride not prejudice: Making diversity work in Bradford', July 2001, hereafter 'Ouseley Report', p. 16 <http://tinyurl.com/7oqnd>.

24 *ibid.*, p. 16. See Note 23.

25 'Nail bomber convicted of murder', *Guardian*, 30 June 2000 <tinyurl.com/8wmr4>.

26 However, given the right conditions, it is possible for community violence (as defined here) to evolve into some form of political violence. It could be argued that this is what happened in Northern Ireland in the period 1969 to 1972, when self-defence groups in Catholic ghettos repelling assaults by Protestant mobs and Protestant police officers developed into the next incarnation of the IRA. If this is an accurate analysis, the catalysts needed for this kind of transformation are: relentless discrimination, high levels of official brutality and lethality, armed vigilantism from the oppressor community, and an intervention by the highest levels of the state on behalf of the oppressor community, leading to a complete loss of confidence in the state by the community under siege. For a first sketch at such an argument, see my article at <http://tinyurl.com/9ddbf>. The implications for the British Muslim community are all too obvious, unfortunately.

14: The Mullah Crew

1 Jon Henley, ' "We hate France and France hates us" ', *Guardian*, 9 November 2005, p. 17.

2 See p. 73.

3 There is a useful discussion of the word and its significance in a *Guardian* blog at <http:/ /tinyurl.com/7tyw4>.

4 Hadi Yahmid, 'French Muslims Address Roots of Riots', Islam Online.net, 20 November 2005 <http://tinyurl.com/dddpt>.

5 'Britain's enemy within', *Scotland on Sunday*, 17 July 2005 <http://tinyurl.com/bnydm>.

6 Nick Britten, 'Muslim tour shows young feel ignored', *Telegraph*, 16 July 2005 <http:// tinyurl.com/ae7vv>.

7 Patrick Barkham, 'Journey through Britain's Muslim divide', *Guardian*, 16 July 2005 <http://tinyurl.com/a8ons>.

8 Britten, 'Muslim tour', *Telegraph*, 16 July 2005 <tinyurl.com/ae7vv>.

9 Barkham, 'Journey', *Guardian*, 16 July 2005 <tinyurl.com/a8ons>.

10 Severin Carrell, 'Islam UK: Anger and sorrow on the streets of Beeston', *Independent on Sunday*, 17 July 2005 <http://tinyurl.com/cxsvm>.

11 Dr Philip Lewis, 'Between Lord Ahmed and Ali G: Which future for British Muslims', Bradford Race Review/Ouseley Report, Section 6, available at <http://tinyurl.com/cxa52>.

12 Dr Yunas Samad, 'Media and Muslim Identity: Intersections of Generation and Gender', *Innovation*, vol 11 (4) (1998), pp. 425-438; cited in Lewis, 'Between Lord Ahmed and Ali G', available at <http://tinyurl.com/cxa52>.

13 M. Macey, 'Class, gender and religious influences on changing patterns of Pakistani Muslim Male Violence in Bradford', *Ethnic and Racial Studies*, vol 22 (5) (1999), pp. 845-866, cited in Lewis, 'Between Lord Ahmed and Ali G' <http://tinyurl.com/cxa52>.

14 Declan Walsh, 'The rescuers', *Guardian*, G2, 9 December 2005, p. 10.

15 *Ibid.*

16 V. Kalra, *From Textile Mills to Taxi Ranks, experiences of migration, labour and social change* (Aldershot: Ashgate, 2000), p. 70, cited in Lewis, 'Between Lord Ahmed and Ali G: Which future for British Muslims', available at <http://tinyurl.com/cxa52>.

17 Ramindar Singh, 'Future Race Relations in Bradford: Factors that Matter', Bradford Race Review/Ouseley Report, Section 8, available at <http://tinyurl.com/djq6t>.

18 Singh, 'Future Race Relations in Bradford' <http://tinyurl.com/djq6t>.

19 G.V. Mahony, 'Race Relations in Bradford', Bradford Race Review/Ouseley Report, Section 7 <http://tinyurl.com/9lscn>. This report was held back from publication for two months, causing something of scandal. See Martin Wainwright, 'Bradford race document leaked', *Guardian Unlimited*, 11 September 2001 <http://tinyurl.com/7oy2r>.

20 Ian Herbert and Kim Sengupta, 'The jihadist who needed no brainwashing to blow up Aldgate train', *Independent*, 10 September 2005 <http://tinyurl.com/crv8f>.

21 See the FBI file released under Freedom of Information legislation, 'The Nation of Islam: Cult of the Black Muslims', 1965, available at the Memory Hole <tinyurl.com/9g84o>.
22 Stephen McGinty, 'Suicide bombers who had it all to live for', *Scotsman*, 14 July 2005 <http://tinyurl.com/aovp3>.
23 Editorial, 'Deprivation breeds hate', *Daily Mirror*, 18 July 2005 <tinyurl.com/cmbxg>.

15: *Umma*

1 Cited in Ron Geaves, *Aspects of Islam* (London: Darton, Longman and Todd, 2005), p. 185.
2 Hamida Ghafour, 'These kids are being told not to listen to their parents', *Telegraph*, 16 July 2005 <http://tinyurl.com/byzp6>.
3 David Leppard and Jonathan Calvert, *Sunday Times*, 17 July 2005, p. 11.
4 Associated Press, 'Friends: Iraq War Spurred Bombers', 15 July 2005 <tinyurl.com/bs4z9>.
5 Peter Foster and Nasir Malick, 'Bomber idolised bin Laden, says Pakistan family', *Telegraph*, 21 July 2005 <http://tinyurl.com/dw579>.
6 Asim Tanveed, 'Bomber "had *jihad* dream"', Reuters (from the *Herald Sun*, Australia), 21 July 2005 <http://tinyurl.com/7qum5>.
7 Josh White and Dan Eggen, 'US admits Koran abuse at Cuba base', *Observer*, 5 June 2005 <http://tinyurl.com/7bb8u>.
8 Asim Tanveed, 'Bomber "had *jihad* dream"', Reuters (from the *Herald Sun*, Australia), 21 July 2005 <http://tinyurl.com/7qum5>.
9 Nick Britten, 'Muslim tour shows young feel ignored, *Telegraph*, 16 July <http://tinyurl.com/ae7vv>.
10 Britten, 'Muslim tour', *Telegraph*, 16 July <http://tinyurl.com/ae7vv>.
11 FCO/Home Office paper, 'Young Muslims and Extremism', April 2004, pp. 4-5, available from the *Sunday Times* website at <http://tinyurl.com/aum6p>, emphasis added.
12 Ron Geaves, *Aspects of Islam* (London: Darton, Longman and Todd, 2005), p. 95.
13 Before it became a book, Huntington's argument was an article in *Foreign Affairs*, Summer 1993 <http://tinyurl.com/2t25q>. A copy is cached at <tinyurl.com/dx65b>.
14 Robert Dreyfuss, *Devil's Game: How The United States Helped Unleash Fundamentalist Islam* (New York: Metropolitan Books, 2005), p. 310.
15 Dreyfuss, *Devil's Game* (New York: Metropolitan Books, 2005), p. 306.
16 Ahmed Rashid, *Taliban*, cited in Dreyfuss, *Devil's Game*, p. 326.
17 Ahmed Rashid, *Taliban*, cited in Dreyfuss, *Devil's Game*, p. 328.
18 Dreyfuss, *Devil's Game*, pp. 328, 329.
19 *ibid.*.
20 Zahid Hussain, ' "University of *Jihad*" teaches students hate and bigotry', *Times*, 15 July 2005 <http://tinyurl.com/862mn>.
21 Ewen MacAskill and Luke Harding, 'Ambassador denies Pakistan linked to bombs', *Guardian*, 18 July 2005 <http://tinyurl.com/cpekm>. Akram also pointed to failures of 'integration': 'You have to look at... what you are doing to the Muslim community and why the Muslim community is not integrating in British society.'
22 Hussain, ' "University of *Jihad*" teaches students hate and bigotry', *Times*, 15 July 2005 <http://tinyurl.com/862mn>.
23 Peter Foster, 'West is to blame for bombers, say mullahs', *Telegraph*, 15 July 2005 <http://tinyurl.com/bsblm>.
24 See p. 56.
25 Olga Craig, 'The path to mass murder', *Sunday Telegraph*, 17 July 2005 <tinyurl.com/b8dhh>.
26 Matt Roper, 'They tried to make me a suicide bomber', *Daily Mirror*, 14 July 2005 <http://tinyurl.com/b6g5m>.

16: *Jihad*

1 Ron Geaves, *Aspects of Islam* (London: Darton, Longman and Todd, 2005), p. 186.

2 Gilles Kepel, *Jihad: The Trail of Political Islam* (London: I.B. Tauris, 2004), p. ix. As well as having to explain to some non-Muslims that *jihad* is not necessarily a violent effort, Kepel also has to explain to some Muslims that 'crusade' is not necessarily either a Christian or a military term.

3 Evan Kohlmann, *Al-Qaida's Jihad in Europe: The Afghan-Bosnian Network* (Oxford/New York: Berg, 2004), p. 36.

4 Fawaz A. Gerges, *The Far Enemy: Why Jihad Went Global* (Cambridge: Cambridge University Press, 2005), p. 60.

5 Gerges, *The Far Enemy* (Cambridge: Cambridge University Press, 2005), p. 61.

6 *ibid.*, pp. 60-61.

7 While there are many important works in this area, the classic texts on US sponsorship of the Afghan insurgency are generally agreed to be Steven Coll, *Ghost Wars: The Secret History of the CIA, Afghanistan, and Bin Laden, from the Soviet Invasion to September 10, 2001* (Penguin, 2004) and John K. Cooley, *Unholy Wars: Afghanistan, America and International Terrorism* (Pluto, 2000). Another important study, with a deeper historical background, is Robert Dreyfuss, *Devil's Game: How the United States Helped Unleash Fundamentalist Islam* (New York: Metropolitan Books, 2005).

8 Kepel, *Jihad* (London: I.B. Tauris, 2004), p. 86. Possibly the key figure in modern jihadism, however, is Abdallah Azzam, whose best-known work is *Defending the land of the Muslims is each man's most important duty.* Kepel, pp. 146-7.

9 Gerges, *The Far Enemy* (Cambridge: Cambridge University Press, 2005), p. 63.

10 *ibid.*, p. 10.

11 Fawaz A. Gerges, 'Planting the Seeds of Al-Qaida's Second Generation', *Foreign Policy In Focus*, 27 October 2005 <http://tinyurl.com/d8482>.

12 Theodore Gabriel, 'Is Islam against the West?' in Ron Geaves, Theodore Gabriel, Yvonne Haddad and Jane Idleman Smith, *Islam and the West Post 9/11* (Aldershot and Burlington: Ashgate, 2004), p. 19.

13 Gerges, *The Far Enemy*, p. 14.

14 Kepel, *Jihad*, p. 273.

17: Fundamentalism

1 Of course Saudi Arabia and perhaps aspects of the Pakistani establishment could also be said to constitute 'armed Islamic fundamentalism', but they are status quo powers, aligned to the United States. If we are going to include such states in this taxonomy, we might describe military action they might undertake or sponsor in the interests of the superpower patron as 'collaborator *jihad*'. The Pakistani involvement in Afghanistan was a mixture of collaborator *jihad* and solidarity *jihad*. Official Pakistani involvement in Islamic fundamentalist armed action in Indian Kashmir, on the other hand, is—putting the very best face on it—support for some mixture of solidarity and perhaps also revolutionary *jihad*. The truth is likely to be less religious and more cynical.

2 Mary Ann Tétreault, 'Contending Fundamentalisms: Religious Revivalism and the Modern World' in Mary Ann Tétreault and Robert A. Denemark eds., *Gods, Guns and Globalization: Religious Radicalism and International Political Economy* International Political Economy Yearbook Vol. 13 (Boulder & London: Lynne Rienner 2004), p. 1.

3 See Santosh C. Saha and Thomas K. Carr, 'Introduction', in Santosh C. Saha and Thomas K. Carr eds., *Islamic, Hindu and Christian Fundamentalism Compared—Public Policy in Global Perspective* (Lewiston: Edwin Mellen Press, 2003), p. 2.

4 Martyn Percy, *Words, Wonders and Power: Understanding Contemporary Christian Fundamentalism and Revivalism* (London: Society for Promoting Christian Knowledge, 1996), pp. 9-12.

5 *ibid.*, p. 13.

6 *ibid.*, p. 8.

7 There is a voluminous literature on the *Qur'anic* treatment of women. See, for one example, Dahlia Eissa, 'Women Living Under Muslim Laws Occasional Paper 11: Constructing the Notion of Male Superiority over Women in Islam: The influence of sex and gender stereotyping in the interpretation of the *Qur'an* and the implications for a modernist exegesis of rights', November 1999 <http://tinyurl.com/878a2>.

8 See p. 78.

9 For an interesting perspective on Ireland, see Theodore W. Allen, *The Invention of the White Race: Volume One Racial Oppression and Social Control* (London/New York: Verso, 1994).

10 Tétreault, 'Contending Fundamentalisms', in *Gods, Guns and Globalization*, pp. 2, 13.

11 *ibid.*, p. 13.

12 Michael Cook, *The Koran* (Oxford: Oxford University Press, 2000), p. 110.

13 I have adopted this usage from Robert Dreyfuss, *Devil's Game: How The United States Helped Unleash Fundamentalist Islam* (New York: Metropolitan Books, 2005).

14 Ron Geaves, *Sectarian Influences Within Islam in Britain—with reference to the concepts of "ummah" and "community"*, Monograph Series Community Religions Project (Leeds: University of Leeds Department of Theology and Religious Studies, 1996), p. 49 n 20.

15 Robert A. Denemark, 'Fundamentalism and the Global Political Economy', in *Gods, Guns and Globalization*, p. 280.

16 Denemark, 'Fundamentalism and the Global Political Economy', pp. 280-281.

17 Geaves, *Sectarian Influences Within Islam in Britain*, p. 78.

18 Cited in Dilwar Hussein, 'The Impact of 9/11 on British Muslim Identity', in Ron Geaves, Theodore Gabriel, Yvonne Haddad and Jane Idleman Smith, *Islam and the West Post 9/11* (Aldershot and Burlington: Ashgate, 2004), p. 128.

19 Geaves, *Sectarian Influences Within Islam in Britain*, p. 78.

20 Jocelyne Cesari, 'Muslim Minorities in Europe', in John L. Esposito and François Burgat eds., *Modernizing Islam: Religion in the public sphere in Europe and the Middle East* (London: Hurst & Company 2003), p. 261.

21 *ibid.*, p. 264.

22 Tétreault, 'Contending Fundamentalisms', p. 13.

23 Rudolph Peters, *Jihad in Classical and Modern Islam: A Reader* (Princeton: Markus Wiener, 1996), p. 130.

24 USC-MCA Compendium of Muslim Texts <tinyurl.com/yreed>.

25 A point emphasized to me by Ziauddin Sardar. Personal communication, 2005.

26 See pp. 61–5 *passim*.

27 Tétreault, 'Contending Fundamentalisms', p. 26.

28 Peter R. Mitchell and John Schoeffel eds., *Understanding Power: The Indispensable Chomsky* (New York: New Press, 2002), p. 50. This footnote (which I have abridged slightly) is appended: 'For polls on Americans' religious beliefs, see for example, George Gallup, Jr. and Jim Castelli, *The People's Religion: American Faith in the 90's*, New York: Macmillan, 1989, pp. 46-48, 4, 14. This study gives the United States a rating of 67 on its "Religion Index," based on various indicators—whereas West Germany, Norway, the Netherlands, Great Britain, and France all had scores in the thirties, and Denmark brought up the rear with a 21.' It also found that nine Americans in ten say they have never doubted the existence of God; and eight Americans in ten believe God still works miracles. Richard Severo, "Poll Finds Americans Split on Creation Idea," *New York Times*, August 29, 1982, section 1, p. 22 (reporting a Gallup poll which found that 44 percent of Americans

believe "God created man pretty much in his present form at one time within the last 10,000 years," 38 percent accept divine guidance of evolution, and a mere 9 percent accept Darwinian evolution - a number not much above statistical error); Noam Chomsky, 'Rollback' Part III, *Z Magazine*, April 1995 <http://www.zmag.org/chomsky/articles/z9504-rollback-3.html>. For passing comments on the 'militia' phenomenon, see Noam Chomsky, *Class Warfare: Interviews with David Barsamian* (Monroe: Common Courage Press, 1996), pp. 83-84.

29 Joe Bageant, *A whore that sitteth on many waters: What the 'Left Behind' series really means*, Coldtype.net, 2005, pdf available at <http://tinyurl.com/byymx>.

30 An investigation by the BBC TV programme *Newsnight* found many unsavoury aspects of the group, but no evidence of involvement in violence. 'Hizb ut Tahrir', *Newsnight*, BBC News Online, 27 August 2003, <http://tinyurl.com/brp2y>.

31 FCO/Home Office paper, 'Young Muslims and Extremism', April 2004, p. 2 <http://tinyurl.com/dmc77>.

32 Gilles Kepel, *The War for Muslim Minds: Islam and the West* (Cambridge/London: Belknap Press, 2005), p. 251.

33 'Muslim women are required, like men, to dress modestly, but women are not told [in the *Qur'an*] to veil themselves form view, nor to seclude themselves from men in a separate part of the house. These were later developments and did not become widespread in the Islamic empire until three or four generations after the death of Muhammad. It appears that the custom of veiling and secluding women came into the Muslim world from [Zoroastrian] Persia and [Christian] Byzantium, where women had long been treated in this way.' Karen Armstrong, *Muhammad*, p. 198.

34 Kepel, *The War for Muslim Minds*, p. 251.

John Tulloch

1 Ros Coward, 'They have given me somebody else's voice—Blair's voice', *Guardian*, 10 November 2005 <http://tinyurl.com/dekl5>.

18: Through The Bombers' Eyes

1 Paul Harris, Nick Paton Walsh and Burhan Wazir, 'The making of a human timebomb', *Observer*, 30 December 2001 <http://tinyurl.com/7utrx>.

2 Vikram Dodd, 'Former grammar school boy gets 13 years for shoe bomb plot', *Guardian*, 23 April 2005 <http://tinyurl.com/99qop>.

3 Emma Brockes, 'British man named as bomber who killed 10', *Guardian*, 28 December 2000 <http://tinyurl.com/8rss8>.

4 Chris McGreal, Conal Urquhart in Jerusalem and Richard Norton-Taylor, 'The British suicide bombers', *Guardian*, 1 May 2003 <http://tinyurl.com/e3zww>.

5 Richard Alleyne, 'Shoe bomber sentenced to 110 years', *Telegraph*, 31 January 2003 <http://tinyurl.com/ey28a>.

6 Vikram Dodd, Jeevan Vasagar and Tania Branigan, 'Polite and caring sons who turned to terror', *Guardian*, 2 May 2003 <http://tinyurl.com/82u4n>.

7 Toby Harnden, 'Israelis are "sickos", say gloating bombers', *Telegraph*, 9 March 2004 <http://tinyurl.com/c7x2e>.

8 'Bomb Britons appear on Hamas tape', BBC News Online, 8 March 2004 <http://tinyurl.com/2675u>.

9 Richard Norton-Taylor and Jamie Wilson, 'Suicide bombers were known to MI5', *Guardian*, 5 May 2003 <http://tinyurl.com/8f8pb>.

10 'Terror suspect admits plane plot', BBC News Online, 28 February 2005 <tinyurl.com/akrrf>.

11 'Explosion plot of "walking angel",' BBC News Online, 22 April 2005, <tinyurl.com/c7oyn>.

12 Stewart Tendler, 'Police success leaves Muslim leaders in shock', *Times*, 1 March 2005 <http://tinyurl.com/de96p>.

13 Mark Honigsbaum and Vikram Dodd, 'From Gloucester to Afghanistan: the making of a shoe bomber', *Guardian*, 5 March 2005 <http://tinyurl.com/b9564>.

14 AP, 'U.K. shoe-bomb conspirator sentenced to 13 years', *USA Today*, 22 April 2005 <http://tinyurl.com/73xz7>.

15 Shan Ross, '13 years for shoebomb plotter who didn't board jet', *Scotsman*, 23 April 2005 <http://tinyurl.com/a3dbu>.

16 Mark Liberman notes the variety of names given by different media outlets within 24 hours of the attacks at <tinyurl.com/7bynp>. An alternative translation is offered: 'The people of the secret organization, Al-Qaeda's *Jihad* Organization in Europe' <tinyurl.com/a8n8z>. Juan Cole suggests that the name refers to the merger of al-Zawahiri's *Jihad* organization with al-Qaeda. ('The time of revenge has come', *Salon* <tinyurl.com/8r2ff>) Perhaps the awkwardness reflects the unfamiliarity of the bombers with the terminology.

17 'Statement claiming London attacks', BBC News Online, 7 July 2005, 13:27 UK time <http://tinyurl.com/9gkbk>; 'Islamic group claims London attack', MSNBC.com, 7 July 2005, last updated 1:37pm ET, US time <http://tinyurl.com/dm3br>.

18 Juan Cole, Informed Comment, 9 July 2005 <http://tinyurl.com/dz6rp>.

19 Juan Cole, '9/11, 7/7 and 8/30', Informed Comment, 11 September 2005 <tinyurl.com/964mt>.

20 Ron Geaves, personal communication, 29 December 2005.

21 Juan Cole, "The time of revenge has come", *Salon.com*, 8 July 2005 <http://tinyurl.com/8r2ff>.

22 'Noted Al-Qaida Ideologue Speaks Out on London Attacks', Counterterrorism Blog, 9 July 2005 <http://tinyurl.com/78zcm>.

23 Juan Cole's translation of the statement is at <http://tinyurl.com/7ark3>.

24 'Statement claiming London attacks', BBC News Online, 7 July 2005 <tinyurl.com/9gkbk>.

25 'London bomber: Text in full', BBC News Online, 1 September 2005 <tinyurl.com/e4emd>.

26 Jason Burke, 'Secrets of bomber's death tape', *Observer*, 4 September 2005 <http://tinyurl.com/73k9s>.

27 Osama bin Laden, 'The Winds of Faith', 7 October 2001, in Bruce Lawrence ed., *Messages to the World: The Statements of Osama bin Laden* (London/New York: Verso, 2005) p. 104.

28 At the time of writing, it was possible (with Windows Media Player) to access a Channel 4 News item incorporating some of the new material at <tinyurl.com/ax7wz>.

19: Revolutionary Suicide

1 FCO/Home Office paper, 'Summary: Young Muslims and Extremism', April 2004, p. 1. The summary and report are available from the *Sunday Times* website, with accompanying correspondence, in four pdfs at <tinyurl.com/dmc77>. As noted earlier, an HTML version of the report is available from GlobalSecurity.org at <tinyurl.com/bttgc>.

2 FCO/Home Office paper, 'Summary: Young Muslims and Extremism', April 2004, pp. 3-5.

3 FCO/Home Office paper, 'Young Muslims and Extremism', April 2004, p. 7.

4 See the BBC programme 'Battle for Islam', made by Ziauddin Sardar, broadcast on 5 September 2005, and summarised in 'Reform is Islam's best kept secret', *Guardian*, 1 September 2005 <tinyurl.com/e29dk>.

5 'Iraq offer receives mixed reaction', BBC News Online, 18 September 2002 <http://tinyurl.com/bzzc8>.

6 'Does the US Intend to Dominate the Whole World by Force: Noam Chomsky interviewed by Andy Clark', Radio Amsterdam Forum, 30 May 2003 <http://www.chomsky.info/interviews/20030530.htm>. The general stance of the US and Britain towards fascism in Italy and Germany is discussed in Noam Chomsky, *Hegemony or Survival: America's Quest for Global Dominance* (New York: Metropolitan Books, 2004),

---

pp. 67-69. The precise reference to Hitler—and Mussolini—as 'moderates' is given in Noam Chomsky, *Deterring Democracy* (London: Pluto, 1991), pp. 40-42. Chomsky quotes the US chargé d'affaires in Berlin who wrote to the State Department in 1933 that the hope for Germany lay with 'the moderate section of the [Nazi] party, headed by Hitler himself... which appeal[s] to all civilized and reasonable people'. In the year this was written, *Mein Kampf* sold 1.5 million copies (it had been published seven years earlier).

7 Ronald W Maris, 'Suicide', *The Lancet*, 2002; 360:319-326 <http://tinyurl.com/cnner>.

8 Canadian Psychological Association, 'Psychology works for Suicide Risk' <http://www.cpa.ca/factsheets/suicide.htm>.

9 This quotation can be found on the website of Scott's academic institution <http://tinyurl.com/bdxxb>. The article itself can be purchased from <http://tinyurl.com/8d8u8>.

10 Jonathan Guthrie and Chris Tighe, 'The eerily ordinary extremists', *Financial Times*, 15 July 2005 <http://tinyurl.com/ckctt>.

11 Cole Moreton, 'The reconstruction: 7/7 - What really happened?', *Independent on Sunday*, 17 July 2005 <http://tinyurl.com/bo2sr>.

12 Fathali M. Moghaddam, 'The Staircase to Terrorism: A Psychological Exploration,' *American Psychologist*, 2005 Feb-Mar;60(?):161-9.

13 Georgetown University press release at <http://tinyurl.com/bmxs6>.

14 I should make clear that this two-stage model does not necessarily correspond to the division between solidarity *jihad* and Great Satan *jihad*. As we saw earlier, *jihadis* are often radicalized during their foreign 'service'. Having set out with a solidarity *jihad* mentality, they tend to adopt a more fundamentalist outlook. It may be that this increasing religious fanaticism partly explains the brutality that some foreign volunteers seem to have brought to *jihad*. For examples of *jihadi* brutality in Bosnia, see Evan F. Kohlmann, *Al-Qaida's Jihad in Europe: The Afghan-Bosnian Network* (Oxford/New York: Berg, 2004).

15 Gilles Kepel, *The War for Muslim Minds: Islam and the West* (Cambridge?London: Belknap Press, 2004), pp. 290-1.

16 According to the theoretician of al-Qaeda, Ayman al-Zawahiri, in his strategy paper, *Knights Under the Prophet's Banner*, if the 'shrapnel' from the battle reaches the homes and bodies of Americans and Israelis, these 'masters' will turn on their servants, the near enemy, the Arab dictatorships. Washington (and Tel Aviv) will 'face one of two bitter choices'. They can either become directly involved and 'personally wage the battle against the Muslims', or they will give up. A rather vague and unreal forecast. The advantage of forcing the US (and Israel) to intervene directly, according to al-Zawahiri, is that then 'the battle will turn into clear-cut *jihad* against infidels'. At this point, presumably, al-Zawahiri thinks the Muslim masses can be roused to mass armed action and victory. Cited in Joyce M. Davis, *Martyrs: Innocence, Vengeance, and Despair in the Middle East* (Basingstoke & New York: Palgrave Macmillan, 2003), p. 166. The unreality of this 'strategy' is an example of fanaticism overcoming rationality.

17 M. L. R. Smith, *Fighting for Ireland? The Military Strategy of the Irish Republican Movement* (London/New York: Routledge, 1995), p. 95.

18 Mark Juergensmeyer, *Terror in the Mind of God* (Berkeley: University of California Press, 2000), cited in Mary Ann Tétreault and Robert A. Denemark eds., *Gods, Guns and Globalization: Religious Radicalism and International Political Economy* International Political Economy Yearbook Vol. 13 (Boulder & London: Lynne Rienner 2004), p. 20.

19 Jessica Stern, *Terror in the Name of God: Why Religious Militants Kill* (New York: Ecco, 2003), pp. 281-2.

20 Huey P. Newton, *Revolutionary Suicide* (London: Wildwood House, 1974), p. 4.

21 See Churchill, Ward, and Jim Vander Wall, *The Cointelpro Papers: Documents from the FBI's Secret Wars Against Dissent in the United States* (Boston: South End Press, 2002).

22 Jessica Stern, *Terror In The Name Of God: Why Religious Militants Kill* (New York: Ecco, 2003), p. 283.

23 Carrick Mollenkamp, 'How a teacher's aide evolved into a terrorist bomber', *Wall Street Journal*, 25 July 2005 <http://tinyurl.com/daqb7>.

20: Timing

1 This was first suggested, to my knowledge, by David Leppard and Jonathan Calvert, 'Focus special: The web of terror', *Sunday Times*, 17 July 2005 <tinyurl.com/93nxx>.

2 University of Southern California, USC-MSA Compendium of Muslim Texts <http://tinyurl.com/36u5p>.

3 Daniel McGrory and Michael Theodoulou, 'Suicide bomber's video confession blames Iraq war', *Times*, 2 September 2005 <http://tinyurl.com/8fclb>.

4 'U.S., UK investigate "bomber tape" ', CNN.com, 2 September 2005 <tinyurl.com/bu4ca>.

5 'Full text: "Bin Laden tape" ', BBC News Online, 15 April 2004 <tinyurl.com/2hgoe>.

6 Gary Thomas, 'London a Refuge as Well as Target for Islamic Radicals', Voice of America News.com, 13 July 2005 <http://tinyurl.com/d5t3h>.

7 Paul Reynolds, 'Bomber video "points to al-Qaeda" ', BBC News Online, 2 September 2005 <http://tinyurl.com/75wf8>.

8 'Britain's enemy within', *Scotland on Sunday*, 17 July 2005 <http://tinyurl.com/bnydm>.

9 I analysed the voting results from an anti-war perspective at <http://tinyurl.com/ae2x9>.

10 This is not, of course, a justification for violence against members of the electorate.

21: Iraq

1 Abd Samad Moussaoui with Florence Bouquillat, *Zacarias Moussaoui: The Making of a Terrorist* (London: Serpent's Tail, 2003), p. 78.

2 Frank Gregory and Paul Wilkinson, 'Riding Pillion for Tackling Terrorism is a High-risk Policy', in *Security, Terrorism and the UK*, ISP/NSC Briefing Paper 05/01, RIIA, July 2005, pp. 2-3. This is available as a 900kb pdf from <http://tinyurl.com/ab2dv>.

3 'The New Al-Qaeda: jihad.com', BBC Two, 25 July 2005 <http://tinyurl.com/a3wca>.

4 Andrew Billen, 'Suicide bombing is a virus that's here to stay', *Times*, T2 section, 2 August 2005 <http://tinyurl.com/a8pea>. Strangely, in subsequent interviews in the British media, Baer failed to repeat his remarks concerning Iraq. See my discussion, with links, at <http://tinyurl.com/85fjk>.

5 Lawrence Freedman, 'A reversal in Iraq will not protect us from terrorists', *Financial Times*, 2 August 2005 <http://tinyurl.com/82yow>.

6 *Financial Times*, 24 August 2005, p. 2.

7 'Profile: Frank Gardner', BBC News Online, June 2005 <http://tinyurl.com/7lnmq>

8 Frank Gardner, 'It will be dangerous to ignore the man in the turban', *Sunday Telegraph*, 7 August 2005 <http://tinyurl.com/8kkro>.

9 John Ware letter, 'Panorama and the MCB', *Guardian*, 23 August 2005 <tinyurl.com/dd6pa>.

10 *Financial Times*, 26 August 2005, p. 15, emphasis added.

11 Polly Toynbee, 'Why was the IRA less of a threat than Islamist bombers?', *Guardian*, 20 September 2005 <http://tinyurl.com/d5z9m>.

12 Joanna Bourke, 'The politics of fear are blinding us to the humanity of others', *Guardian*, 1 October 2005 <http://tinyurl.com/8gzkg>.

13 Shahid Malik, 'Muslims must do more than condemn terrorism', *Financial Times*, 14 July 2005 <http://tinyurl.com/cmfvj>.

14 'Clare Short interviewed by Steve Richards: Interview with GMTV Sunday Programme', transcript on epolitix <http://tinyurl.com/7f4va>. Originally seen in *FT*, 16 July 2005.

15 Alan Travis, 'British imams to tackle radicals in mosques', *Guardian*, 23 September 2005 <http://tinyurl.com/95uym>.

16 See pp. 9–10.

17 'Major defends police in shooting', BBC News Online, 25 July 2005 <tinyurl.com/bs994>.

18 Douglas Hurd, 'You cannot divorce Iraq from the terror equation', *Independent*, 28 July 2005, p. 27 <http://tinyurl.com/acqxj>.

19 Greg Hurst, 'Blair warned of extremist threat from his policy on Middle East', *Times*, 29 August 2005 <tinyurl.com/9cwnn>. This misrepresented Tony Blair ever so slightly.

20 Nigel Morris and Colin Brown, 'Senior Tory says that suicide attacks are "totally explicable" ', 3 August 2005 <http://tinyurl.com/bos4x>. The interview can be streamed from the *Today* programme website (with RealPlayer) at <http://tinyurl.com/d68qe>.

21 Carla Power, 'The Lost Generation', *Newsweek International*, 7 August 2005 <http://tinyurl.com/8scjw>.

22 Jonathan Petre, 'Muslim students lay the blame on No 10', *Telegraph*, 1 September 2005 <http://tinyurl.com/dp3bf>.

23 Sean O'Neill, Helen Rumbelow and Ruth Gledhill, 'Muslim "task force" criticised for being too establishment', *Times*, 20 July 2005 <http://tinyurl.com/9tjes>.

24 *Financial Times*, 19 August 2005, p. 2.

25 Vikram Dodd, 'Radical plan to stop Muslim extremism', *Guardian*, 17 September 2005 <http://tinyurl.com/dd4do>.

26 'Ministers and Muslims at odds on tackling terror', *Financial Times*, 22 September 2005.

27 *ibid.*

28 'No inquiry into 7 July bombings', BBC News Online, 14 December 2005 <http://tinyurl.com/ctooa>; 'London bomb survivors launch campaign for public inquiry', *Wikinews*, 18 December 2005 <http://tinyurl.com/absf3>.

29 Philip Johnston, 'Clarke considers a public inquiry into Muslim extremists', *Telegraph*, 23 September 2005 <http://tinyurl.com/9zma8>.

30 Alan Travis, 'British imams to tackle radicals in mosques', *Guardian*, 23 September 2005 <http://tinyurl.com/95uym>.

31 'No inquiry into 7 July bombings', BBC News Online, 14 December 2005 <http://tinyurl.com/ctooa>. 'London bomb survivors launch campaign for public inquiry', *Wikinews*, 18 December 2005 <http://tinyurl.com/absf3>.

32 Madeleine Bunting, 'Muslim voices have been lost in the rush to make headlines', *Guardian*, 10 October 2005 <http://tinyurl.com/btgcv>.

33 *'Preventing Extremism Together' Working Groups – August-October 2005*, Home Office, October 2005, pp. 90, 92, 93. A 2Mb pdf of the report may be downloaded from the Home Office website via <http://tinyurl.com/amnoq>.

34 Anthony H. Cordesman, 'Iraq and Foreign Volunteers: Working Draft: Updated as of November 18 2005', Center for Strategic and International Studies, pdf downloaded from <http://tinyurl.com/bbj7j>.

22: How To Stop The Bombers

1 Tony Blair interviewed on the *Today* programme, BBC Radio 4, 29 August 2005, emphasis added. Listen by streaming with RealPlayer from <http://tinyurl.com/7ze2q>.

2 Gaby Hinsliff and Martin Bright, 'The crackdown', *Observer*, 7 August 2005 <http://tinyurl.com/9d4lk>.

3 'Blair vows hard line on fanatics', BBC News Online, 5 August 2005 <http://tinyurl.com/bmhb6>.

4 Gaby Hinsliff and Martin Bright, 'The crackdown', *Observer*, 7 August 2005 <http://tinyurl.com/9d4lk>.

5 To take only one example, on-the-spot fines for 'drunken louts'. See 'Blair backs down on fining "louts"', BBC News Online, 3 July 2000 <http://tinyurl.com/853jw>.

6 Richard Ford and Daniel McGrory, 'Blair's 12-point plan to tackle terror fails to get full marks', *Times*, 28 December 2005, p. 6 <http://tinyurl.com/97cng>.

7 A document was displayed on the screen, headed 'Special Immigration Appeals Commission', quoting the evidence of a British intelligence officer who had interviewed Abu Qatada several times: 'I fully expected him to use that influence, wherever he could, to control the hotheads and ensure terrorism remained off the streets of London and throughout the United Kingdom'. 'Why Bomb London?', *Dispatches*, Channel 4, 8 August 2005 <http://tinyurl.com/8b32b>.

8 'A British jihadist', *Prospect*, August 2005, No. 113, pp. 20, 23 <http://tinyurl.com/d76uq>.

9 'Why Bomb London?', *Dispatches*, Channel 4, 8 August 2005 <http://tinyurl.com/8b32b>.

10 Michael Clarke, 'The contract with Muslims must not be torn up', *Guardian*, 26 August 2005 <http://tinyurl.com/cxjzz>.

11 David Leppard and Jonathan Calvert, 'Focus special: The web of terror', *Sunday Times*, 17 July 2003, p. 13 <http://tinyurl.com/93xrs>.

12 David Leppard and Robert Winnett, 'Focus: Blair's extremism proposals attacked as the hunt continues for terror's new breed', *Sunday Times*, 7 August 2005 <http://tinyurl.com/a6yd5>.

13 Sean O'Neill and Daniel McGrory, 'Detectives draw up new brief in hunt for radicals', *Times*, 28 December 2005 <http://tinyurl.com/9g84u>.

14 Jason Bennetto, 'Revealed: MI5 ruled London bombers were not a threat', *Independent*, 17 December 2005 <http://tinyurl.com/9n3xw>.

15 Sean O'Neill and Daniel McGrory, 'Detectives draw up new brief in hunt for radicals', *Times*, 28 December 2005 <http://tinyurl.com/9g84u>.

16 Michael Evans, 'Pre-Budget Report in Brief: More money to fight terrorism', *Times*, 6 December 2005 <http://tinyurl.com/cxttt>.

17 Michael Buchanan, 'London bombs cost just hundreds', BBC News Online, 3 January 2006 <http://tinyurl.com/cga7m>.

18 Kim Sengupta, 'The police's nightmare: home-grown terrorists', *Independent*, 13 July 2005, p. 7.

19 Richard Norton-Taylor and Jamie Wilson, 'Suicide bombers were known to MI5', *Guardian*, 5 May 2003 <http://tinyurl.com/8f8pb>.

20 Nasreen Suleaman, 'Biography Of A Bomber', BBC Radio 4, 16 November 2005.

21 Robert Baer, 'This deadly virus', *Observer*, 7 August 2005 <http://tinyurl.com/7pb37>.

22 Kate Connolly, 'Germans to put Muslims through loyalty test', *Telegraph*, 31 December 2005, p. 13.

23 Simon Kuper, 'Theo van Gogh's killing exacerbates the Muslim-bashing in Holland', *Financial Times* magazine, 3 December 2004. A cached version can be found at <http://tinyurl.com/arsq8>. Van Gogh was killed largely because of a film he made about Islam. Kuper comments: 'Van Gogh's film, *Submission*, showing abused female bodies superimposed with misogynist texts from the Koran, was broadcast on Dutch television in September. Few pointed out that he could have made a similar film with misogynist texts from the Bible. Rather, it spoke to the growing belief that Islam is incompatible with Dutch society.' This is precisely the point made earlier in this book: that Western non-Muslims are finding it very difficult to respond rationally to Islam, and to the actions of Muslims.

24 Ben Russell, Nigel Morris and Marie Woolf, 'Fringe: Party must reconnect with voters, say ministers', *Independent*, 27 September 2005 <http://tinyurl.com/cbpd6>.

25 Patrick Barkham, 'Journey through Britain's Muslim divide', *Guardian*, 16 July 2005 <http://tinyurl.com/a8ons>.

26 Dorothy Rowe, 'Frequently Asked Questions' <http://www.dorothyrowe.com.au/dr_faq.htm>. Dorothy Rowe's best-known work is *Depression; The Way Out of Your Prison* (London: Routledge, 1996).

27 Julia Stuart, 'I'm baffled why my best friend Kathy leapt to her death', *Independent*, 8 January 2006 <http://tinyurl.com/bn2c3>. See also *The Times* <tinyurl.com/b8fuj>.

28 For a discussion of individual-oriented unexpected suicide, see David Canter, Susan Giles and Catherine Nicol, 'Suicide Without Explicit Precursors: A State Of Secret Despair?', *J. Investig. Psych. Offender Profil.* 1 (2004). To explain events such as 7/7, this model needs to be expanded to include larger collective and political experiences.

29 'Protocol Additional to the Geneva Conventions of 12 August 1949, and relating to the Protection of Victims of International Armed Conflicts (Protocol I), 8 June 1977' <http://tinyurl.com/9xnz7>.

30 'Michael Scheuer, ex-CIA bin Laden Unit Chief, Explains Why Insurgents Are Willing To Die Fighting Us...Maybe It's Not Our Freedom They Hate...', *BuzzFlash*, 5 January 2005 <http://tinyurl.com/4kvdd>.

31 Matthew Tempest and agencies, 'Straw urges patience over Iraqi constitution', *Guardian Unlimited*, 30 August 2005 <http://tinyurl.com/9a9p8>.

32 Harith al-Dari, 'No elections will be credible while occupation continues', *Guardian*, 15 December 2005 <http://tinyurl.com/dlfdv>.

33 Yasmin Alibhai-Brown, 'Cultural integration is a two-way street', *Independent*, 1 August 2005, p. 31.

34 Martyn Percy, 'Editorial', *Liberal Theology in the Contemporary World*, Volume 43:1 (2002), p. 2.

Notes

1 Cited in Maulana Wahiduddin Khan ed., *Words of the Prophet Muhammad: selections from the hadith* (New York: Al-Risala Books,1996), p. 9.

Index

1 Cited in Ron Geaves, *Aspects of Islam* (London: Darton, Longman and Todd, 2005), p. 185.

According to Anas ibn Malik,
when God's Messenger said: 'Help your brother,
irrespective of whether he is the oppressor or the oppressed',
a man said: 'O Messenger of God, I can help the oppressed,
but how can I help the oppressor?'

The Prophet replied:
'Stop him from committing an act of oppression.
That in itself is a form of help.'[1]

Glossary

Ahl as-Sunnat wa Jamaat—Sufi Sunni Muslim tradition, often referred to as Barelwi
Barelwi—Sufi Sunni tradition originating in South Asia, contains several Sufi *tariqas*
biradari—network of the extended family
Deobandi—revivalist Islamic movement opposed to Sufism
halal—'what is lawful'; in non-Arabic speaking countries, usually refers to food, and to the
    ritual form of animal slaughter in Islam in particular; similar to *kosher* in Judaism
hadith—a saying or deed of the Prophet Muhammad collected after his death
Hizb ut Tahrir—an international Islamic fundamentalist movement
Islamophobia—fear and hatred of Islam and Muslims
jihad—struggle in the way of God; can be nonviolent, spiritual or armed
jihadism—a commitment to armed struggle for avowedly Islamic purposes
kufr—unbelief
madrasa—Islamic school focused on the memorization of sacred texts, and theology
mujahideen—someone engaged in *jihad*
Qur'an—Muslim holy book ('Koran'); literally 'recitation'
salafism—fundamentalist form of Sunni Islam, related to Wahhabism
salat—the five daily prayers of Islam; one of the five 'pillars' of Islam
sharia—Islamic legal system (not merely criminal law)
Sufism—conventionally refers to a mystical strand of Islam; also refers to Traditional or
    'folk' Islam, found within Shia Islam, Sunni Islam, and as a separate tradition
Sunna—the example and teachings of the Prophet Muhammad
tariqa—Sufi order or association
umma—the global community of Muslims
'urubah—'Arabness', 'Arabism'
Wahhabism—fundamentalist form of Sunni Islam found mainly in Saudi Arabia
zakat—the religious duty within Islam to donate a proportion (usually 2.5 per cent) of one's
    wealth or income to needy Muslims every year; one of the five 'pillars' of Islam

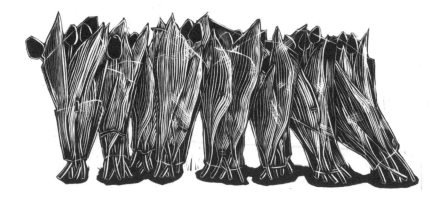

Index

For more information on 7/7,
please visit the website for this book:
<www.thelondonbombings.info>

'A word of truth
uttered in the presence of an unjust ruler
is a meritorious form of *jihad*.'
The Prophet Muhammad[1]